Advance Praise for *X-Plan Parenting*

"This is so much more than a 'plan.' . . . This book is relevant to all of us, wherever we are on our journeys, and invites us to trust we are not alone, to trust in God's grace, and to trust above all that we are loved, just as we are."

—Reverend Jacquelin E. Compton, pastor,
Central Christian Church (Disciples of Christ)

"A book that parents of every faith can use. In this new era of pervasive social media and instant information, *X-Plan Parenting* integrates ages-old wisdom with fresh insights to help us guide our kids on their life journeys to become strong and responsible adults . . . who can still love and respect 'good ole Mom and Dad' for their efforts."

—Darrell Fetty, Emmy-nominated, award-winning
producer, writer, actor . . . and parent

"Fulks's *X-Plan Parenting* presents specific strategies and real-life situations for those looking for wisdom, strength, and the faith to face those challenges head on. This book is engaging, authentic, transparent, and beautifully written and is certain to boost the confidence of any parent."

—David Hermon, PhD, LPC, professor,
College of Education and Professional
Development, Marshall University

"A Christ-centered guide bursting with humor, refreshing honesty, and wisdom. Using his own missteps as cautionary tales,

Fulks reminds readers that conscientious parenting requires self-awareness, humility, and the flexibility to course correct."

—Marie Manilla, award-winning author of *Shrapnel*
and *The Patron Saint of Ugly*

"*X-Plan Parenting* focuses as much, if not more, on what to do about ourselves as human beings as it does on what to do about the kids we parent."

—Reverend Joseph Bruce Allen Hill, district superintendent,
United Methodist Church, former director of
Christian Education and senior pastor

"With grace and wisdom, Fulks reminds us that 'the life they [your children] are meant to lead may not be what you have in mind.'"

—Mary Calhoun Brown, author of *There Are No Words*,
winner of eleven literary awards

"Bert Fulks is a storyteller who uses honesty and vulnerability to help guide parents to cultivate their own child's God-given authentic self. . . . Parenting is a joint venture between parent, child, and God, and with his book, the reader is left feeling hopeful that his wisdom and encouragement can be incorporated in their own X-Plan venture."

—Margaret Dempsey, PhD, licensed psychologist

"Bert Fulks's book explores the intense and often complex relationship that adults have with children and the importance of raising them to be open, self-reliant, and successful."

—Eliot Parker, author and West Virginia
Literary Merit Award winner

X-PLAN
PARENTING

X-PLAN PARENTING

Become Your Child's Ally—a Guide to Raising Strong Kids in a Challenging World

Bert Fulks

HOWARD BOOKS

New York   London   Toronto   Sydney   New Delhi

Howard Books
An Imprint of Simon & Schuster, Inc.
1230 Avenue of the Americas
New York, NY 10020

Copyright © 2019 by Bert Fulks

First Howard Books trade paperback edition June 2019

HOWARD and colophon are trademarks of Simon & Schuster, Inc.

For information about special discounts for bulk purchases,
please contact Simon & Schuster Special Sales at 1-866-506-1949
or business@simonandschuster.com.

The Simon & Schuster Speakers Bureau can bring authors to your live event. For more information or to book an event, contact the Simon & Schuster Speakers Bureau at 1-866-248-3049 or visit our website at www.simonspeakers.com.

Interior design by Davina Mock-Maniscalco

Manufactured in the United States of America

10   9   8   7   6   5   4   3   2   1

Library of Congress Control Number: 2018048026

ISBN 978-1-9821-1201-1
ISBN 978-1-9821-1202-8 (ebook)

For my parents and my kids—
I'm grateful for the journey.
All of it.

Contents

X-PLAN PARENTING

χ

The X-Plan

Home for lunch, my wife, Laura, was about to head back to work.

"Babe, will you give this a quick read?"

I handed her an article I'd just finished. She proofs everything I write. I trust her judgment and keen eye, but many of my topics are personal and gritty, so I need her permission to put our lives on display. She's never said, "No, don't publish this," but I still ask. Almost three decades of marriage have taught me a few things.

Laura read *X-Plan: Giving Your Kids a Way Out*, a short piece about giving teens an escape from rough situations using a simple text message. It's a plan we developed for our younger son, Danny.

"It's good," Laura said as she handed me the pages, "but if you submit this, won't it screw it up for Danny when people read it?"

I laughed. About twenty years prior, I'd left my teaching job to be a stay-at-home dad and write full-time. My brother had scoffed: "I give it six months, and the only thing you'll be writing is a suicide note." In some ways, he was right. My fledgling writing career was lost to my real full-time job: raising kids.

As they became older, I eventually returned to the keyboard. My readership had grown over time, but remained just a sarcastic smidge below best seller status.

"Honey"—I flipped my X-Plan article in the air—"nobody's going to read this."

We now laugh about that.

———

Technology glitch, I thought at first. My blog's stats were screwed up—they had to be! Within twenty-four hours of my publishing the X-Plan, traffic exploded from thousands of readers to millions. It wasn't until I started receiving phone calls, emails, and private messages from total strangers that the reality hit me—this thing was everywhere.

They're talking about your article on K-LOVE, a friend texted me.

Much like parenting, sometimes God's blessings feel like more than we can handle. In truth, I wasn't prepared for the popularity of that piece. God apparently had more faith in me than I deserved.

Friends, I have a confession: just one week before, I was ready to quit writing.

I'd been to a Colorado retreat for a week of prayer, and I was struggling. Walking along a hardpack road, the gravel crunching beneath my boots and wind hissing through the aspens, I was pushing in on God with an all-too-familiar question: "Where are you leading me?" I felt a change on the horizon, but I was adrift and unclear about direction. It's hard to navigate when you don't know the destination.

Writing had delivered some success, but it wasn't paying any bills. Plus, we'd just survived a cancer scare that felt like a wake-up call. (What would become of us if anything happened to Laura?) I'd been considering going back to school and finishing my master's degree in counseling. Our hometown was crying out in need, and I suspected God was calling me into that arena. The drug epidemic had become a hurricane with no eye, and I was surrounded by its destructive force. I missed a friend's funeral because of my Colorado trip. He had gotten himself clean, remarried, landed a good job, was walking with God . . . but one slipup killed him. That hit me hard, because if this guy couldn't make it, who could?

My oldest son, Ben, once found himself stuck on a ladder. Halfway up, fear grabbed him, and he froze. That's exactly what I was feeling at this time—stuck, unable to go back and too afraid and confused to go forward. With my background in teaching and ministry, maybe God was asking me to add the final piece to my trinity: a counseling degree. Maybe that was the final ladder I'd have to climb.

Walking alone on that mountain road, I paused long enough to light a cigar. Leaning against a split-rail fence, I studied the rock faces on distant snowcapped mountains. A hawk circled above me. I was in the heart of beauty, but it gave me no peace. It somehow spurred the disquiet in my soul.

How could I not hear from God in this place? I'd traveled across the country to come to the mountaintop! I'd been wrestling with my life's direction for some time, but now it seemed urgent. There was much at stake, and I needed God's counsel. But the answer I wanted wasn't coming.

Where are you leading me? Is it counseling? Just yes or no— *ANSWER ME!*

At some point, my eyes closed and I slipped deep into prayer. The world around me faded.

Father, talk to me! Whatever the answer is, I swear I'm okay with it . . . but I need help here. Is it counseling? Is that what you're saying? Is that what's next? Father, PLEASE!

About an hour later I opened my eyes, clouded by tears. There'd been no answer. I wasn't sure God was even listening . . . or ever had been.

"Thanks for your help," I said to no one. "I guess I'll figure this out on my own."

I turned back toward the road. Then I saw it. Hanging on a metal gate right in front of me was a brilliant red sign.

STOP

"The good Lord works in mysterious ways," my mother says.

I almost collapsed as something rushed over me. It felt like falling into a pool on a spring morning—it steals your breath as every nerve in your body comes alive.

God was here in this place, all around me, within me.

STOP

Stop striving, he said. *Stop looking for the next ladder to climb, the next title to validate you. I have you where I want you. Keep doing what you're doing. That's your mission. Trust me.*

After flying back to West Virginia, the next thing I published was the X-Plan . . . which eventually brought us together here.

When Laura learned that I finally—after twenty years— had a book deal, she cried with me. "God called you to this so long ago," she said, knowing what a long climb it had been. "But he wanted you to write about being a father, and he needed twenty years to give you that story."

God is many things, friends, but when you're willing to trust and obey (as the old hymn goes), he is always faithful.

———————

"Bert, your X-Plan is being shared and discussed around the world," the interviewer said. "Why has this sparked so much attention?"

I almost said, *The blind squirrel found a nut?* I didn't. I was sitting in my living room for this Skype interview, but I didn't want sarcastic, silly me to get too comfortable and derail a serious discussion.

"Two reasons," I said. "One, I tapped into a universal constant—people worry about their kids. Two, there's urgency now like never before. Our kids confront issues on a daily basis that are potentially fatal. It's not like sneaking a beer at Billy's house anymore. One bad decision and that's it, game over. The stakes are too high, and everyone is looking for ways to help their kids survive."

I was thinking of friends who had already buried their kids, the teens I see each week in recovery, and my own. My eyes scanned the room, studying my kids' pictures: Katie Jo in her ballet costume. A close-up of Danny's tiny baby feet. Ben with his buddies in their baseball uniforms.

One slipup and . . . gone.

"Tell me about your kids," the producer said. I was happy to.

I talked about their integrity. Compassion for others. Their sense of fair play and dedication. Their willingness to come to us with questions and have frank discussions.

"I think they're just old souls in young bodies," I laughed. "Laura and I are pretty blessed."

"Bert," the reporter pressed, "there are millions of parents who would love to know how to end up with kids like that. Can you share some secrets?"

I wasn't prepared for that question. My mind flooded with memories—some hilarious, others beautiful, and several more awful than I care to admit.

Holding our sobbing teenager in the midst of betrayal, loss, and devastation. Our deserted first grader (who didn't believe we'd actually leave her) screaming through tears as she chases the family minivan down the street. Laughing around the campfire. My son sobbing on his birthday over something I'd said. Slamming doors. Badminton championships and gutter-worthy smack talk. Homework battles. Boyfriend and girlfriend drama . . . So many teachable moments and life lessons. So much joy. And pain.

This was a fifteen-minute interview, and I couldn't answer that question in a few seconds. There was too much to say.

"I don't know," I fumbled. "If I could bottle it and sell it, I would."

What you're now holding is the answer I wanted to give. As parents, Laura and I have nailed a lot of stuff . . . and we've failed miserably many times. I'm going to show you the good and the bad—we can learn from both.

At the core, I hope you see God's fingerprints throughout, because when it comes to parenting, none of us can do this without his guidance and grace.

In the next few pages, I'll share the original X-Plan article. God used it to reach millions of parents. If you've read it, feel free to skip ahead. But before we dive in, I want to share something with you.

Although I've spoken on this subject more times than I

can count, there's only one question I've never been asked: "Why the letter X?" I can't decide if that's because it's obvious or no one sees what's there. For me, the X represents three things:

First, at the heart of the X-Plan is that old algebraic unknown: the letter X, that thing we solve for to balance the equation. As parents, the X is the mystery of who each child is meant to become. It's the expression of one's identity, the authentic self, the awesome, peculiar way each of us reflects the image of our creator. Laura and I know our kids are not blank slates where we get to write our own scripts. Rather, each child is a unique unknown waiting to be revealed. And once that authentic self begins to shine through, it unleashes the special ability to stand, fall, and rise again in a world full of pitfalls.

But how do we cultivate that in our kids?

Consider the shape of that X. We see two lines going in different directions that come together in one, distinct point. You are one leg of the X. Your child is the other. Your separate journeys come together in that blazing moment of temporary eternity we call parenthood. At the heart of the X-Plan is the parent-child relationship.

Ultimately, though, I chose the letter X for a specific reason.

X (chi) is the first letter in the Greek word for "Christ." For Laura and me, our relationship with Jesus is the key to our relationships with our children. My kids' only hope of me fathering them well comes through my own healing. My best parenting moments reflect my walk with Christ. My worst moments— and there are many—have bled out from my own brokenness, the dark, fractured places that are yet to be restored. And I'm okay with that admission. It leaves a lot of space for grace, something we all need.

Any time our kids need help, I pray they know they can come to us . . . and that we continue to point them to Jesus with our words and actions.

That's our X-Plan.

X-Plan: Giving Your Kids a Way Out (#xplan)

(As featured on Today Parents, Good Housekeeping, People, Her View From Home, Scary Mommy, Huffington Post, Mamamia, Moms-Everyday, K-LOVE, *and numerous social and news media outlets.)*

FEBRUARY 23, 2017 / BERT FULKS

Friends, as most of you know, I spend an hour each week with a group of young people going through addiction recovery. Yes. Young people. I'm talking teenagers who are locked away for at least six months as they learn to overcome their addictions. I'm always humbled and honored to get this time with these beautiful young souls that have been so wounded by a world they have yet to understand. This also comes with the bittersweet knowledge that these kids still have a fighting chance while several of my friends have already buried their own children.

Recently I asked these kids a simple question: "How many of you have found yourself in situations where things come up that you weren't comfortable with, but you stuck around because you felt like you didn't have a way out?"

They all raised their hands.

Every single one of them.

In the spirit of transparency . . . I get it. Though I'm in my midforties, I'm still in touch with that awkward boy who often felt trapped in the unpredictable currents of teenage experiences. I can't count the times sex, drugs, and alcohol came rushing into my young world. I wasn't ready for any of it, but I didn't know how to escape and, at the same time, not castrate myself socially. I still recall my first time drinking beer at a friend's house in junior high school—I hated it, but I felt cornered. As an adult, that now seems silly, but it was my reality at the time. "Peer pressure" was a frivolous term for an often silent, but very real thing, and I certainly couldn't call my parents and ask them to rescue me. I wasn't supposed to be there in the first place. As a teen, forcing down alcohol seemed a whole lot easier than offering myself up for parental punishment, endless nagging and interrogation, and the potential end of freedom as I knew it.

X-Plan

For these reasons, we have something called the "X-Plan" in our family. This simple but powerful tool is a lifeline that our kids are free to use at any time. Here's how it works.

Let's say that my youngest, Danny, gets dropped off at a party. If anything about the situation makes him uncomfortable, all he has to do is text the letter X to any of us (his mother, me, his older brother or sister). The one who receives the text has a very basic script to follow. Within a few minutes, they call Danny's phone. When he answers, the conversation goes like this:

"Hello?"

"Danny, something's come up and I have to come get you right now."

"What happened?"

"I'll tell you when I get there. Be ready to leave in five minutes. I'm on my way."

At that point, Danny tells his friends that something's happened at home, someone is coming to get him, and he has to leave.

In short, Danny knows he has a way out; at the same time, there's no pressure on him to open himself to any social ridicule. He has the freedom to protect himself while continuing to grow and learn to navigate his world.

———

This is one of the most loving things we've ever given him, and it offers him a sense of security and confidence in a world that tends to beat our young people into submission.

However, there's one critical component to the X-Plan: Once he's been extracted from the trenches, Danny knows that he can tell us as much or as little as he wants . . . but it's completely up to him. The X-Plan comes with the agreement that we will pass no judgments and ask no questions (even if he is ten miles away from where he's supposed to be). This can be a hard thing for some parents (admit it, some of us are complete control freaks), but I promise it might not only save them, it will go a long way in building trust between you and your kid.

(One caveat here is that Danny knows if someone is in danger, he has a moral obligation to speak up for their protection, no matter what it may cost him personally. We teach our kids that we are our brother's keeper, and sometimes we have to stand for those too weak to stand for themselves. Beyond that, he doesn't have to say a word to us. Ever.)

For many of us parents, we lament the intrusion of technology into our relationships. I hate seeing people sit down together at dinner and then proceed to stare into their phones. It drives me nuts when my kids text me from another room in our house. However, cell phones aren't going away, so we need to find ways to use this technology to help our kids in any way we can.

Since first publishing this piece, I've seen a lot of discussion about the pros and cons. Here are some of the questions folks have had:

Does this encourage dishonesty?

Absolutely not. It actually presents an opportunity for you as a parent to teach your kids that they can be honest (something *did* come up, and they *do* have to leave), while learning that it's okay to be guarded in what they reveal to others. They don't owe anyone an explanation the next day, and if asked, can give the honest answer "It's private and I don't want to talk about it." Boom! Another chance for a social skill life lesson from Mom and Dad.

Does this cripple a kid socially instead of teaching them to stand up to others?

I know plenty of adults who struggle to stand up to others. This simply gives your kid a safe way out as you continue to nurture that valuable skill.

What if this becomes habitual?

If you're regularly rescuing your kid, hopefully your family is having some conversations about that.

If you don't talk about it or ask questions, how do they learn?

If you're building a relationship of trust with your kids, they'll probably be the ones to start the conversation. More important, most of these conversations need to take place on the *front* side of events. Ever taken a cruise? They all make you go through the safety briefing in case the boat sinks. They don't wait until the ship's on fire to start telling you about the lifeboats. Talk with your kids. Let them ask questions and give them frank answers.

If they're not where they're supposed to be, shouldn't there be consequences?

Let's be honest. A kid in fear of punishment is a lot less likely to reach out for help when the world comes at them. Admitting they're in over their heads is a pretty big life lesson all by itself. However, don't get so caught up in the details. This isn't a one-size-fits-all scheme. Every parent, every kid, and every situation is unique. What it might look like in your family could be totally different from mine—and that's okay.

I urge you to use some form of our X-Plan in your home. If you honor it, your kids will thank you for it. You never know when something so simple could be the difference between your kid laughing with you at the dinner table or spending six months in a recovery center . . . or (God forbid) something far worse.

At the end of the day, however, the most important thing is that you're having open, honest discussions with your kids. Keep building a relationship of trust. This isn't the same world we grew up in. Our kids face things on a daily basis that—given one bad decision—can be fatal. Don't believe me? I've been to funerals for great kids from awesome families.

Friends, it's a dangerous world. And our kids are out in it every day.

Prayers for strength and compassion to the parents out

there as we all try to figure out this whole parenting gig—it never gets easy.

I beg you to share this piece. Talk about it with your kids. If this somehow gives just one kid a way out of a bad situation, we can all feel privileged to have been a part of that.

#xplan

Blessings, friends.

The Wonderful, Terrifying Climb

I'm on the roof looking down at my eleven-year-old son. Halfway up the ladder, he's frozen.

"Ben, one hand at a time," I tell him again. "One foot at a time. Come on. You can do this."

"Dad, I'm scared!"

He doesn't need to tell me. I see him shaking. His body is pressed into the rungs, hugging them, and his white-knuckled death grip is impossible to ignore.

"Ben," I assure him, "you're almost here. Two more steps and you can touch my hand."

"I'M SCARED!" His cry bounces off the hillside.

I understand—I really do. Now a grown man, I'm still not fond of heights. As a boy, I was terrified just like Ben. Even so, I overcame my fear. That's part of becoming a man, and that's something I need to help my son unravel. I've been afraid for too much of my life, and I refuse to let Ben remain all twisted up, enslaved by fear.

"Son"—I try to sound calm—"look up here."

His eyes find me. They are rimmed with tears.

"You were excited to climb up here and—"

"I'm going back," he says. He takes a timid step down the ladder.

"No"—I become stern—"you're not. You're afraid to go on. I get it. But it's not scary up here. I promise. This ladder is safe. There's no way you'll fall." That sounds convincing to me.

"I don't want to come up anymore, Dad!"

"Okay." I grab my tool bag and start across the roof. "But here's the deal. For the next hour, that's a one-way ladder. It only goes up. You're going to have to decide if you want to climb up and join me or stay right where you are until I'm finished. But if you go back down, you're grounded for two weeks."

"What?" Ben's voice cracks. "That's not fair!"

"Fair or not, that's the way it is."

I walk to the far side of the roof, calling over my shoulder to my son, who is now out of sight, "Stay where you are or take a few more steps. Your call, son."

In this—one of my mishandled moments as a father—I somehow manage to ignore the shards of my own brokenness.

For both father and son, times like these feel like we're performing without a net.

Such is parenting.

PART 1

IT'S NOT ABOUT YOU

The original X-Plan article sparked thousands of comments all across social media. Among them were criticisms like these (paraphrased):

> *"This is a great way to raise kids who can't stand up for themselves and think Mommy and Daddy will just take care of everything."*

> *"Good parents don't need this. You should never let your kid go where you aren't one hundred percent sure they'll be supervised and safe."*

I share these because they highlight two dangerous attitudes toward raising strong kids. The first suggests kids should be left on their own to figure out a confusing, dangerous world. The second waves the banner of control. Both extremes leave kids damaged and lost.

We should always be engaged in our kids' lives, but we've got to give them space to experience life's challenges, make mistakes, and still know they can come to us for support and guidance.

Ultimately, our kids need to know we're in this together.

As you read, you'd do well to not expect a "how-to" book. It's not. I don't have all the answers. And I'm not sorry about that. My kids and I are still traveling our journey. I've learned a lot, but God is still growing me up alongside my kids. My aim is to challenge you as a parent, awaken some things hidden deep within you, and get you to view your relationship with your child from different perspectives. If you're able to do that, you'll benefit . . . and so will your kids.

Keep a journal as you read through the book. Write down your reactions, questions, memories that come up—explore these! Pray about it. I promise, God will move if you're honest and vulnerable. I'll provide some questions before each section to help get you started. However, before setting out, ask God (and keep asking), "Father, what do you want me to see here?" . . . and then open your heart.

QUESTIONS TO X-PLORE

1 Think back to your teen years. What are some things you kept hidden from your parents? Why couldn't you share those things with them? What does that say about your relationship? As a teen, did you believe your parents trusted you? Did you trust them?

2 In his book *Dangerous Wonder*, Mike Yaconelli talks about "dream stealers," adults who crush a child's hopes and passions. Were your parents ever dream stealers (possibly without realizing it)? How has that affected you?

3 How did your parents deal with failure when you were a kid? Did it come with shame? Regret? Punishment? Recall times you screwed up as a kid. How did you feel about it at the time? Now? Did your parents ever (over-) protect you from mistakes or failure? Are you now a risk taker or do you play it safe? How do you feel about that?

4 To what extent did your parents praise your successes as a child? How did it make you feel? Did you learn to chase applause and/or avoid failure? As an adult, do your accomplishments ever come with a dark anxiety that you might not be "good enough" to deserve praise?

5 How will your kids answer these questions in thirty years?

Mom and Dad, questions one through four are important.
Number five is crucial.
Because when it comes to parenting, it's not about you.

CHAPTER 1

Why Trust Matters

To be trusted is a greater compliment than to be loved.
—George MacDonald, *The Marquis of Lossie*

But even after all he did, you
refused to trust the Lord your God.
—Deuteronomy 1:32 (NLT)

Say this with me: "I can't trust my kids."

How's it feel to admit the truth? Does it hurt? It used to destroy me to recognize that cold, harsh reality. My kids know I value few things above honesty, but they still hide the truth from me at times . . . and that might not be their fault.

You want another fun challenge?

Say this one out loud and notice your emotional reaction as the words roll off your tongue: "It's not my child's responsibility to earn my trust."

Feel that knot twisting up in your gut? A bit unsettled by the notion? I hope so, because those emotions are invitations to get to work on your relationship with your kid.

"You want to make it interesting?" I ask.

Danny doesn't need to say a word. The nine-year-old's fiery

eyes tell me he's game. *Bring it on, Dad*, he silently confirms with a single nod. *I'm your huckleberry.*

I reach into my pocket and fish out a crusty penny: ruddy bronze with corrosion eating across Lincoln's face like mold on a corpse. I wish I had a shiny new one—it would be easier to see—but this will do. Plus, it increases the level of difficulty, which always adds to the excitement.

Between my thumb and forefinger, I hold the penny in front of my son's face like a magician about to dazzle his young imagination.

"One shot at a time," I tell him. Danny studies the coin . . . my face . . . and then the coin again. "First one to hit it wins."

I can see him working things out in his head. "And the loser?" he asks.

We're a competitive family. To the victor go the spoils, and losing comes with a cost. I am prepared for his question.

"The loser has to do a lap around the house . . ." The morning sun is climbing high and it's already getting warm—a fine day for baring it all. The birds must know my next line, because they're chatter-laughing before I even finish the sentence. ". . . in nothing but his underwear."

"Oooooh," Danny says as an ambitious grin crawls up his cheeks, reducing his eyes to slits. "You are so on!" *The young gunslinger is filled with foolish vanity, and he's about to be shot down by Wyatt Earp*, I'm thinking. Tempering fantasy is a time-honored task when it comes to parenting, and I'm about to remind the boy why I'm the boss.

We lean our BB guns against the deck rail, and Danny scampers off to the garage to fetch some tape. I consider grabbing the video camera. This might be worth recording. Footage of Danny running around the house nearly naked will be great material for his graduation or wedding reception video. Might come up in therapy someday, too, but I'm hopeful the experience won't damage the boy too much.

Danny returns with the tape and meets me in the yard. The cardboard box we've been shooting for the past hour looks like Swiss cheese. We manage to find a solid spot, Danny hands me a piece of tape, and I secure the penny in place.

"One shot at a time," I remind him as we walk back to the deck. The grass has come in thick this year, and we're two riflemen walking across the prairie. In my mind, I can hear our spurs jangling. "First shot wins. I'll even let you go first."

Danny takes hold of his rifle, pumps it five times, and then leans against the deck rail as he takes aim. *Laura probably won't like this*, I'm thinking, picturing the boy taking his lap of shame in his superhero boxer shorts. *Man, I hope he's wearing The Flash! That will be poet—*

My thought is interrupted by a metallic *PING* that echoes through the entire neighborhood. It's like a bell calling everyone to church . . . or a public hanging. That beautifully awful sound will echo in my brain for eternity.

My son. The one who struggles so much to find his place in the world. The boy who usually avoids risk altogether or gives up too early because—even at nine years old—he's learned to anticipate failure. The very first shot. A solitary BB. He nailed Lincoln right in the head, but unlike John Wilkes Booth, Danny did it from an impressive distance.

"Yes!" My little marksman pumps his rifle into the air, and all I can do is smile. It was an incredible shot, and I couldn't be happier for him. Until he turns and takes aim at me, that is.

"Drop 'em, Dad!"

I suddenly remember a Brian Tracy[*] quote: "The glue that holds all relationships together [. . .] is trust, & trust is based on integrity."

Trust suddenly becomes the topic in my inner dialogue:

Surely I don't have to run around the house in just my underwear to gain my son's trust.

You do if you want to keep it. If Danny can't trust you with the little things, will he be able trust you in the heat of battle, when it really matters?

It's a beautiful day! Everyone's outside—kids playing, people working in their yards, there's a young couple walking their dog. Someone will call the police . . . or think I'm crazy.

Trust me, they'll see it's you and think nothing of it.

"Mom!" Danny yells through the screen door into the kitchen. "Dad has to run—"

I don't give him a chance to draw a larger audience. I throw my shorts down and jump out of them as I yank off my shirt. I leap from the deck and take off in a dead sprint. Arms pumping like a maniacal train gone off the rails, I circle the house. My feet barely touch the ground. As I steam around the corner, my headlights bring into view my oldest son, Ben, and one of his friends standing in front of the garage. They scream and dive out of my path as they cower in terror, arms over their heads.

I clear the steps to the deck in one jump, scoop up my clothes, and disappear into the house. Standing in the kitchen, my hands on my knees as I gasp for breath, I realize I'm not alone.

---

[*]Brian Tracy (@BrianTracy), "The glue that holds all relationships together–including between the leader & the led is trust & trust is based on integrity," Twitter, April 10, 2014, 8:51 a.m., https://twitter.com/briantracy/status/454285587600932867.

"We've been together for over twenty years," I hear Laura say. She's standing at the window that looks out over our front yard. "I had no idea you could run that fast!"

Danny is back on the deck, now laughing as he tells Ben about our BB-gun challenge and his single shot.

Trust demands vulnerability. But it's hard to look like a noble, trustworthy father when you're sucking wind in your underwear.

––––––

Take a moment and consider every shattered relationship in your past. Without knowing any details, I guarantee every story that comes to mind has one thing in common: a loss of trust. Whether or not there is betrayal, when you lose faith in someone's motives and intentions toward you, the relationship can never be the same.

"I don't trust you."

A friend said that to me several years ago, and her words still haunt me. We'd worked in ministry together and fought side by side through several intense spiritual battles. We'd shared more laughs and tears than I could count, so her unsuspected confession landed like a sucker punch.

As she explained her feelings, I felt myself becoming defensive. A couple of years prior, I'd gone through some life changes and pulled away from several organizations and obligations, some of which my friend remained passionate about. However, that wasn't the source of her pain. She was wounded because she felt I hadn't been transparent with her about what was happening in my world. She'd been getting second- and thirdhand information, and the conclusions being drawn weren't kind. Remember the old telephone game? The message gets distorted as it moves through the channels. Same thing here. In hindsight, I could've handled it a lot better, but I'd never said or done anything deliberate that should have caused her to lose faith in me. But that didn't change how she felt—betrayed. In fairness to her, I should've been more intentional in defending our friendship.

Webster's Dictionary defines "trust" as "firm reliance in the honesty, dependability, strength, or character of someone or something" and a "reliance on something in the future: hope."

Trust lost the ability to hold us together, and our friendship fell apart. We occasionally see each other and exchange social pleasantries like strangers on a bus. It's both awkward and painful. I think of her often and pray she's doing well, but I'm quite certain I've lost a friend forever, and we're both the less for it.

———

According to psychologist Erik Erikson, our personalities are shaped through psychosocial developmental stages of conflict resolution. That's a mouthful of jargon that basically means we go through a series of personality conflicts throughout life: struggles like industry versus inferiority and identity versus role confusion. Think of each "conflict" as a linear scale with each possible outcome at opposite ends. How you resolve each conflict shapes your personality, according to Erikson. The person who ends up closer to inferiority than industry is less likely to take risks and try new things; she won't be very industrious (it's the old "not good enough" mentality). However, the person at the extreme of identity will likely be so hardheaded and sure of herself, she'll never accept the challenges of new ideas; she won't risk admitting she might be wrong.

The first conflict we experience as babies, Erikson proposed, is a question of trust versus mistrust. Are the world and the people in it consistent and reliable? If a baby cries when she's hungry, will Mother appear promptly to meet her needs? Our ability to trust is one of the most basic, fundamental elements of who we are as individuals.

When it comes to trust versus mistrust, either extreme is dreadful, and most of us end up somewhere in the middle, risking our hearts with certain people while keeping others at a safe distance. Think of the people you know. Some folks are natural skeptics and can't believe anything without solid proof. Others are dangerously gullible and will fall for anything. Imagine a clown standing beside his 1978 Chevy van at the city park. The windows are heavily tinted. *Free Candy* is spray painted on the sides of the van. Do you want your kids to trust that clown? No way! But you don't want them to live in fear, doubt, and isolation, either. You hope they learn to trust certain people in certain situations. But how do you navigate those murky waters?

Start here: Can your kid trust you? You should always be wrestling with that question as a parent.

> Can your kid trust you? You should always be wrestling with that question as a parent.

Consider your faith in money. You're in a store and pick out a shirt you love—it's perfect! Right size, color, and price. You've got enough cash in your pocket, so you know you can head to the register with confidence, pay for your shirt, and stroll out with no hassle. But what if the value of your money fluctuated each day? A dollar was worth a hundred credits yesterday, but the value plummeted this morning. It might only be worth forty-five . . . or just five credits. You can't be sure you have enough to buy that shirt until the cashier tells you how trustworthy your money is.

Can you imagine the anxiety of every single purchase if you constantly had to wonder if you could trust the value of your own money?

Trust allows us some security in an unpredictable world.

I want my kids to know they can trust me (for their sake and not my own ego). To achieve that, we have to constantly nurture that confidence, because the world is out to destroy it. Trust is always the primary target of evil, and has been since the beginning of time.

———

Imagine the dawn of creation.

Adam and Eve are strolling in the cool of the garden. Foliage so lush it's like a velvet painting. Greens and yellows and oranges and reds. Birds singing as they dart through the trees. A herd of deer is drinking at a crystal stream.

Adam pulls a thick, violet fruit from a vine and bites into it. The juice runs down his chin and onto his chest. Eve smiles as her *ezer kenegdo*—her helper, her intimate life mate—offers her a bite. Brushing her hair from her face, she takes a delicate nibble.

Paradise . . .

God has provided for every need and offered his constant companionship. All of creation belongs to Adam and Eve to explore. They don't know struggle and drudgery, and they get to revel in the adventure of each new day.

And then evil enters the story.

"Hey." A whisper rises from the brush, so soft it could be

the wind or maybe just Eve's imagination. *"If you think that's good, you should try this. It will change . . . eeeeeeverythiiing."*

Eve's gaze follows the voice and lands on a tree so full of fruit, the branches almost touch the ground. Their father has given them the entire world to enjoy, save one thing: a solitary tree, the only boundary placed upon an otherwise limitless existence. Without understanding why, the woman wants it at once, an unknown craving so desperate it hurts. She takes a step toward the tree, but stops. Something deep within her tells her, *NO!* She lingers . . . suddenly unsure . . . confused . . . lost.

"He's lying to you, you know." The voice kisses the dark corners of her mind like a lover's whisper. *"He says you'll die, but that's not true, and you know it, don't you? That is the best thing he created, and he just doesn't want you to have it. But you'll actually be doing him a great kindness, because you won't need his protection anymore. You can unlock everything he's hidden from you so you never have to rely on him again."*

She reaches out and takes hold of a fruit so ripe that her fingers leave indentions. It will be rotten tomorrow.

She hesitates only a moment, and then bites into it— *Quick, before you lose your courage!*

Lies, she thinks as an unexpected bitterness fills her mouth.

Adam stands passively at her side the entire time. He does nothing to defend what will be lost forever.

Trust.

I can't imagine the spell that overcame Adam and Eve. To be in the presence of an evil so timeless and cunning that our minds can't begin to fathom—it must have been torturous. Psychological warfare at its worst.

Most of us know the story of Adam and Eve, Satan, and the fall. We've known it since the earliest days of Sunday school. The story is ingrained into our broader culture, too. But have you ever considered how original sin came to be? Most people point to desire as the linchpin. This is why so many Christians think we need a litany of rules and regulations to keep people in line—*we can't be helped; we're slaves to desire!* Sadly, that attitude has done more harm than good—it's robbed more life than it's given, that's for sure—and it ignores the real crux of what happened to Adam and Eve.

Satan didn't attack them with desire. He struck a more sinister blow by targeting their trust.

If you reduce the fall of man to its most basic element, original sin came through a loss of trust. *"You can't trust him . . . He's lying to you . . . hiding things from you . . . His motives aren't as pure as he would like you to believe."* The entire world belonged to Adam and Eve. God had already provided an answer for every desire they would ever have, and Satan knew it, but if he could just get them to doubt God's motives and intentions . . .

Satan knew if he could plant a seed of mistrust that would grow just a little, it would blow the whole thing apart. It would drive a wedge so deep that Adam's relationship with God would be splintered forever. And he was right. The evil one is old and wise. He knows that an adversary is easy to defeat if he can scatter their forces. In the garden, evil's assault on trust was the entire battle plan, and just like Danny's epic BB-gun victory, it only took one shot. That's how fragile a commodity trust is.

After the fall, no more walks with God in the cool of the day. No more peace. Confidence, shattered. Adam and Eve are left with soul-sucking feelings of isolation, fear, doubt, and anxiety. Just look at what happens next.

God comes walking through the garden, calling out to Adam: "Adam? Adam? Where are you?"

And where is our hero? Hiding in the bushes.

"*I was afraid, so I hid*," he admits to God.

Think for just a moment the psychological truth in that statement. When we are afraid and unsure, when we've lost our confidence in ourselves and others, we hide. Perhaps not always physically, but emotionally and relationally, we certainly do.

This has become part of our wiring since that epic fall.

Notice, however, that God did nothing to betray Adam's trust. He didn't deserve the doubt that was planted in Adam's and Eve's hearts, but their relationship was shattered nonetheless.

Now, Mom and Dad, I ask you: How might your kid be hiding from you?

I know my kids play some things close to the vest. I realize there's a lot they don't share with me (it would be unhealthy if they did). However, I don't want them to hide from me. I don't want them to live with a crippling fear that they're ultimately alone in this world. It's an awful thing for a kid to grow up believing it's them against the world *and* them against their parents. They need to know I have their backs and we're in this together.

They need to be able to trust me.

————

I can remember a time when, as a youngster, I lost some faith in my parents. First let me say that my parents are incredibly loving and caring people. Mom would wear herself ragged trying to care for everyone but herself. I can't count the number of times I saw Dad* hand ten bucks to a homeless guy, no questions asked (and we rarely had ten dollars to spare). However, one incident splintered our relationship, and they never realized it.

To help pay the mortgage, Dad had sectioned off the second floor of our home and turned it (plus the garage) into apartments. One day a young black couple came to see one of the vacant units. They were very nice people, and I remember being mesmerized by their dark skin. (We didn't see many black people in our part of town.) Mom graciously showed them the apartment and chatted as if they would become fast friends. After they'd taken the tour, Mom asked them to write down their names and a phone number.

"I have someone ahead of you who wants it, but if they change their mind, I'll call," she told them.

She was lying, and I knew it. No one else had come to see the apartment.

After they left, I asked Mom why she'd lied to them.

"Honey." She struggled to find the words. "Some of our renters don't like blacks. They'd move out. They pay well, and we can't afford to have them leave."

As an adult, I now understand some of the difficult compromises my parents had to make. I've made more than my share. As a boy, though, the hypocrisy smacked me across the face. Mom had seemed so open and loving with that couple, but had no intention of renting to them. Witnessing that lack of authenticity shook my faith in my parents. Where else were they being less than genuine? What lies had I swallowed? Could

---

*For clarification, my parents split up before I was born. Mom remarried before I turned one. I call both men Dad. However, unless otherwise noted, "Dad" refers to my stepdad.

I trust someone who hides the truth out of convenience and self-protection?

Growing up in the east end of Huntington, West Virginia, I experienced a lot of grown-up moments long before I was ready. I once asked Mom about sex (going to Dad wasn't an option). I suspected how it might go over, so I framed the question as delicately as possible: "Mom, will you tell me about the birds and the bees?"

She blushed, and then hid behind her humor. "Sure!" she said. "The birds go tweet-tweet, and the bees go buzzzzz!"

"Mom! I'm serious."

So was she. She didn't want to talk about it. "You're too young to be thinking about that stuff."

That was the only sex talk I ever received. Everything I wanted to know, I learned on the streets, and I became sexually active at a young age.

Mom and Dad weren't perfect. They made mistakes—fewer than I have as a parent—but they always wanted the best for my siblings and me. I know that. Still, my trust in them eroded over time, and that bond would have come under assault even if they'd done everything right. God never betrayed Adam and Eve's trust, but Satan still sabotaged the relationship with a seed of doubt. These seeds are so easily planted; we have to constantly be on guard to nip them in the bud. Maintaining any relationship requires a constant effort of weed and feed—pluck the invading weeds before they take over, and nurture only what you're trying to grow. It's a constant, exhausting effort, but your enemy isn't taking a break. Neither should you.

I once did a phone interview with Chicago's *Bill and Wendy Show*. Wendy laughed about her relationship with her boys:

"My husband and I told them they could come to us with any questions about sex, drugs, and rock-'n'-roll and we'd shoot it to them straight. I'm kind of regretting that now"—she laughed—"because some of the things they've asked . . ."*

I suspect my smile could be heard across the phone line. "Wendy! God bless you for that!"

Once, during a late-night talk with one of my teenage sons (I'll let you guess which one), the subject came around to sex. I was advising him about respecting women and avoiding situations where he could be accused of some awful things even if he'd done nothing wrong. As we talked, he began to open up, and I felt safe going deeper—I trusted his teenage maturity.

"Son," I said, "I'm not so old or ignorant to not understand the stuff you're facing. Your body is raging with hormones, and it's normal to get aroused. But let me warn you, those hormones can overtake your brain if you let them. You're going to find yourself in situations—there will be kissing and rubbing and heavy breathing—and all of a sudden something you know is a really bad idea is going to seem like a really good idea. Listen to me—it's a bad idea. Trust me. Don't let an erection steal all the blood from your brain. You're not ready to deal with everything that comes with that. Just know that you're normal. It's okay to feel the stuff you feel. But you need to reel it in so it doesn't cause you and someone else a lot of problems. And don't listen to your stupid friends. If you've got questions—*anything*—you come to me and I'll be totally honest with you."

He sat there in awkward silence for quite a while. Finally, he spoke up.

"Dad, I do have one question."

---

*https://wgnradio.com/2017/04/03/bert-fulks-the-x-plan/

"Okay," I said. "Fire away."

"Well, I hear my friends talking about this, and it's kind of embarrassing because I don't know exactly what it is. I think I know, but I'm not sure."

Honestly, I was expecting something about girls getting their period.

"Well . . ." He fumbled for the words.

"Just ask," I reassured him.

He briefly looked me in the eye, then looked down. He was on the precipice. Could he trust me with his own vulnerability? Finally, he took a leap of faith.

"What's a blow job?"

Laura will tell you that I handle uncomfortable situations with humor. Like Adam behind his fig leaf, witty sarcasm is where I hide, and into the bushes I ran.

"Son," I said with a smile, "I've been married for almost twenty years. I don't remember."

The birds go tweet-tweet and the bees go buzzzzz!

I couldn't do that to my son. As uncomfortable as it was, we talked about it, and I explained it to him. I gave him space to ask more questions—he did—and was glad to see that he felt safe enough to ask them, and he trusted my answers.

———

Like Adam in the garden, too many kids learn to hide from their parents. Too often they don't trust their parents' words or motives.

Don't let that be your kid. Not for your sake, but theirs. The world is scary enough without feeling like they have to hide from you, too. They need to have the confidence they can reach out to you at any time with anything. That kind of trust is delicate and you have to defend it every chance you get. Remember, the world is constantly trying to damage that trust. You don't even have to do anything to lose it. You can just stand by like Adam did, and it will all be lost before you realize it.

I'm not talking about giving your child everything they want so they'll like you. I have a lot of people I like very much and enjoy hanging out with them, but there's no way I'd ever trust them with some of my heart's fragile places. George MacDonald writes, "To be trusted is a greater compliment than to be loved." Indeed. There are times my kids loathe the sight of me. There have been times they've been so upset with me that I need a coat and mittens to survive the icy environment. The other night Katie Jo and I were laughing about what we now call her *I hate Dad* phase. But I believe my kids all know deep down that my number one concern is always their well-being. Even when I'm wrong in my methods and judgments (which happens often), I pray they trust my motives.

To build that kind of trust with your kid, you need to constantly question your motives. I pulled out one of my old developmental psychology books from college and came across this quote: "Trust depends on the parents' own confidence, on their sense that they are doing things right."* In other words, kids are very intuitive. They sense weakness, pettiness, and warped motives. It's like vomit in a pool, and they'll swim away from it as fast as they can. If you want your kid to trust you, you've got to be strong and confident in your pursuit of their hearts. When your strength is authentic, you can allow yourself to become

---

*William Crain, *Theories of Development* (Englewood Cliffs, NJ: Prentice Hall, 1992).

vulnerable to their questions, no matter how uncomfortable and confusing they might be.

When I published the X-Plan article, it wasn't a success because it reached millions of readers. For me, the accomplishment came from so many parents having open, honest, uncomfortable conversations with their kids. Relationships were strengthened as parents reached out for their kids, telling them, "I want you to know that I've got your back, no matter what." That gives a kid a ton of confidence to find their place in the world. It builds trust. And any time you can advance your forces on that battlefield, evil—and its intent toward your kid—is defeated.

I know some of you would be horrified to have been in my shoes for the oral sex question. I also know many of you would have handled it completely differently. That's okay. The important question to ask is, "Does my kid trust me enough to come to me with that question?" Some parents have told me, "I just don't have that kind of relationship with my kid." I suggest you work on that.

Laura and I once knew a young lady who'd landed in trouble. She came to us instead of her parents. We were glad to help, but sorry she couldn't go to her parents. They're great people, but they would have dished out a heavy dose of reprimand and *I told you so* in a situation that had already delivered its own punishment and life lesson. This young lady couldn't endure any more, so she hid from her parents.

Rule number one in teacher training is "You're not an encyclopedia, so don't act like it." If you want to lose your kid's trust, act like you know it all. Little kids might buy it, but not for long. No one has all the answers, and when people around us act like they do, our BS alarms begin to sound.

Your kids are going to have runs-ins and questions about things you have no experience with. Realize that. Don't fake it. It's okay to say, "I don't know," and then work to figure it out together. I'd rather my kids find out early that *Dad doesn't know everything* and still come to me rather than hide from me because *Dad doesn't know everything, but fakes it and acts like he does and makes me feel like an idiot.*

> Your kids are going to have runs-ins and questions about things you have no experience with. Realize that. Don't fake it. It's okay to say, "I don't know," and then work to figure it out together.

There's a powerful scene toward the end of the movie *The Last of the Mohicans* (1992). In the midst of the French and Indian War, Alice Munro, youngest sister to the tale's heroine, has been taken captive by Magua, the leader of a Huron tribe. Moving along a cliff, Alice finds herself standing on the edge, hundreds of feet above jagged rocks and a churning river. Magua reaches for her, motioning for her to step away from the ledge, to come to him, to safety. Alice hesitates only a moment as she looks deep into Magua's eyes, searching. A haunting expression on her face reveals that she can't trust the man or his intent. Alice steps off the cliff and falls to her death.

Alice had an immediate choice—certain death or a chance for survival (though likely a painful one). It seems to be part of our nature to choose the devil we're sure of rather than one we can't trust. Just like Alice, we will choose deadly, destructive paths over the ones we've lost faith in. We hate uncertainty, and in our sinful quest for control, we avoid it, even to the point of death. When kids can't trust the person reaching for them, they sometimes step off some tall cliffs.

Danny recently blindsided us with deceit. He'd done something stupid and hidden it from us. Naturally, our trust in him took a hit, so we have to work that much harder to strengthen his trust in us. Just like God, who keeps pursuing us even when we're not faithful, we have to keep pursuing our son's heart.

Too many times we worry about being able to trust our kids.

Friends, turn that around. How much can your kids trust you?

CHAPTER 2

The Way They Should Go

*Like no one else, parents can unlock the door to a child's
uncommonness. As parents, we accelerate or stifle, release
or repress our children's giftedness. They will spend much
of life benefiting or recovering from our influence.*
—Max Lucado, *Cure for the Common Life*

Let's have some fun. Write down all of your hopes and dreams
for each of your kids on a piece of paper. If your imagination
serves up specific details, include those.

Now, go outside with your paper, strike a match, and burn
that sucker to ashes.

Friends, one of the most common ways we damage our
kids comes through our misguided desires for their lives. This is
also why so many parents become disconnected from their kids.

I recently had a young man tell me how his father would
beat him if he found the boy watching kids' shows like *Barney*.

"He thought it would turn me gay," he said with a
heart-numbing shrug.

Though most of us cringe at the thought of hurting our
kids, probably all of us inflict deep wounds with foolish desires
wrapped up in good intentions.

———

A friend said to me during a recent election season, "Social media has plundered almost all of my friendships. I used to be able to pass people on the street, stop and say hello, and feel good about the interaction. But now, thanks to Facebook, I know what people really think. I see their stupidity, and I just can't like them anymore."

I laughed, but I get it. I was once an intellectual elitist and had a problem with morons who struggled to get a D in high school history having a vote equal to mine. I taught world history, economics, psychology, sociology, geography, politics . . . I could debate the faulty precepts of Keynesian economics, and yet my vote was canceled out every election by some knucklehead.

If you don't have a college education and read a minimum of eighteen books a year, then you shouldn't get to vote, I'd think. *Sorry. Not sorry. I'm tired of the village idiot having an equal say to Stephen Hawking or Maya Angelou.*

And then God gave me Danny, leaving no doubt that our Father has a loving sense of humor . . . and the grace to reveal my own stupidity.

Laura and I were both A+ honors students, so I expected our combined DNA would only produce academic overachievers.

First we had Ben. Wild and energetic, but a hardworking people pleaser. Straight-A student. Holding his own at a private college as a student athlete on both academic and baseball scholarships. He can throw out a speedster trying to steal second base or debate the socioeconomic underpinnings of Beethoven's Third in comparison to Springsteen's *Jungleland*. Ben is a Renaissance man.

Katie Jo came next. I don't even understand her intelligence. She digests books like popcorn, handfuls at a time. If her teachers don't challenge her, she gets bored and agitated. Now a senior in high school, she's receiving invitations from elite universities, urging her to apply.

Meanwhile, Danny is in the garage with a hatchet and two logs trying to construct a homemade crossbow. He'll probably lose a finger. I'm now thinking of the time he came limping across the road from his cousins' house with blood streaming down his leg. They'd had a knife-throwing contest and Danny had somehow managed to throw the knife into his own leg.

The kid is not what I'd expected. He radiates what Max Lucado refers to as "uncommonness," and that's how Danny's intelligence and giftedness shine.

————

"Danny," I said to my son, "you'd be stupid to go to college."

I never thought I'd say that, but God continues to grow and change me.

When she'd learned that he was joining the high school vocational-technical program, Danny's girlfriend tried to shame him. She'd even told him she couldn't be with someone who didn't have the education to make a lot of money. Danny had taken that to heart.

"Maybe I want to go to college," Danny argued, but Laura and I knew he was being motivated by two of man's biggest pitfalls: women and money.

"Danny," Laura said in her mothering tone, "honey, you hate to read. Studying for a test is misery for you. You put off assignments until the very last minute. It's okay if academics aren't your thing. But you've got to realize you'd hate college—it's all the things you despise."

Danny's path might one day lead him back to college, but that's not where he's headed now. He's passionate about mechanics, how things work. Since he was a baby figuring out how to drop the side of his crib and open cabinet child locks, Danny has always been the kid who takes things apart and reassembles them. Give him a set of tools, some spare lawn mower parts, a glue gun, and a roll of duct tape, then just stand back and watch the magic happen. Danny will dream up a machine that will trim your beard, make margaritas, and walk your dog all at the same time.

I write that jokingly, but he truly amazes me with his mechanical mind. His ability to see beyond what something is supposed to do and imagine what it *might* be able to do is a rare gift, and one we have to nurture.

It's a shocking about-face for me to admit this, but it would be foolish to push him toward college prep work. As a loving father, why would I push the anxiety of becoming something he's not made to be upon my own child? That would only damage him.

Laura and I toured our local vo-tech facility with Danny. We left with a sense of not only peace, but excitement that we'd never expected. We knew Danny was gifted with a mechanical mind, but watching him on that tour—interacting with the other students, talking with the instructors about electrical engineering and auto mechanics—we saw a spark of life in our son. It all excited his young heart.

———

One of my favorite Biblical examples of typical parenting is how Jesse fathers his young son David.

Jesse's older boys are away from home, fighting in King

Saul's army. Concerned for his sons, Jesse sends David to check on his brothers.

"Take them some food, find out how they're doing, then get back to the fields where you belong," Jesse tells David. *"There are sheep to tend, and you're going to be a shepherd, boy."*

Can you imagine if Jesse would have had his way?

Never in Jesse's wildest dreams would young David defeat a giant. David was made to be a shepherd, Jesse assumed. However, God had made the boy for something else: he was to become a warrior king—perhaps the greatest of all kings.

Jesse failed to see the greatness in his own son because it didn't fit the story line he was trying to write for the boy. Too often we do the same to our children.

***

It was a Sunday afternoon when Laura's uncle Jim called.

"Bert," he said, "does Ben have any interest in playing baseball? I'm helping the guy in charge of minor league this year, and I wondered why Ben isn't signed up."

It took everything I had to not make a snarky comment about my loathing for baseball. My most endearing memory of baseball from my own childhood was my brother busting me in the face with a fastball and me falling into a rosebush. I'm still not sure what hurt the most: the busted lip, the thorns ripping my flesh, or the suspicion he'd done it on purpose (I was often the target of his pranks). Anyway, I grew up hating baseball, mostly because I was afraid of the ball. With the memory of a wounded animal, baseball represented only pain and humiliation for me.

"Who was on the phone?" Laura asked after I hung up.

"Jim," I scoffed, "wanting to know if Ben wants to play baseball."

"Well, does he?"

I didn't reply. I didn't have an answer. I'd never asked Ben. He'd tried basketball, soccer, gymnastics, and football, but I'd never offered to sign him up for baseball. It wasn't part of the petty script I was writing.

I'll never forget Laura walking into Ben's bedroom and asking if he wanted to give baseball a shot. Meanwhile, a silent scream—*NOOOOOOOO!*—erupted inside of me as visions of busted lips and shredded skin tortured my brain. I hated baseball.

He said, "Sure!" and the terrified boy inside of me sobbed. Honest to God, I was overcome with dread.

A month later, Ben was playing baseball, I was soon roped into coaching, and our family's journey took a course I could have never charted. We are now a baseball family. I went on to coach Little League, All-Stars, Babe Ruth, and a state tournament team. We plan vacations around the sport and buy Cincinnati Reds ticket packages. Baseball has brought more life to our family than I ever thought possible, all because it's part of our son's DNA—an integral part of who he is. If I'd had my way, however, I would have robbed him (and us) of that gift.

––––––––

In Psalm 127:4, God hands us a tremendous parenting tip, and most of us miss the heart of the message. We're told that children are "arrows in the hands of a mighty warrior" (NIV).

Think of an arrow. When that verse was penned, an arrow was simply a wooden stick.

God's word says your children are like arrows. But they're not so simple.

How an arrow flies depends on how it's been shaped, the type of arrowhead and fletchings, and where the arrow is aimed. Ultimately, however, the type of wood is critical. Two nearly identical arrows will fly differently if one is made from balsa and the other from hickory. It's the same with people. God has made us all from different spiritual stuff because we each have a different purpose and a unique flight path.

In 1 Corinthians 12, Paul talks about the unique gifts of the Spirit. He compares these gifts to various parts of the human body. In the grand scheme, each part has a specific job, and when it functions as designed, the whole body benefits. However, if the brain is thrust into the role of the heart, the body dies. If one part suffers, the whole body suffers. It's the same with our kids and the overall health of the family. We have to help each of them discover the unique part they're supposed to play, and that is often beyond our own expectations and desires.

> One of the greatest acts of faith is accepting that God has placed your child here for a specific reason, and the life they are meant to lead may not be what you have in mind.

I can't expect Ben, Katie, or Danny to be like me, their mother, or one another. They were each made differently. One of the greatest acts of faith is accepting that God has placed your child here for a specific reason, and the life they are meant to lead may not be what you have in mind.

Scripture confirms this in Proverbs 22:6. "Train up a child in the way he should go and when he is old, he will not depart from it" (KJV). A key phrase is *the way he should go*. Notice it doesn't say, "the way you think they should go" or "the way you would have them go." We are commanded by Scripture to actively pursue what each child is made for and then nurture those gifts and encourage those paths, no matter how much it breaks the mold we've designed for them.

We recently spent our kids' spring break touring colleges as Katie Jo decides her future. I'll be honest: it's a challenge for me. I have a friend who received a grant to study the mathematics of black hole development (I wonder if she's sickened by the thought of my vote being equal to hers). I'm pretty sure my Katie Jo carries as much intelligence as that gal. Katie is smart enough to be a biochemical engineer. I suspect she could create life with a math equation. She might be able to cure cancer. But she wants to dance and sing and act. We spent a week visiting colleges for the performing arts, weighing the best programs that will fit her needs. I feel like I'm watching Einstein audition for an ensemble role in community theater . . . and I couldn't be more proud of my daughter. She's following her passion. Katie Jo comes alive when she talks about theater and dance. For her birthday, we took her to see *Hamilton*, and you would have thought we'd given her a key to the universe.

One might argue, *If her IQ is part of her spiritual gifting, it would be foolish to squander it on performing arts.* A part of me still wrestles with that notion. However, I've got to give God some space to reveal where and how he wants to use my daughter's gifts. How do I know it's not onstage? Or maybe theater isn't the destination, but a critical part of her journey, her flight path.

But what if this is all just a silly distraction from her true calling?

Father, how do I aim my daughter toward the target you've set for her?

I constantly ask those questions. But more important, I listen for his answer.

———————

In high school I won the accounting award for my work in an honors business program (I know, nerd alert). That directed me toward a free ride to Marshall University's College of Business. However, after a few semesters, I was bored out of my skull. My business classes felt like running on a treadmill in a dark room—endless drudgery with no scenery. Meanwhile, Dr. Palmer's Western Civilization class was rocking my world. At the same time, Laura and I were working with our church youth group, and I loved it. Those two things gave me enthusiasm I just couldn't get from accounting, marketing, and management classes.

Was God using my passions to draw me toward his path?

Enthusiasm.

In his book *Primal*, Mark Batterson writes, "Those who follow in the footsteps of Christ ought to be the most passionate people on the planet. The word *enthusiasm* comes from a combination of two Greek words: *en* and *Theos*. It means 'in God.' And the more you get into God, the more passionate you become."[*]

God calls us all into life, friends, and his voice echoes in the things that make us come alive.

In a moment of sheer madness, I transferred out of business

———————

[*]Mark Batterson, *Primal: A Quest for the Lost Soul of Christianity* (Colorado Springs, CO: Multnomah Books, 2009).

and into a comprehensive social science education program. I was going to be a man of letters, teach social studies, and spend my life working with kids. To this day, I still feel the vitality that came with that decision. I felt like an explorer as his ship pulls away from the dock—anxious for what might be out there, yet fully aware I was made for this adventure.

"Honey," my mother said when she learned what I'd done, "why would you do that? You're so smart. You can do anything. You could be a doctor. Anyone can be a teacher."

I'll never forget the sting of her words. They were well-intentioned, but they drove a wedge between us. In her defense, she spoke out of love and concern—she wanted the best for me—but she failed to realize what made my heart come alive and for what I was made. What she was saying was, *I want you to reach your fullest potential*, but what I heard was, *If you become a teacher, you'll be a disappointment.* Friends, don't let your kids hear that message—you'll regret it, and so will they.

Arrows are made to fly. Period. End of story. And they never reach their potential until they are fully released.

Moms and dads everywhere, hear me. Give up on control. It's not about you. It's not about what you did or didn't have growing up. Not about your hopes and dreams. Your kid is a unique individual made with something irreplaceable, and your job is to help him realize what that is and release him onto his path. Even

Give up on control. It's not about you. It's not about what you did or didn't have growing up. Not about your hopes and dreams. Your kid is a unique individual made with something irreplaceable, and your job is to help him realize what that is and release him onto his path.

when that goes against everything you think you know, you have to trust that God has placed within your care something sacred that isn't yours to control.

Think of how many times in the Bible a kid has to leave home to realize his destiny. Moses is sent down the river in a basket. Joseph is sold into slavery. David goes off and defeats a giant with a slingshot. Jesus goes missing and is found teaching adults in the temple.

To be clear, I'm not talking about hands-off parenting and leaving kids to find their own way. Remember, they're arrows. If you don't help shape and point them in a particular direction, someone else will. However, if you're petty, shortsighted, and shackled by your own broken desires, they will suffer. I'm praying you're not any of those things. Hopefully you're considering your child's unique journey and your role in supporting that.

If you've never shot an arrow, let me clue you in on the process. The archer must know if the arrow is constructed of fir, maple, or cedar—they all fly differently. That will affect how the arrow is aimed—high with a falling arc or straight ahead. You have to compensate for variables such as changing winds, temperature, and obstacles. You also have to be strong and steady, or else you risk sending your arrow onto a deadly path. Finally, you have to let go. I say again . . . You. Must. Let. Go. In the early stages, this is from a short distance. Send them off and see what happens. How successful was the flight?

Danny and I shoot at bales of straw stacked in front of a block wall. Sometimes a poorly aimed arrow misses the target and hits the wall. It always ends up broken. Take that to heart as you think about both your aim and the target. Forcing your kid into a direction they weren't made to travel could damage them beyond repair.

Parenting is about perfecting your archery skills: letting that thing fly, knowing when to retrieve it when it misses the mark, figuring out what went wrong, making adjustments, correcting your aim, and then—if you get it right—increasing the distance.

After Ben's first semester of college, he was overwhelmed. He was homesick, unsure of himself, and terrified of what another semester would be like. He didn't want to go back. In a moment of emotional pleading, Laura and I almost caved in. I held my young man in my arms and we shared some tears. Voices in my head cried, *Bring the boy home!* but I couldn't do that to him. I wanted him home, to be sure. I missed him something awful. But I knew Ben was on the right path, and the fear of the unknown—those lonely times of flight when anything could happen—are part of growing up and realizing who and what you are.

"Son," I said to him, "you've got this. You're stronger than you think you are, and you're going to be okay. I promise." With that, I released him and let him fly back into the world. It was one of the most painful things I've ever done, but one of my best parenting moments. It came from a place of strength, intentionally focused on my son finding his place in the world. I'd done all I could do up to that point. I'd honed him, sharpened him, and directed him as best I knew how, but he would never reach his destined target if I didn't let him go. A year later, Laura and I found ourselves marveling at the man Ben had become in such a short amount of time. Had we given in to our fears and retrieved him midflight, we would have crippled him forever and denied him what has become a beautiful flight path.

Friends, you have two pretty big road signs when it comes to finding your place in the world. One is your natural gifting. Some folks are good with their hands; some are intellectuals, some musicians, while others have a knack for working with people. We're quick to figure out what we suck at, but we sometimes lose sight of what we're really good at—what natural talents we've been given. If you can figure that out, you've got one arm of the goalpost.

Next, what makes your heart come alive? What are you passionate about?

Most of us waste a lifetime lamenting the paths we never took. We call it sacrifice and commend ourselves for abandoning our passions, but it's really more about fear—a lack of courage to risk following our hearts. We chalk it up to growing up and accepting responsibilities, and then we think we're doing our kids a favor by forcing that mentality upon them. I see too many parents demanding their kids just "grow up!" Meanwhile, Jesus is saying, *You won't find life until you become like children.*

> Too often we ask God to bless our children instead of seeking out how he already has.

Too often we ask God to bless our children instead of seeking out how he already has.

Jeremiah 29:11 tells us that God has a plan for us. This verse evokes an array of emotional responses in me—from hope to despair to bitterness. I'll be honest, very little of my life has felt like a well-ordered plan of divine purpose. I have a buddy who says life is little more than a series of regretful events that lead you to say, *I'll never do that again!* For most of us, that packs a lot of truth. When I look back on my story, it's the screwups, the betrayals, and the missed opportunities that steal most of the spotlight.

But what if we change the question from *Where did you screw up?* to *When did you experience true joy?*

Let's revisit Proverbs 22:6. *Train up a child in the way he should go . . .*

Great advice. Unfortunately, much is lost in translation.

Train up? I trained my dogs to sit, stay, and come. I can tell our retriever, Cleveland, to "Go get the ball!" and he'll disappear on a mad hunt and won't return until he's found a tennis ball. The Bible—the quintessential parenting book—reveals raising kids to be as simple as training dogs: just teach them to follow commands and meet your expectations, and they'll be okay.

Yes, that's sarcasm.

The philosopher John Locke once suggested that each child is a *tabula rasa*: a blank slate that enters the world ready for its destiny to be prescribed by others. Too many parents worship at the altar of this notion, believing they can mold their kids into whoever they want them to be. However, *tabula rasa* parenting is in direct conflict with Jeremiah 29:11, Proverbs 22:6, and the X-Plan.

I once worked with a teacher who had a crazy educational philosophy: "Kids come into the world equipped with everything they're meant to have," she would say. "It's not our job to crack open their skulls and dump in a bunch of rules and information. That's brutality. Education should be a process of drawing out something that's buried deep inside—and that's different for each kid."

Jeremiah 29:11 tells us we've each come into this world

for a purpose—we're actually made for something. Sadly, that divine spark gets buried beneath the rubble of misunderstanding that comes with Proverbs 22:6—kids just need to be trained.

. . . and Jesus wept.

In *Cure for the Common Life*, Max Lucado blows apart the whole warped notion of how adults should "train up" children. In the original text, the root word for "train up" reveals how most of us have screwed this up and failed our kids in the process. "To train up," Lucado writes, "means to awaken thirst."* We're not training and domesticating wild animals. We're supposed to be helping our kids figure out their unique talents and passions—the things they were made for, the things that make them come alive!

> We're supposed to be helping our kids figure out their unique talents and passions—the things they were made for, the things that make them come alive!

Can you imagine how different your life might be if someone had done that for you?

Very few of us had that blessing. Most of us were just taught to survive, play the game, and achieve some socially prescribed definition of success. Good glory, no wonder so many people feel lost, disillusioned, and bitter (and are slaves to peer pressure, starving for validation).

Danny once had to listen to me harangue him about a disaster in the garage. He'd cut apart a ride-on toy, taken some

---

*Max Lucado, *Cure for the Common Life: Living in Your Sweet Spot* (Nashville, TN: Thomas Nelson, 2005).

scooter parts, and, along with some old plywood, created some kind of Frankenstein-monster-death-trap-machine that he wanted to race down our hill. The only possible outcome was a trip to the emergency room and a lawsuit from the neighbors.

"Danny . . . son," I lamented, "what were you thinking?" (I've asked him that question many times over the years.)

"Dad," he replied with all the dignity he could muster, "I had a plan. It just didn't work out. Sometimes you try things that don't work out."

Laura was biting the insides of her cheeks, trying not to laugh. She'd seen plenty of my screwups. A part of me wanted to laugh as well, but in that moment, something in Danny's words pierced my heart.

I'd quit taking chances. I'd abandoned the risky search for what my life's plan (not *my* plan, but *the* plan) might actually be. I'd reduced my life to meeting expectations, playing it safe, hoping for approval . . . and slowly dying inside. Colin Hay's song, "Waiting for My Real Life to Begin," began playing in my mind, a song about holding back, hiding, and completely missing life's beautiful adventure. The worst part was how I'd also been suffocating my son's heart instead of helping him unearth and harness his unique gifting.

I can now look back and help Danny recognize his unique abilities and joyous moments. I should be trying to awaken my son's deep thirst and directing his gifting so he can learn to live out of his heart (without killing himself or anyone else in the process).

In a family of college folk, Danny is headed into vocational-technical training, and I'm excited for my son's journey. Unlike most adults, he's got a clue about what he's good at and what brings him joy. He's discovering the plan for his life. And that will provide him great strength.

Revisiting your own life story will reveal your heart's purpose and path. It's never too late to rediscover who you were made to be. And the best trail marker is the answer to the question, *What's something you do well that makes your heart come alive?*

> It's never too late to rediscover who you were made to be. And the best trail marker is the answer to the question, *What's something you do well that makes your heart come alive?*

When you can marry your talents with your passions, you'll have lightning in a bottle, and you'll illuminate the plan for your life. Don't dismiss anything as trivial or stupid. Maybe a part of your life's purpose is cooking. That doesn't mean you need to open a restaurant to fulfill your destiny. If you just press into that gifting and let yourself be lost in the joy of it, you'll be amazed at how life can be unleashed (for you and the people orbiting your world).

If we can do this now as adults and recapture even a flicker of life, think what it could mean for our world if we help our kids on their journeys, long before they're as lost, afraid, angry, and confused.

Looking back on your own journey, can you see where your life remains unfulfilled because you failed to recognize both goalposts (your talents and desires)? Both are crucial to finding the space in between, the sweet spot for your life. Pick only one and you've got less than a 50 percent chance of scoring. Pick them both and aim for the middle, and you've got a fighting chance to find your destiny.

Until we're in the grave, I believe we all have a chance to re-direct our lives onto the path we were meant to follow. My kids see me in my forties, still writing every day, following my heart with my humble talents. I hope it encourages them to never give up. At the same time, I'm trying to help each of them realize their goalposts and aim for the middle with everything they've got. I can't score for them from the sideline. All I can do is coach them up, celebrate with them when they succeed, and comfort them when they miss their target.

They are arrows.

Train up a child in the way he should go . . .

What's something you do well that makes your heart come alive?

Too often we ignore this question and ask instead what the world expects of us. As Howard Thurman says, "Don't ask yourself what the world needs. Ask yourself what makes you come alive, and go do that, because what the world needs is people who have come alive."*

Rich Mullins, the contemporary Christian artist, once said that he hoped he could be an arrow that points other people to God. Indeed.

Father, I pray you help me point my children in the ways they should go.

That's core to X-Plan parenting.

---

*As quoted by Gil Bailie, *Violence Unveiled: Humanity at the Crossroads* (New York: Crossroad, 1996).

CHAPTER 3

Love Them Enough to Let Them Fail

Winners are not afraid of losing. But losers are.
Failure is part of the process of success.
—Robert T. Kiyosaki

You build on failure. You use it as a stepping-stone.
—Johnny Cash

There's a deep part of me that celebrates when my children struggle and fail.

I suspect that comes from someplace holy.

A veteran teacher once told me a heartbreaking story.

Polly Parent calls the school to speak with Mr. Denton, her daughter's math teacher. The secretary takes a message, assuring the agitated mother that, yes, Mr. Denton will receive the message, and yes, he will call today.

He returns the call, but without the world's-on-fire urgency Polly demanded. He knows what this is about.

"Mr. Denton," Polly says, "my daughter is a straight-A student. She has always been a straight-A student. But on her report card, you gave her a B. I am assuming that is a mistake."

"No, ma'am," Mr. Denton assures her. "No mistake. Polly-anna earned a B in my class."

For the next half hour, the teacher listens to Polly Parent vacillate between praising her daughter's excellence and making thinly veiled accusations about what a hard-hearted hack of an educator he must be. Mr. Denton explains Pollyanna's grades and describes what Pollyanna can do to earn that coveted A and become a better student.

"Pollyanna's a great kid," Mr. Denton assures the mother, "but she's not an A student in my class. I know she plans to go to college, and it's my job to help prepare her for that. Giving her a grade she hasn't earned doesn't help her."

After a moment of silence, Polly Parent hits the rewind button and pushes play again.

"Pollyanna is a straight-A student . . ."

After some time, the embattled teacher sees this conversation going nowhere and offers a solution.

"I tell you what," he says, "I'll change the grade, and make sure she gets an A for the rest of the year . . . but only on one condition."

Polly Parent's silence answers for her: *And that is . . . ?*

"The condition is I never hear from you again, and your daughter never sets foot in my classroom again, because you clearly care more about that grade than your daughter's education."

I laughed when I first heard this story.

"Did you get in trouble for that?" I asked him.

"Oh yeah," he said with a grin. "I landed in the principal's office for that one." He shook his head, rolling his eyes. "Mom got her daughter's schedule changed, and she ended up in somebody else's math class. But"—he lifted a sharp finger—"Mom didn't do that kid any favors."

Early in my teaching career, I had a student in my world history class who absolutely drove me nuts. Alan had a black-and-white, categorical mind. In my classes, however, I didn't teach history as facts to memorize, but events to interpret. I challenged my students to think. I didn't lecture for hours about the French Revolution. Instead, I gave them letters and documents from that time period and had them figure out what was going on. I wanted my students to actually *do* history, not just regurgitate names and dates.

Alan wanted nothing to do with it. For an entire school year, I had to endure his complaints (although, to his credit, he remained respectful). He just couldn't understand why I was asking them to read and think instead of just having them memorize the usual stuff in the textbook. I had two meetings with his parents that year. They, too, were frustrated. Alan didn't have as high of a grade in my class as he was earning in his other classes. However, they were at least willing to trust (or tolerate) me and my methods. They voiced their concerns, but ultimately agreed that Alan had to learn to face new challenges in life . . . and my class was one of those hills to climb.

A few years later, I bumped into Alan and we had a great time catching up.

"Fulks," he said, "when I went to college, my very first history class was nothing but reading and deciphering primary sources. Everyone in that class struggled." He smiled like Sylvester the Cat with a mouthful of Tweety Bird. "Everyone but me." He pumped his fists and laughed. "Yes, I got this!"

I wanted to hug the young man. Not for my sake, but his . . . and his parents'.

"Man, I fought you so much on that stuff, but you really prepared me for college."

I wonder if Polly Parent's kid ever got to say that to one of her teachers. I doubt it, because Polly overprotected her daughter from challenges and possible failure (as if that B—

above average—were a mark of failure and shame). The Polly Parents of the world want their kids' trophies on the shelf and pictures on the wall so they can brag when company arrives. However, when truly challenged, those kids often end up suffering a life of performance anxiety and mediocrity (the very thing Polly Parent forbids). Meanwhile, parents like Alan's let their kids slog through some discomfort and confusion, experience what it's like to get punched in the mouth and get back up off the mat. Alan and I came to intellectual and psychological blows many times over the course of that year, throughout which his parents supported him, but didn't extract him from the trenches or fight the battle for him.

Alan's now a successful architect and urban planner. I'm certainly not tooting my horn or taking credit for that; I'm just happy for a young man who now makes his living by constantly taking on new, creative challenges. Alan had some pretty cool parents who let him learn to live in a world that doesn't bend to his every whim and desire. They loved him, and they proved it by letting him wrestle with frustration and possible failure.

———

A few weeks ago, Danny was in the garage with some construction paper, duct tape, and cardboard. Against my better judgment, I asked what he was doing.

"I have some engine cartridges left over from my model rocket kit," he said. "I'm going to design and build my own rocket and try to launch it."

There was no way this could end well. A part of me suspected Danny would end up blowing his face off and/or burning down someone's house. For a moment, I thought of telling him, *No. Clean up that nonsense.* Or pushing him away and taking charge. *Let me show you how do to that.* However, I resisted every ounce of logic and parental yearning for control, and I let him go.

About an hour later he called us all out to the backyard, where he had constructed a launch platform. His homemade rocket was perched and ready. Danny had fashioned a piece of poster board into the shape of a rocket. He'd scrawled *EXPLORER 1* down the side of the fuselage. The fact he'd named it *EXPLORER 1* told me that Danny anticipated the rocket's fate would require other attempts. He was hopeful, but was also prepared to head back to the drawing board if (when) this launch failed. A pair of wires stretched across the yard to a sparking device that Danny would use to ignite the engine.

"Okay!" he yelled from the yard. "Ready?"

We watched from the deck, a safe distance away from the likely explosion or impaling. Danny was a bit closer to the danger zone, but as parents, we sometimes have to give Darwinism a chance to function for the greater good of mankind.

"Mom, will you video this?" Danny asked. Of course, Laura already had her phone in hand to record the coming disaster. I wondered if Child Protective Services might use her video as evidence mounted against us.

"Here we go! The official launch of Explorer One!" Danny then began the countdown. "Ten! Nine! Eight . . ." His enthusiasm was infectious. He finally made it to "one" and then bellowed, "BLASTOFF!" I held my breath as Danny pushed the red control button. A tiny spark and a puff of smoke belched from the rocket's base. And then . . . nothing.

He'd failed. It didn't work. *EXPLORER 1* stood in defiance on the launch platform beneath the cruel, blazing sun in monumental mockery of Danny's hopes, dreams, and best efforts.

I half expected Danny to pull a Clark Griswold, lose his cool, and annihilate his Frankenstein of flight. He didn't. Instead, he calmly approached the rocket and bent over to inspect it. If there were ever a time he risked blowing his face off, this was it.

"Danny!" I yelled from the deck. "Back away from that, son." At that point, I joined him in the yard. I didn't plan to solve his problem and make his rocket fly, but I wasn't going to let him think I didn't care. We traced his wire connections, and I helped double-check his work. It looked good. I couldn't explain why the rocket had failed to ignite, and I told him so.

"Son, it looks like you did everything right," I said with a shrug, hoping to reassure and encourage him.

"Maybe the ignitor is a dud," he said, and off he ran toward the garage. I looked at the rest of the family on the deck. Laura's expression revealed her ever-hopeful disappointment for our son. Success has never come easy to Danny, and I think it weighs more heavily on Laura than it does on him. Katie was trying to be patient, but she couldn't help her teenage inclination to roll her eyes.

Danny reappeared from the garage, installed a new ignitor in the base of *EXPLORER 1*, and the whole production began again.

I didn't have the heart to tell him his idea of making a homemade rocket would probably never work and he should just resign himself to making a paper airplane.

"Ten! Nine! Eight . . ."

I was already preparing my spiel, ready to pull the spotlight away from Danny's failure and try to focus instead on the effort. I needed to water the green spots and celebrate his ingenuity and effort.

"One!" Danny yelled. "Ignition!"

This time the tiny spark was followed by an angry hiss, and *EXPLORER 1* shot toward the heavens.

He'd done it. Danny had taken paper, cardboard, duct tape, and paper clips and constructed a rocket that was now soaring through the sky.

That's the kind of trophy worth keeping, the ones that commemorate when your kid risks total failure and ridicule, but achieves victory in his refusal to quit. Unfortunately, we couldn't do that. Danny had failed to design and install a parachute into the nose cone of his rocket. *EXPLORER 1* disappeared into the woods and was lost to the annals of space travel.

Still, we celebrated with him. We also laughed with him over *EXPLORER*s *2* and *3*, which were utter disasters. And *EXPLORER 4*? Perfection.

> When it comes to our kids, the potential for failure is always part of the deal. We have to learn to embrace that risk.

When it comes to our kids, the potential for failure is always part of the deal. We have to learn to embrace that risk.

A tremendous obstacle to growing strong children is the notion that your kids are (for better or worse) a reflection of you. I once heard Christian author and counselor John Eldredge say, "Your kids are not the report card on who you are." Make no mistake, much of what we do as parents can lift up or cripple our kids, but there's no more selfish parenting motive than worrying about how others perceive you when they look at your kids.

I once coached baseball against a guy who made everything about him. I can always tell the guys on the baseball field who are the most broken. These guys live in fear of being exposed as failures. They're always the loudest, attention-seeking blowhards around. Again, not bad guys. Just broken. Like the rest of us.

Coaching against this guy one day, one of his players took a wild swing at a pitch that was way over his head. Everyone at the ball field knew the kid regretted the swing at once. He'd taken a stupid risk (yes, some risks should be avoided) and struck out. The poor kid's shoulders slumped and his chin dropped to his chest. However, instead of helping that kid work through his failure, the coach made it all about how he, the adult, looked in the eyes of the crowd. Ah, peer pressure.

From his third-base coaching box, he screamed at the defeated kid, "Jimmy! Why would you swing at that?! I taught you better than that! I taught you better than that!" He slapped his hands together in disgust and repeated one more time, but even louder and more emphatically, his hand claps pounding along with each word: "I—TAUGHT—YOU—BETTER—THAN—THAT!"

It's important to let kids experience failure, but how we coach them through it is equally important. Being thrown under the bus by an adult was more defeating to that kid than whiffing at a high pitch. Jimmy couldn't know that his coach was struggling with his own sense of worth and his broken need for validation. It was pretty transparent for most of the adults, though. I have no doubt the coach's behavior drove a wounding message into that kid's heart: *You're an embarrassment to me.* That's the message many kids hear in the ways we respond to their failures, and that is always crippling.

I wonder if Pollyanna heard that same message when she showed her mother the B from Mr. Denton's class, even though

Mom had the best of intentions when she stepped up to fight for her daughter.

We all want our kids to succeed, but too often it's from warped motives. That desire for success can be easily twisted. I remember Ben's first year playing Little League baseball. One of the other dads said something about his son that still echoes in my mind: "Whatever he does, I love and support him. That's my job. But his successes and failures are all his, not mine." As parents, we have to be careful about pinning wins and losses on our kids. The downside can be a dangerous sort of independence, arrogance, or even withdrawal and isolation from an unhealthy fear of failure. However, this dad had a healthy perspective when it came to his son's life. He was expressing the required altruism of a loving parent: *This isn't about me.*

When your kid knows you've got her back (win or lose) and you're proud of her heart, she'll develop a healthy faith in you and in herself, and she'll learn to embrace new challenges and thrive, even in the face of failure.

Even God—the ultimate parent—refuses to insulate us from potential disaster. We often see him put folks on a path where failure is not only possible, but probable.

Hey, Jeremiah, deliver this message. People won't listen and they'll ridicule you and despise you for it, but do it anyway.

Moses, go tell the most powerful ruler in the land that you're taking his slaves and walking out of town.

Esther, defy every law and custom and risk your life by lobbying for the protection of my people.

Gideon, you're outnumbered by almost four to one. Not terrible odds . . . so let's make it interesting. Scale your forces down until it's closer to four hundred fifty to one and let's see what you've got.

Jesus, head into the wilderness and confront an evil that dwarfs the imagination . . . and then set out to heal and restore mankind's brokenness.

I could go on and on. The audacity of God to not only allow us, but also encourage us to risk failure is tantamount to who he is and how he loves us. Walking with God never comes with comfort and security, and there's a reason for that. God invites us to risk and not play it safe because if we allow him, he uses those situations to develop something crucial within us. This might be faith, strength, trust, hope, endurance . . . Whatever it is God wants to reveal in us, through us, and for us usually can only surface in the midst of our struggles. If we deny him the opportunity to do that for our kids, we're not protecting them from failure; we're crippling their authentic strength.

––––––––––

When it comes to our kids' successes and failures, there's an assumption that rewarding only victories will encourage the development of winning attitudes and behaviors. I once wrote a blog in favor of participation trophies and I was saddened by the amount of people who were angry at the notion of rewarding effort, as if love and grace toward a child develop slackers who won't appreciate what it takes to be a winner. However, studies have revealed something else.

In one study, four hundred fifth graders were given a test. Afterward, some were praised for their intelligence ("Wow, you must be smart!") while others were praised for their effort ("Wow, you worked really hard!"). The kids were then asked to take another test, but they had a choice: an easy test that guaranteed success, or a more challenging test. Most of the kids praised for being a winner ("You're so smart!") chose the easier test, while a whopping 92 percent of the kids who were praised for their effort actually risked failure by embracing the tougher challenge.* Now you tell me: Who will experience more growth, the kid who learns to avoid failure, whose identity and self-worth are wrapped up in wins and losses, or the kid who looks challenges in the eye and says, *Bring it on!*?

I'll give you a hint—it's the one who reflects the image of our Father, the wild, dangerous, risky one who always finds a way to use every perceived failure as a stepping-stone to something greater.

Too often we live under an unholy agreement that we have to look like a success story, that we're in control and have it all figured out. That cancerous charade poisons the way we parent, and it eventually stunts the growth of our children. Without realizing it, we end up chaining our souls to a fear of

Too often we live under an unholy agreement that we have to look like a success story, that we're in control and have it all figured out. That cancerous charade poisons the way we parent, and it eventually stunts the growth of our children.

---

*Jason Powers, "Science Says Participation Trophies Are a Big Win for the Little Ones," *Huffington Post*, August 28, 2016, https://www.huffingtonpost.com/jason-powers/science-says-participation_b_8054046.html.

failure, and we transmit that fear deep into the hearts of our children. These kids end up living unfulfilled, restless lives of anxiety and regret—all the things that lead to dangerous, addictive behaviors of self-medication.

One of my friends played major-league baseball for a number of years. One day we were chatting about the pinnacles and pits of his career, his struggles and achievements, the many years spent chasing a dream that remained out of reach for longer than most guys could imagine, let alone endure. "I think I was just too stupid to quit," he laughed. But it wasn't that really. The guy had heart. He bounced around in the minors for what seemed an eternity, occasionally getting called up for a brief stint before getting sent back down. But even though he kept failing to break into the majors, he never quit. Instead, he used each failure as a stepping-stone (as Johnny Cash once said), until he eventually found himself pitching in the World Series.

While that's a perfect enough ending to a discussion on risking failure, there's something else my friend shared with me that I've never forgotten. As a pitcher, he was never expected to do much when he got the chance to bat. His value to the team didn't rest on his successes and failures at the plate. On that topic, he shared with me the best advice he'd ever been offered by a major-league hitting coach:

"Swing hard. You might actually hit it."

That's not a bad motto to teach our kids.

Risking failure is the lifeblood of the X-Plan journey.

CHAPTER 4

I'm Not Your Trophy!

Some friends recently went through a nasty divorce. My buddy Tim screwed up in a big way and was trying to piece together his life and the damaged relationships with his three kids. Two were open to his advances. However, Jon (the oldest), wasn't letting his dad back in. Jon refused to see his dad, wouldn't take his calls, and would disappear when he knew Tim was coming to visit.

"I've tried everything," Tim said to me. "I just don't know how to reach him."

I knew what I wanted to say, but I wasn't sure Tim was ready to hear it. In a lot of ways, he was still playing the victim. After a moment of silence, I said, "I'm going to overstep my bounds and risk being way off base, but I'll tell you what I see."

"Please do."

I went on to explain my outside-looking-in observations. "Jon is an extraordinary athlete—as you were—and that's been one of the strongest links in your chain. He also has the most fragile ego of any kid I've ever seen. Even when he was a little boy, when things went his way, he was an unstoppable force. But when the wheels came off, he was the first one to completely shut down."

"I know," Tim said, "he's always been sensitive."

"It's more than sensitive. Jon's not disappointed when he strikes out. He reacts as if he IS a disappointment. It's the flip side of the same coin. Heads, he's worthy. Tails, he's not. Right now, Jon is the coin, getting flipped. When he's heads-up, you celebrate. But when he's tails . . . Do you see what I'm getting at?"

"Yeah, but—"

"Tim," I continued, "everything about Jon is performance-based, and I think he's living with some warped notion that his only value as a human comes from his athletic performance. And, like it or not, you've encouraged that in how you've always celebrated his success. His life feels like tails right now—it's flipped upside down. You need to be honest and vulnerable to that and stop cheering for the fleeting moments of heads."

Silence.

"Tim, I see your social media posts about Jon. I realize you're trying to reconnect, but look back at your posts. Every single one of them is a celebration of some accomplishment on the field. You're trying to lift your kid up like a trophy, but I think he needs to be pursued as your son—just for who he is and not for his latest home run or touchdown, a young man whose world has shifted and he's left feeling unsure, betrayed, and angry. I'll be honest with you. My biological father left when Mom was pregnant with me. The few times I would see him and he tried to brag about my accomplishments, it ticked me off. He'd left. He wasn't around for the hard stuff, so I refused to be his trophy that he could show off before putting me back up on the shelf to ignore."

"I hear you," Tim said, "but I was always around."

"You're right, but from my vantage point, your relationship was always sports-related in one way or another. You broke your kid's heart, man, and you're trying to plug back into that same port—but it's fried right now. You've got to pursue Jon in other ways if you want to heal those wounds. In fact, I'd ignore everything performance-based for a while and find new ways to connect outside of that."

I could tell he was processing my words. Finally, he said, "You're right. I'd never thought about that."

Two days later Tim was on Facebook posting about Jon's game-winning shot. And the boy dove deeper away from his dad.

———

As I write this, our seventeen-year-old daughter, Katie, is tee-tering on the edge of a stroke. Maybe not literally, but she is the most driven, hardworking, self-critical person we know, and it worries us. In school she's taking all AP and honors courses. She's wrestling with college choices. She's been cast as prima ballerina in an upcoming ballet. She acts, sings, dances, cho-reographs, and student-directs local stage productions. She is a paid vocal performer. But no matter how much she achieves, it's never good enough in her own eyes; the stress she lives with, the blind crusade to outperform even her own insane expecta-tions, is nothing short of cruel, and this is largely our fault as her parents.

Katie has always been incredibly intelligent, talented, and wise beyond her years, and we probably praised her too much when she was little. Yes, praised her too much.

Here's a video of my nine-year-old nailing a Broadway tune.
Straight As again! Nothing below a 99 percent!
Can you believe she did the choreography for that show?

She killed her audition and has been invited to NYC to workshop a new musical.

She's so mature—so intelligent and wise beyond her years. Read this article she wrote!

Looking back, I now see what we were doing. Laura and I were telling Katie that we loved her achievements, and with imperceptible glacial speed, the silly heart of our little girl became buried beneath layers of production and performance.

"When she really fails," I once told Laura, "I don't think she'll be able to handle it."

The addictive power of praise can leave you doubting yourself even after a great performance. After a while, you start to distrust all praise and gratitude, because something inside feels shattered and unworthy. Trauma counselor Dan Allender once said, "We struggle with gratitude because we are not used to dealing with delight."* Many of us learn to deflect praise because we ultimately believe we're undeserving. *Not good enough.* I agree with Allender's assertion that "evil hates the echo of praise, joy, and love," but I think evil uses those very things to further wound us and tear us apart.

When your sense of self-worth is tied to the applause of others, you surrender control of your own joy—indeed, your life—and put it in the uncaring hands of strangers. Think of how Facebook and other forms of social media work: you post something, and the more "likes"

> When your sense of self-worth is tied to the applause of others, you surrender control of your own joy—indeed, your life—and put it in the uncaring hands of strangers.

---

*The Restoration of the Heart Conference, Colorado Springs, CO, 2016.

you get, the better you feel—right? I run several pages, and I used to drive myself nuts trying to figure out why one post would draw dozens (or even hundreds) of positive responses and something else would sit there like a turd in a punch bowl. And the worst part—it really did affect how I felt about myself and my work.

How twisted is that?

We live in such a performance-based society, life feels like an endless struggle for approval, and what people want to see and hear changes by the moment.

Laura and I now realize we helped feed the not-good-enough monster that is eating away at Katie, causing her to burn the candle at both ends in her maddening race to the top of some mountain that has no summit. We bragged about her successes, put her on a pedestal, and reinforced the silent message that her value does not rest comfortably in her own authenticity, but rather in what she accomplishes. Through our praise for our wildly gifted daughter, we've done some damage, and that breaks my heart. I think Katie remains blind to her intrinsic awesomeness. She has internalized the fictional expectations of some unseen audience, given them control of her happiness, and often feels inadequate as a result.

Hoping it's not too late, we are now more deliberate with our praise, celebrating the person rather than the performance. We now tell Katie we love to see her joy in her dance. We delight in her passion that shines through when she sings. We are making concerted efforts to engage her heart when we tell her, "We don't care if you succeed or fail in anything you do. We are proud of you because you're ours, and we love just being around you when you're doing the things you love."

Some of my best times growing up were Wiffle-ball games in the backyard. We competed like it mattered while exploring our abilities, but failure brought no misery because there was no audience to praise our successes.

In an informal, three-decade survey, kids were asked their least favorite thing about playing organized sports. The most popular answer: *the ride home.* Let that sink in for a moment.

In his book *Play Baseball the Ripken Way*, Cal Ripken Jr. tells about watching his son's youth baseball team in a game they were losing. The other team was on fire, and those kids' parents were going nuts with over-the-top cheering. However, just like in life, an error was made . . . followed by another . . . and the wheels came off the bus. Ripken recounts how the once-screaming fans grew quiet, and the silence was as deafening as a downpour of boos. The parents stopped cheering for their own kids, who were struggling, sending the overwhelming message that success is the only thing that makes us proud and brings us wild joy. When the crowd grows silent, it's not much different from someone screaming out expletive-laced threats.

That's heartbreaking. If we're not careful, we set our kids up for a lifetime of seeking validation through their performances. Kids don't have the capacity to differentiate between their intrinsic value and their applause-seeking efforts. No wonder kids like Jon (who are so used to the crowd going wild) fall apart when the fanatical cheering stops.

Ripken applauds one youth league that has "Silent Sundays." The kids come to the field and play their games, but the spectators remain quiet. This removes the emotional manipulation and control of adults; it allows kids the freedom to learn and grow without the added pressure that comes with a cheering crowd. "They [cheering adults] can drive the kids' emotions way up and they can help them crash,"* Cal writes. Whether they succeed or fail, Ripken argues that parents must support their kids "at a consistent level," and child psychology experts agree with baseball's "Iron Man."

Praise can actually damage your children and cripple their development. In a performance-based reality, they become emotional slaves to the crowd. "Praise," writes psychologist Robin Grille, is merely "the sweet side of authoritarian parenting."[†] If you're not careful, you risk crushing your child under the weight of your applause. It's too easy for them to equate their performance with your approval . . . and your love. They also soon suspect that you're only trying to control them or boost your own damaged ego. Grille sees the fallout in kids who walk away from their natural talents "because they are repulsed by their parents' gloating."

If we're not careful, every clap can become an abusive slap across the face.

————

Throughout Scripture, God only speaks audibly a handful of times. Twice, he praises his son, Jesus. Parents should notice what is said and what isn't, and learn by example from someone who seems to know the formula for raising a strong kid.

As Jesus is just beginning his public ministry, he goes to his cousin, John, at the Jordan River. Feeling unworthy, John reluctantly agrees to baptize Jesus. John takes hold of God-in-flesh

*Cal Ripken Jr., Bill Ripken, Larry Burke, *Play Baseball The Ripken Way* (New York: Random House, 2004).
†Robin Grille, "Rewards and Praise: The Poisoned Carrot," The Natural Child Project, https://www.naturalchild.org/robin_grille/rewards_praise.html.

and submerges him in the cool waters. As Jesus comes out of the water, God speaks (I'm paraphrasing, but every translation shares the same heart of the message): *This is my son. I love him so much, and he brings me tremendous joy.*

Parents, notice what isn't said. God doesn't say, *This is my son, who taught in the temple as a boy and made me so proud . . . and just wait until you see his miracles!*

There's none of that.

This is my son. I love him so much, and he brings me tremendous joy.

God expresses his love and pride in who Jesus is. There's no crowing about his accomplishments.

Be honest, what would you give to go back in time and hear your parents say, *You are mine—mine!—and I love you. I'm so proud of who you are. You are my joy!* No conditions. No qualifiers. Just, *I love you for your heart.* How much would that message have changed the trajectory of your life for the better? How much torture have you endured trying to win approval and applause, even from your closest family members?

This is my son. I love him so much, and he brings me tremendous joy.

Friends, after God speaks those words, Jesus sets out to confront evil in the wilderness. God knew that his son would go toe-to-toe with Satan, and he spoke an essential truth into Jesus's heart that the man needed to hear. God repeats the same audible message during the transfiguration on the mountaintop (Matthew 17:5)—*This is my son. I love him so much, and he brings me tremendous joy.* God doesn't speak out loud much, so when he does, that's a decent clue that what he's saying is important. God realizes his son needs to hear this . . . and if Jesus needs to know his father loves him and is proud of him for who he is and not what he does, how much more do we—and our kids—need to know it?

During Ben's first year of college, he injured his arm and had to sit out baseball season. Months of rehab were followed by the revelation of deeper, undiagnosed injuries. A looming shoulder surgery was going to set him back at least another year. This was a lot to handle for a young man away from home and trying to figure out college life. A couple of times Ben mentioned walking away from baseball. Ben's anxiety was tangible, and our discussions felt tense. I think we both sensed one wrong word might ignite a smoldering argument. I took a lot of time and prayed about this, asking God to help me support and guide my son with wisdom. What he showed me wasn't pretty.

I came to realize something I'd been doing to my son since the end of high school. Whenever I spoke about him being away at college, I was quick to mention to folks that Ben was on a baseball scholarship. He'd actually been awarded baseball and academic scholarships, but I only touted the baseball part. I was very proud of my son's hard work and dedication that had brought those opportunities. I thought I was celebrating him. I was wrong.

Ben was struggling with whether or not he could come back from shoulder surgery and another year away from the game. What made it worse was his father's distorted message: *I'm proud of you* because *you play college baseball.* Nothing could have been farther from the truth, but that's what my ignorant expressions of pride were saying. Once I realized what my praise had been doing to my son, I acted at once to correct my mistake.

During our next discussion about school and baseball, I

laid it out in no uncertain terms: "Son, I love you. I'm proud of you because of who you are, and there's nothing you can do to change that. I don't want you to regret missing the chance to play just once, fully healthy, but it's your journey. Your decision. Baseball helps pay your tuition, so you'll need to pick up a part-time job or work-study to help make up the difference, but all I want is for you to follow your heart. I'm proud of the man you're becoming, and that has nothing to do with baseball. You're my son and that makes me happy. I have your back no matter what you do."

Yes, that's part of our X-Plan. Kids must know we've got their backs, no matter the circumstance. We celebrate who they are, not their performances.

> Kids must know we've got their backs, no matter the circumstance. We celebrate who they are, not their performances.

Ben had the surgery and is just now throwing the ball again for the first time in nine months. Home on break, he asked me to pass a baseball with him in the backyard. As we threw the ball, I saw a passion and joy in his face I hadn't seen in a long time, and I now know that I'd almost stolen that from him. He'd become convinced that he had to play baseball to earn my blessing. Once that lie was uprooted and I stopped crowing about baseball, Ben shrugged off the invisible weight of his father's conditional delight.

This is my son. I love him so much, and he brings me tremendous joy.

That is what my son needed to hear, so that's what I told him.

PART 2

OKAY, IT MIGHT BE ABOUT YOU

Children learn more from what you are than what you teach.
—W. E. B. Du Bois

I'm all broken.
—Ernest Hemingway, *A Farewell to Arms*

One of my favorite Stephen King books is *Pet Sematary*. In this horror story, a child is killed in a tragic accident. In senseless desperation, the child's father buries the boy deep in the woods, in a place with terrifying powers, where the dead eventually claw out of the grave and come home. However, the child isn't restored to life. What returns is cruel and inhuman, and it destroys the family.

This story haunts me.

It reminds me of the times the broken child I've buried somewhere deep inside has crawled out of some unholy place and terrorized my own children.

As the X-Plan gained worldwide popularity, I was heartbroken by some of the responses. I saw a *lot* of hostility toward children and what should be regarded as beautiful and sacred: a childlike nature. It reminded me of how children were depicted in art for centuries—kids weren't painted with childlike qualities, but presented to look like miniature adults. That attitude still haunts us, largely because we struggle with the kid buried inside each of us; the weak, frightened, injured child who screams out from a shallow grave: *Never let this happen again!* (Whatever "this" may be—it's different for all of us.)

Jesus wants to heal the broken and restore our childlike nature. Our refusal to allow that grace only damages our kids in ways we can't even imagine. We've got to face some of our own young, tender places. Until we let Christ revisit and redeem some of our backstory, we'll struggle to lead our kids forward.

The loudest X-Plan critics seemed upset by kids who didn't act like adults. But—oh, dear ones—instead of struggling to get kids to act like miniature adults, parents need to find the courage to become like children again.

The X-Plan is about rescuing the child. So, in this case, it might be about you. Left unhealed, your brokenness will wound your kids.

QUESTIONS TO X-PLORE

1 Did your parents ever (unknowingly or knowingly) do or say something that hurt you in some deep, fragile place? Has it lingered in your soul? How have you learned to handle the memories of you as a child?

2 We often hear, "Experience is life's best teacher." Can you remember any childhood experiences that wounded you inside? Do you now find yourself striving to guard your own children from the same pain? Can you look back and recognize painful fragments of childhood your parents carried inside?

3 Did you ever feel unknown by the ones who should've known you best? Were there times when your parents simply failed to recognize or understand your worries, fears, and struggles? At the time, how did you feel about that? And now?

4 Can you remember a time when your parents did something completely spontaneous and playful with you? What effect did that have on your young heart?

5 How will your kids answer these questions in thirty years?

CHAPTER 5

The Damage We Do

A vicious creature lives in the shadows of our home. Over the years, I've come to realize all families have similar monsters that lurk in the darkness. Their ill-defined, almost invisible bodies leave spiritual slug trails of anxiety, rage, fear, and depression. Sometimes we catch a glimpse of them in the mirror.

These cruel beings haunt every parent. They linger around us and wait for us to reach for our kids, and then—with blinding speed—they force weapons into our hands, devices that leave deep but invisible cuts in young, innocent flesh.

Parents nearly always remain oblivious to these wounds, and the children will spend a lifetime self-medicating pains they don't even understand.

Even your best efforts to parent your children can leave them traumatized. The sooner you start to prayerfully consider how your children are being assaulted—and how YOU were assaulted—the sooner you can invite healing and protection into the parent-child relationship.

One of my own scars just recently came to light.

I'm standing in our kitchen . . .

The tight fist in my chest confirms my readiness.

If she says a word—even one word—I will turn into Bruce

Lee, leap over the kitchen counter, and deliver a roundhouse kick to her face in one *Matrix*-like movement.

I open the drawer and lift a few items with such delicacy you might think I'm diffusing a bomb. I move with a surgeon's precision, life and death in my hands, as I try to ignore the thunder of my own heartbeat—a gathering storm that swells every time I open this drawer. This time, I'm looking for my truck keys.

Most people have a junk drawer in their kitchen: a place where everything gets deposited when the counters need clearing. Got to hide the mess and maintain the façade that everything is in place, well ordered, and under control. But don't call ours a junk drawer. That makes Laura angry. It may have something to do with growing up in a house that was quite unlike our own: organized, showroom neat, and tidy. Our on-the-go, chaotic lifestyle simply won't allow for that sort of order, and it eats at Laura. She desires a display-worthy house, and it grates on her for us to suggest that we have a "junk drawer." And for the love of everything holy, don't let her catch you "digging" through it!

I feel her looking at me. Her stare becomes an unseen hand that reaches down my throat and squeezes my windpipe. She's strangling me. My heartbeat pounds in my ears.

Don't say one word to me! Please, God, muzzle her!

"Honey," Laura says, the agitation bleeding from behind the word's innocence, "I just straightened that drawer. Please don't dig. Just tell me what you're looking for."

"My keys," I hiss.

"They're not in there. I haven't seen them."

I close the drawer with sinful calm, spin on my heels, and march out of the house. I have to. If I stay another second it will get ugly (as it has so many times before). Every time my fingers touch the knob on that stupid drawer, it's like flipping a switch that turns on the fighting. And I'm always ready for it. Laura doesn't even have to say anything; her words haunt my memory: *I just cleaned and arranged everything in there—don't you dare mess it up!*

Some terrifying rage erupts inside of me every time I open that drawer.

I'm trying hard to control my breathing, but my white-knuckled grip on the steering wheel betrays my emotions. Laura is silent beside me. Neither of us has spoken more than a few sentences in the past three hours. She knows I'm vexed, and the tension inside the truck is smothering. In marriage, we are often prisoners in a fragile peace.

Finally, I risk it.

"Babe"—I take a deep breath—"I need you to understand something. When I was a boy, we weren't allowed to touch anything in the kitchen without permission—I couldn't even get a drink of water unless I asked first."

I can feel Laura looking at me, and this time it feels like delicate fingers on a gaping wound.

"Every time I open that drawer and you say something to me about it, it's not me you're talking to. All of a sudden I'm a scared, six-year-old kid, sneaking through the kitchen, praying no one hears me and I don't wake anyone up and get in trouble . . . just because I'm thirsty." Tears begin to rain down onto my shirt, leaving dark stains like bullet wounds. "And that kid feels like an unwelcome guest in his own home!" I break down.

How could Dad have ever known that forty years later his attempt to teach us limits, manners, and respect would become twisted into something grotesque and plague my marriage? I'm suddenly reminded of a terrified boy desperately clinging to a ladder and the father who'd left him there, forbidding him to go back down as he taught the boy a "valuable lesson." *My God, what have I done to my children?* I can still see Ben's white knuckles clawed around the rungs.

"Honey"—Laura touches my arm, and it burns with a healing passion—"I am sorry. I didn't know. I will never say anything about that drawer again."

She never has.

———

Ben was home from his first semester of college. It was good to have the whole family together again. We were playing games at the kitchen table, poking fun at one another—everyone is fair game—as we laughed at old stories and new confessions.

"Danny, do you know what actually happened to your *Wall-E* blanket?" Ben chuckled.

Danny's face went blank as his eyes swelled. "No."

"Dad took it during one of his cleaning fits and forgot to give it back to you. It's in a trash bag in the attic."

"What?" Danny cried, "Dad! I thought I'd lost it somewhere!"

"Well, you did," Katie laughed.

"I always wondered what happened to *Wall-E* . . ." Danny's voice trailed off as he raced from the kitchen and pounded up the attic steps, driven by echoes of his siblings' laughter.

Ben and Katie then shifted their attack. They started in on me and my militaristic demands about keeping their stuff picked up. They mocked me with hilarious accuracy.

"Clean up your room or I'll clean it for you."

"If you don't pick it up, I will."

"Well, I guess you don't want this anymore."

They made me sound like an ogre.

In fairness, I sometimes gave them thirty minutes or more (sometimes a whole day) before I showed up for the harvesting. But when time was up, I entered the room with silent determination and began chucking anything left out into a black, fifty-five-gallon garbage bag.

"Here comes Dad with his garbage bag," Katie chortled, pumping her arms to mimic my march, "and we'd all be like, '*NOOOOOO!*'"

At the time, they'd believed their stuff was going out with the trash. However, I always intended to give it back little by little as they demonstrated some ability to keep their rooms tidy. Sometimes I forgot. I just recently came across a bag full of Ben's stuff I'd gathered from his bedroom floor about ten years ago. In the case of the *Wall-E* blanket, Ben had found a bag of Danny's childhood belongings that I'd tossed into the attic three or four years prior and forgotten.

Danny hadn't mentioned his blanket (or the rest of his stuff) for years. I guess when something is taken from us, we just learn to live with the mugging after a while.

"Dad." Ben looked at me, still smiling, but seriousness had crept into his expression. He began shaking his head like an old man remembering something painful. "You used to scare the snot out of me. I'd hear your feet on the stairs, and my blood pressure would shoot up. *Oh no! Is there a cup or bowl sitting out? A pillow on the floor?* I'd look around the room as if I only had a few seconds before you'd walk in and start screaming at me for something ridiculous."

Katie nodded in agreement, smiling. But it was a sad smile.

I laughed, but my children's honesty broke my heart. Is that really what they felt when they heard me approaching? How many times had I gone in loving pursuit of their hearts and they—like Adam and Eve—were hiding in fear? In how many other ways were they still hiding from me because of that fear? What had I done to them?

————

My childhood home was a stately two-story yellow brick house with a full attic and finished basement. My great-grandparents had built it in the 1920s. Dad purchased it (his childhood home) after they passed. To help pay the mortgage, the upstairs had been sectioned off as apartments for rent.

It was a huge, creepy mansion with dozens of windows that seemed like the watchful, menacing eyes of some alien creature. Always awake. Missing nothing. Judging. Keeping score and calculating punishment. Yes, I grew up in a haunted house, and I was a scared little kid.

The bedroom I shared with my older brother was at the end of a mile-long hallway. In this boy's mind, that corridor of death was draped with shadows where monsters and vampires climbed the walls. We had one light switch at the beginning of this valley of shadow and death. Each night, I would flip the light on, scan for out-of-place silhouettes, flip it off, and then run like crazy for my bedroom. It was a nightly horrifying few seconds that I can still feel in my chest. It makes me want to puke. I never went to bed without horror.

Mom and Dad knew I was afraid, but they couldn't imagine the depths of my terror. Something in that house was going to kill me, I knew it. Sometimes Mom would let me leave the hall light on until I made it safely to my room. She'd turn it off when she'd come to tuck me in. Dad, on the other hand, didn't cater to such nonsense.

One night as I prepared for my death race, Dad was standing in the kitchen watching me linger at the edge of the haunted passageway. I turned on the light.

"You don't need that," he said. "You know where your room is."

My heart lodged in my throat.

"Honey," Mom said to him, "he's scared."

She meant well, but hearing the truth somehow made me feel worse. On top of my dread, I was suddenly ashamed for being weak and afraid.

"There's nothing to be scared of," Dad huffed. He must have seen my hand still at the switch, because he quickly repeated, "You don't need a light." This time, his tone made certain his command. This night, there would be no hall light. I swear I could hear silent laughter from the creatures waiting to devour me.

I peered into the darkness. My mind served up images of tentacles and claws and teeth waiting to rip into my chubby body. I took a hesitant step into the shadow as I gathered strength. The house became silent. This was it. I flexed my leg muscles, preparing for the horrible quickstep that would shift into a sprint at the first sign of whatever ghoul was hiding behind a door. I told myself I could do this—I had to! One more step. And then another. My thighs were shaking.

Suddenly a noise exploded behind me—giant metallic jaws with jagged glass fangs biting at me. I screamed and tore into a mindless dash as some mechanical devil chewed up the carpet behind me. I punched my bedroom light switch and flew across the room and then disappeared beneath my covers. Shuddering and sobbing in terror, tears soaking my Superman pajamas, I waited for the creature to tear off my covers and sink its rusty fangs into my throat. I was going to die.

I think a part of me did.

I was still howling when Mom came in to try and comfort me.

I later learned that Dad, having just come up from his workshop in the basement, had been holding a glass baby food jar filled with metal washers. I know he never meant to wound me as deeply as he did when he rattled that jar behind me. Had he expected a laugh? Maybe he intended to shock the irrational fear out of me. I don't know. But to this day, it is still the loudest, most terrifying sound I've ever heard.

How could I not run for my life? And keep running.

I wonder if Ben still feels stuck on that ladder.

———————

A couple of years ago our family took a road trip to New Orleans with friends. I wanted to fly. My buddy Steve wanted to drive.

Steve's enthusiasm for the journey seemed borderline crazy to me. I love being on vacation. However, I hate getting to vacation. As I thought more about Steve's odd affinity for the road, I began to realize what I'd become—a person who lives for the destination but is always anxious about the journey. I prayed about this, asking Jesus to flip on the hall light and reveal what was hiding in the shadows. What he showed me was a man who was addicted to end points but terrified of the unknown elements between points A and B. I began to realize that the only comfortable places in my life were just a few pins on a map. Sad to say, I'd rarely been able to enjoy the voyages to those places. All my life, I'd learned to plot a destination, and out of fear and a warped sense of inadequacy, I would lower my shoulders and run for my life, leaving others behind or drowning them in my wake.

I can't begin to count the times Laura has looked at me during a trip and asked, "Why are you in such a hurry?"

Because something's coming for me.

Too much of my life has felt like racing through a haunted hallway. *I have to get under cover—a place where I can hide—before I'm exposed and destroyed.* In so many ways, I've been running for years, too afraid to stop and look around because I might actually see the fanged horror that's hunting me.

I'm not saying Dad created this anxiety by shaking washers in a jar. He had his flaws—Don't we all?—but he was a good man with good intentions. I know if he'd had even a clue about the seemingly innocent things that left deep scars, he would have never done them. However, without meaning to, he'd tapped into some irrational, childhood fear that was already lurking inside of me like a dormant cancer, just waiting for the chance to come alive and grow.

Dad never intended for me to be afraid. He wanted me to be brave and secure. I know that now. He never meant to make me feel like an illegal refugee in our home, either. He was just trying to teach us boundaries and respect. Not bad lessons. However, the messages I took from those lessons—you're unwelcome, unsafe, alone, weak, inferior, and you're going to be chewed up by the world—were whispered by a more sinister source. My parents never saw how their good intentions were often used to traumatize and haunt a young boy. But that's where evil works—in the darkness.

Not long ago, Danny said to us, "You almost got divorced

because of me, didn't you?" When Danny was younger, Laura and I fought a lot. We've had plenty of time to work through it, and we now see it for what it was: evil in the darkness.

"No, Danny, that wasn't about you. That was about us."

Some of my mom's siblings were lost to tragedy at young ages. She knows how fragile life is, and it showed in her smothering care of me. Her desire to protect me from the world always made me feel weak, reinforcing the unspoken message that I would never be man enough to survive a dangerous world, that I need to hide in the bushes and hope to never be exposed. Just like Adam.

For a long time, I saw this overprotection in Laura's (s)mothering of Danny.

Danny was our unplanned (not our "accident," as he says) child. We weren't trying to have a third child, but we weren't doing anything to prevent one, either. Danny came along, and we soon realized that God had given us a mini-me. I see so much of myself in Danny that it's disorienting, like looking in a carnival fun house mirror. Neither of us could talk before the age of three. We were both awkward children with vivid imaginations that others either laughed at or dismissed because of their inability to comprehend our unique view of the world. With a penchant for drama and comedy, we both love to entertain but hate to be noticed (an odd but not uncommon mix). We fluctuate between thriving in the universe of the imagination and hiding from the real world before our eyes.

Many times Danny and I simply react to each other like magnets. Some parts of us are drawn together, but the sameness forces us apart. With the best of intentions, I tried to father my son, strengthen him, and harden him to the fear, anxiety, and insecurity I'd known as a boy. Laura, however, interpreted my frustrated attempts with Danny as resentments toward a child she believed I'd never wanted. That was an unspoken lie that haunted the darkness of our home, but when the spiritual fog sets in, it's hard to see the truth, especially with your high beams on.

Friends, you need to realize that the most damaging, untrue thoughts come from unholy places. If left to fester, they will poison your family.

As we worked our way through this, Laura began to awaken to some of her own childhood wounds—damaged places longing for nurturing and acceptance. She shared with me a time when she'd gone to an air show with her dad. Laura had been born with severe hip dysplasia and had several childhood surgeries. She walked with a limp and constant pain. At this particular air show, her dad was anxious to share his passion for airplanes with his little girl. They walked around and looked at planes for hours.

"I was tired and hurting so much," she told me, "and I remember feeling like Dad was mad at me for being a baby and spoiling his day. I don't think he knew how much I was hurting."

Laura buried that experience deep inside, but every time she saw me instructing or disciplining our son, that hurting little girl came to life and swooped in to protect Danny's fragile heart against an uncaring father. I'll add here that, like my own, Laura's father was anything but uncaring, but at the core of our childhood wounds, lies feel true, and they linger, taking up residence in the deepest parts of our hearts. Laura's childhood brokenness was leading her to overmother, and the resentment and tension between us grew. Any time I tried to father Danny, it seemed Laura would violate our rule that we'd never question each other in front of the kids.

To be sure, I played my part in this mess. As much as Laura tried to protect Danny, I was doing my own share of damage; because of my insecurities, I thought I had to toughen him up. If only I could help him to be stronger and smarter than I'd been, he might avoid the soul-crushing humiliations I'd known . . . but my own wife was working against me, crippling my son, making him even more fragile in a world that would chew him up.

Laura was overmothering, and I was overfathering. Because of our childhood brokenness, husband and wife found themselves on a collision course as we went to war over the son we both love.

Meanwhile, Danny found himself in the middle of a battlefield. He didn't see two people at odds over their immense love and concern for him. The lie whispered into his heart was devastating: *You were an accident. They didn't want you. You're a screwup, and you screwed up this family—they're going to split up because of you—and everyone resents your existence. Even Ben and Katie despise you.*

Friends, it is healing to revisit these broken places in your own childhood, not looking for someone to blame, but to unearth the messages that wounded you and still haunt you. Trust me, they're lurking in the shadows.

Can you think of things your parents said or did that cut you to the core? Things they still say or do that cause some awful reaction inside of you?

In the finest Appalachian heritage, my mother learned to show her love through food. She was always cooking and baking, mostly comfort foods that leave you bloated and fat. Not so ironically, when we were kids, a hot topic in our house was my sister's weight. With the most loving intent, Mom wanted to help Jennie slim down so she wouldn't be too fat to make cheerleader or majorette. I can remember having massive plates of chicken and dumplings for dinner, but Mom would wait until Jennie left the kitchen before she pulled the chocolate cake from its hiding place behind the television in the living room.

Mom wanted to help my sister look and feel pretty. However, the calorie-rich message that Jennie swallowed only nourished deep lies and accusations: *Fat . . . ugly . . . embarrassing . . . unlovable . . .* Before long, my sister went, as the old song goes, "looking for love in all the wrong places." She ran away from home and was married before she'd even graduated from high school.

Mom didn't intend for those things to happen, but what we hear doesn't have to be said or even implied. I am horrified at the damage I've done to my own kids. Some I realize. Most I'm sure remains hidden. But none of it was ever intended.

The best parents in the world damage their kids on a daily basis. Sorry to break that news. Life is like a day at the seashore, only the beach is filled with broken glass and the ocean is teeming with sharks. Even with your best efforts, there will be blood in the water, salt in the wounds, and everyone who goes for a swim will get bitten.

I don't mean to seem fatalistic, but this is something we need to be honest about. If you don't start to explore the ways you were hurt as a child, you'll never wake up to the damage you're doing to your own kids. Don't dismiss this. Be vigilant and prayerful about it. With every interaction comes an un-

> If you don't start to explore the ways you were hurt as a child, you'll never wake up to the damage you're doing to your own kids.

spoken message, and if you're not discerning what those messages might be, you won't be able to defend your kid against them.

As my brokenness is being restored—*O God, we have so far left to go!*—I'm learning to be more intentional in the messages I deliver to my children. My words and actions will still become twisted—this I know—but I'll limit the damage as much as I can. Meanwhile, I'm learning to care less about reaching the end of the hall. I'm taking my time and enjoying the journey, embracing the risk and adventure, and learning to live in the moment with a full heart that I no longer need to hide and protect like a wounded animal. Jesus is healing me. Repairing me. Restoring me. I hope that shows in how I parent my kids.

I pray it does the same for you.

Hurt people hurt people.

I don't want to hurt anymore.

And I pray my kids don't hide from me when they need me.

CHAPTER 6

Unbroken Parenting

It's a sunny spring afternoon. A father and his six-year-old son are throwing a baseball in the backyard. The ball arcs through the pastel sky like a wingless bird as the boy yells out the count after every catch.

"Three!" He throws the ball back to his dad. Father snatches it and then launches a high one. The boy has to sprint but manages to get under the ball and make the catch.

"Four!" Dad bellows. "Well done!"

Mom waters her flowers along the deck, watching her men . . . her *boys*. She knows the fragile strength they both carry.

She can't help but smile, happy for her son, who's just learning the game of baseball. He's doing so well. There's untapped talent beneath that hand-me-down Spider-Man T-shirt. This will be Ben's first year playing, and she knows how important it is for him to succeed.

Ben adjusts his Cincinnati Reds cap, pulls the ball from his glove, and then wings it back to his dad. The ball goes off-line and sails into the neighbor's yard. Dad shrugs at his son as if to say, *Oh well, you know the drill*, and trots to retrieve the ball. From the next yard, Dad blasts another one into the sky—a deep shot to center field! The youngster takes flight, losing his cap, and makes a diving catch worthy of a seasoned twelve-year-old all-star.

The boy hops up, glove held high. "*SportsCenter* play of the day!" he cries. His infectious joy spreads to the deck, where mom is clapping.

"Great job, Ben!"

Ben looks to his dad, now walking back toward him. "Good catch," Dad agrees, and then motions for the ball. "That's one."

"One?" the boy pleads, arms collapsing at his sides.

"You know the drill, son. Ten in a row before we quit. That means ten good catches and ten good throws. Your last throw was awful. A giant with ten-foot arms couldn't have caught that."

"Dad!" he yells before picking up his cap. "Please!"

"Nope. Sorry. Ten good ones—catches *and* throws."

Frustrated, the boy fires the ball at his dad, spinning fast enough that the red stitching disappears. The kid's going to be one heck of a ballplayer. But, again, the ball sails into the next yard.

"I'm not getting that one," Dad says. "You get it."

"Fine!" Ben throws his glove on the ground and marches past his father. He's trying not to cry.

"And we're back to zero."

The man looks to his wife. Shaking her head, she shows her disapproval before withdrawing into the house.

About an hour later—sixty war-torn minutes—Ben completes ten exchanges in a row (and Dad made sure none of them was easy). The boy celebrates his final catch as if he's just won the World Series. Dad congratulates his son, telling himself that Ben's long ordeal—the frustration and tears—was a necessary trial of manhood. *No matter how angry Laura is, she'll soon see it was all worth it. The boy will be ready for baseball. He has to be.*

Well done, Dad. Way to stick it out to help your kid. Most fathers would have given up after ten minutes of the complaining and caterwauling.

———

This scene could have been a pivotal moment in Ben's life. Perhaps it may still be . . . if it comes up in therapy someday.

To my surprise, Ben continued to play baseball. He became a top player at every level. He and I have talked many times about those long, miserable hours in the backyard, throwing that ball back and forth until it was so dark neither of us could see it. He thinks it made a difference: it taught him to never quit, keep working hard, and that through your own never-say-die grit, you can grab life's reins and ride it like a rodeo cowboy. There's some truth in that. However, I need to confess: "Son, I am filled with regret. Your achievements are entirely yours—you have a strong, courageous heart. In my weakness as a parent, through my own brokenness, I risked forever damaging the core of who you are, and I am sorry."

Now, well into my forties, I can still hear the deep-throated cries of frustration from my young son after a less-than-perfect throw or missed catch. Although I'm thankful for the hundreds of hours spent coaching my son, I'm ashamed at my petty ambition and warped motivations.

Forcing a six-year-old child to make ten perfect catches and throws all those years ago had very little to do with Ben and everything to do with me.

I am embarrassed to admit that I was parenting out of weakness. My own childhood humiliations were still raw, unhealed, and that tainted how I have handled my kids on more occasions than I can count.

———

As a kid, the end of summertime was both dreadful and thrilling. Spelling tests, reading books, and social studies projects loomed heavy on the horizon. But it also came with intrigue. What would the new teacher be like? Would there be any new students this year? A fresh crop of pretty girls?

The end of summer was also a lonely time. Many of my friends played football and would disappear into the practice fields a few weeks before school started. I didn't play for two reasons. First, football wasn't a thing in my family—no one had ever played. Second, Mom wouldn't allow it. Her baby would get hurt, she was sure of it, and she was determined to protect me.

As my buddies banged helmets and shoulder pads, I had to find something else to fill those long final days of summer.

We lived across the alley from Emmons Elementary School. The teachers usually started appearing a couple of weeks before the first day of classes. They would spend hours each day in their classrooms, decorating and arranging, organizing books and supplies, and preparing their battle plans for whatever we blue-collar hooligans could throw at them.

I would ride my brother's old Huffy bike around the school yard, waiting for the cars to start filling the parking lot. Once they did, I would make my appearance in the office.

Ms. Baldwin, the secretary, was especially fond of me for some reason. She would welcome me in, give me an embarrassing (but awesome) hug, and ask about my summer. I never realized then how cool it was to have an adult actually care about me and want nothing in return. After the pleasantries, I would ask about my new teacher.

Once that sensitive information was secured, the schmoozing mission was on. I would head off to find my new teacher and offer my services for anything she might need. (Trust me, it paid dividends. You wouldn't believe the nonsense I got away with because of a little investment of time.)

Year in, year out, this was how I spent the last days of my summer break.

However, one year, things changed. Although I pleaded every year, my mother's defenses failed in the summer before fifth grade. She agreed to let me try football.

The following day I was helping Ms. Adkins hang alphabet posters above the chalkboard. I waited for the best possible moment, and then (chest puffed and chin high) I casually dropped the bomb that I knew would devastate the poor woman.

"I'm sorry, Ms. Adkins, but I won't be able to help tomorrow."

"Oh?" Behind her desk, she steadied herself. The nine-year-old boy was all too aware of her looming heartbreak. I wasn't sure she would be able to go on without me.

"I have . . ." I took a deep breath and let my next words ooze out like a paramour's seductive whisper. ". . . fooootbaaaaaall praaaaactiiiiiccccccce." The words floated in the air, but I knew the weight of them would detonate on impact and destroy Ms. Adkins, her classroom, and probably the whole dang school. It was a bombshell.

As I recall, the old gal handled it admirably.

―――――

Remember, I'd never played football before this. No one in my family had ever played. Although many of my best friends were gridiron veterans, I knew very little about the sport. However, it didn't take long for me to learn two important things: I was overweight and I was weak.

For five days a week, two hours a day, I would sweat it out in practice, refusing to drink water in my attempt to shed pounds. I had to lose weight. Otherwise I had two options—ride the pine or move up to the next division (where the kids were even bigger, stronger, and faster). Neither sounded good.

Coach suggested I wear a thick plastic lawn bag under my shoulder pads to drain my body of as much sweat as possible. I pilfered one from the garage and cut holes for my head and arms. In those days, dehydration hadn't yet been invented.

Exhausted, stumbling around in a physical and mental fog, I became an affable blocking dummy for the healthier, more athletic kids. But that was okay. I could take it. I was playing football. And the pounds started coming off—*Hoo-wah!*

The day of our first game, I woke up early, peeled off my *Star Wars* pj's, and climbed on our bathroom scale. It was close, but I wasn't sure I would make weight. I'd endured too much to be left watching from the sidelines, forbidden to play. Apparently, fat kids were hazardous to the athletes, and league officials were tyrants on the matter. I had to figure something out. Fast.

After some coaxing, I talked Mom into helping me. I wish I hadn't.

On any other Saturday morning, I would've been in my pajamas in our family room, eating a bowl of off-brand Froot

Loops, and watching cartoons. However, that childish nonsense was left behind. I was a football player now. That came with a cost, and it was time to man up.

The determination to prove myself delivered a chubby, nine-year-old kid to his bathroom floor. Flat on my back, knees pulled to my chest, eyes squeezed shut, I pretended to not be horrified at the thought of my mother shoving a water hose up my rear end. Growing-up moments can be costly. This one came with an enema.

Three hours later, I made weight. I was eligible to play in my first football game.

For those who aren't football savvy, there's only one place to put awkward, slow kids who don't know what the heck they're doing: on the line. Mandatory play time wasn't a reality then, but my coach wasn't a total jerk. He tried to get everyone into the game for at least a play or two.

It was a Sahara Desert kind of day. Temperature already in the eighties long before noon. What little grass remained on our field was a sickly pale yellow, half dead and starving for water, not unlike *number twenty-four—that Fulks kid.*

The game began. I stood on that sideline and watched. And waited. I had no clue what was actually going on, but there was running and tackling and whistles and cheers and groans and clouds of dust . . . and me. Finally, after an eternity of baking in that sideline oven, my number came up.

"Bert!"

Coach was in the middle of field, motioning for me. Game time!

I ran onto that field like I'd already made the play that wins the championship.

We huddled up. The coach hissed out the play. The center—I

think it was Andy—snapped the ball. David, our quarterback, handed it to Lance, the meanest kid in town. The kid I was supposed to block spun me around like a turnstile and hammered Lance in the backfield, driving him hard into the ground.

As we reconvened in the huddle, Coach was livid. He was trying to scream at me, but he couldn't find me. Apparently (and I didn't know this at the time), every player has a specific place in the huddle. That way the coach can find him quickly and scream at the idiot. It's an efficient system.

Coach scanned the huddle and yelled, "Where the heck is Bert?"

I was hiding behind him. "Here, Coach."

The next part is a slow-motion sequence that's branded into my soul.

Coach spins, reaches out with huge talons, and grabs hold of my face mask. Like a scolded puppy that's just soiled the heirloom rug, I am yanked headfirst and dragged around the huddle—in front of all of my family and friends—as that giant continues to berate me. Held up only by my face mask snared in his massive grip, my feet stumble over the dusty ground. Coach slams me into my assigned spot. Once there, he rips me apart for missing the block that cost his team three yards.

My friends were quiet about it, but they were laughing at me. All except for Lance—I think he wanted to kill me.

I knew I'd missed my block. However, honest to God, I had no clue that I had a particular place to stand in the huddle. No one had ever told me that.

Humiliated? Yep. Heartbroken? You know it.

I toughed it out for a couple more weeks of trash bags and enemas, but I eventually quit. For a while, it was hard to look my friends in the eye. I was in no way ready to play football. And that was an awful truth.

I'm telling you this because I want you to realize what a pivotal moment this was in my life. Although I didn't realize it at the time, a deep part of me made a solemn vow that day: *I will never be unprepared again. I will study harder and work harder than everyone else. I will know everything there is to know. And I will hide on the sidelines until I know that I'm the one who gets to do the humiliating.*

That crippling vow stayed intact for decades, robbing a man of countless joys. Out of that secret vow came a bitter, sarcastic control freak. I became a man who would waste hours on the Internet exposing strangers for their ignorant beliefs and attitudes . . . a Christian man who would scour the Bible—not listening for God's heart, but searching for information to prove others wrong.

Years later, my innocent son found himself victimized by the cruelty of a humiliated, broken child who will never forget the degradation of a grown man dragging him around a football field by his face mask.

I never wanted Ben to know the terrible humiliation of not being prepared. I wanted him to be tougher and smarter than everyone else. I wanted him to know the victory that can only come through blood, sweat, and tears (as cliché as that is). Although I had the best of intentions (so I thought), it is only through God's grace that I didn't destroy my son during these times.

––––––––

If I had to point struggling parents to the best piece of parenting advice in the Bible, I would urge them to wrestle with a father's desperate plea as told by Matthew (9:18–26), Mark (5:21–43), and Luke (8:40–56). Here we find Jairus—a synagogue leader with Pharisee ties (remember, those guys hated Jesus). Crossing political lines, Jairus asks Jesus to heal his dying child. In another example of God's weird timing, the little girl dies before Jesus makes it to Jairus's home. When the devastating news reaches Jesus, he tells the father (I'm paraphrasing), "Relax. It will be okay. I can fix this." The crowd laughs at that. Unbelief at its best. But Jesus does exactly as he promised, and the child is restored to life.

I hope parents recognize the crux of this story: an adult steps up, goes against everything he knows, and asks Jesus to heal a child believed to have been lost to time. And Jesus does it. Scandalous. Over and over again, we see his incredible, rule-breaking compassion for children. However, I reference this tale for what I hope is becoming obvious: you are walking around with fragments of a broken child inside of you. You are haunted by a little boy or girl you think you've buried. That wounded child is alive, hiding in the dark corners of your soul, and whenever that kid feels threatened, he rises up in ugly ways.

Think of painful childhood moments as fragments of broken glass, littered across the landscape of your soul. If left unhealed, they will cut deeply those you love the most. With the best of intentions, we think we're preparing our children for the future, making them tough, and/or protecting them; but most often we're handing the reins and a whip to the damaged child inside of us—and our children bear that wrath.

Isaiah 61 reveals the heart of Jesus's mission:

The Spirit of the Lord God is upon me;
    [. . .] he hath sent me to bind up the brokenhearted,

to proclaim liberty to the captives, and the opening of the prison to them that are bound (KJV).

———

Friends, we all are the brokenhearted. The Hebrew text for "brokenhearted" is *shabhar lebh*, which means a spirit that has been crushed and shattered. We have many fractured places within us: young versions of ourselves now held captive by painful memories. Although you've tried to lock them up and throw away the key, those fragments of your soul still exist deep inside of you. As long as we leave them there, we remain broken and weak. Jesus has come to heal—to bind up—those severed pieces of us. That's his purpose. He's come for you.

> Jesus has come to heal—to bind up—those severed pieces of us. That's his purpose. He's come for you.

Understanding Jesus's perilous mission for your own heart is crucial to what kind of parent you will become. He wants to heal your brokenness—that wounded child—and make you whole. You have to ask him to reveal where you've been damaged and invite his healing and restoration. Until you do, you will continue to parent from a wounded heart . . . and no matter how much you love your kids, these broken pieces will cut them.

The sins of the parents . . .

My revelation about the face-mask incident from nearly forty years ago came to me after a night of prayer with friends. Talking about childhood experiences and the damaged places within all of us, we prayed, inviting Jesus into our memories. For me, he answered with one word: *football.* Days passed before I began to suspect what he was after—a memory of a lost boy. With some hesitance, I finally asked Jesus to take me to that chubby, awkward nine-year-old kid I'd tried so hard to bury.

He's not dead, Jesus was saying. *He's lost and afraid. May I heal him?*

In one of the most soul-crushing moments in my spiritual life, this witty, sarcastic (and often bitter) man became vulnerable to God's terrifying grace. I invited Jesus deeper into my story. With loving skill, Jesus put me face-to-face with nine-year-old Bert, still in his game uniform, face stained with tears behind a beat-up face mask. I never realized the loathing I'd developed toward that poor kid, and until I could have some compassion toward him, I would never be able to love my own children in the ways they needed.

With healing comes strength. In parenting advice, I often say that it's not about you, but in this case it *is* all about you. Behind our many efforts to help our kids succeed, the story of a fractured child is revealed: a girl who believes she's not beautiful or special; a boy who hides—he knows you think him a failure, an embarrassment.

Think of the things you want for your children, both now and down the road. Consider all of life's arenas: school, relationships, sports, performance activities, even religion. . . . Now pray about it. Ask Jesus, *Is this really about me? Why do I want this for them? What's my motive here? Is this really about a scared, humiliated child that I've tried to bury in the past? Jesus, will you reveal that wounded child in me? Will you take me to her? Please save her. Will you heal her? Please give me the wisdom and courage to tell her how special she is, and that she doesn't have to hide anymore.*

Exodus 34:7 reveals the urgency when God tells Moses, "I lay the sins of the parents upon their children" (NLT). At the core, your sins are the ways you turn away from God and try to go it alone, as if you have it all figured out and don't need healing. Consider the ways you self-medicate to numb the pain still felt by that younger version of you. Don't dismiss these tender places. Our most overlooked sin is usually that we don't let Jesus do the very thing he came for—to heal us and make us whole.

Remember, an *X* is formed when two lines headed in different directions come together. X-Plan parenting acknowledges how the condition of one affects the other.

Friends, develop some space in your life for your own restoration. There's no better parenting tip I can give you. As hurt people hurt people, we need to recognize the ways we've been hurt. Until we honor the young, tender places inside of us and invite Jesus's healing, our own children will suffer the fallout. And they deserve something better. It is a dangerous, hurtful world, and now—more than ever—our kids need parents who have been made whole and can love them with strength. And no matter how old your kids are, no matter how far you've traveled, it's never too late for healing and redemption. Just ask Jairus. His kid was dead. Until Jesus showed up with his X-Plan.

> And no matter how old your kids are, no matter how far you've traveled, it's never too late for healing and redemption.

I bet Jairus became a different father after that.

CHAPTER 7

Don't Provoke Them

One of my worst parenting mistakes has been trying to make my kids feel better when they're struggling and upset. I've come to realize that much of my desire for their happiness has more to do with my brokenness than hope for their well-being. When I fail to be sympathetic to whatever may be swirling around in their young souls, I risk provoking something ugly (or even deadly) that's lurking inside of them.

Katie Jo (our seventeen-year-old) is up early. I find her curled up in the family room recliner, brooding over her first cup of coffee as she stares blindly at her phone. Dawn's early light slices through the blinds and reveals the suspended dust particles that haunt every home, no matter how much you clean.

"Mom showed me videos of last night's rehearsal," I say from the doorway.

Preparing to take her first leap as prima ballerina in a full production of *Romeo and Juliet*, my baby girl is staring into a spotlight that might be an oncoming train. She's grateful for the opportunity (she's worked for years to get this chance, wearing out pointe shoes at a painful rate), but she puts such insane pressure on herself that she can't enjoy it. Few superstars could live up to my JoJo's dangerous, self-loathing expectations.

"It's really coming together, babe." I move toward her to caress her hair. "Beautiful." But I stay my hand, knowing at once that my touch is not welcome. *She thinks she's unworthy, unlovable . . . not good enough. Her walls are up, and she's inside, beating up on herself.*

I see tears form in her eyes. "No," she says as her lower jaw stiffens. She takes another sip of coffee and hides behind the giant fishbowl of a mug. Like most young ladies, my daughter struggles with wanting to hide and be known at the same time.

Right now, her ballet performance is all that matters to her, and she's listening to the treacherous voices that are assaulting her: *You're going to blow it and then you'll be exposed, and they'll see—they'll all see—that it was a ridiculous mistake to think you could do this. Not good enough . . .*

I'm trying hard not to let myself care too much about this ballet. I do care—naturally—because it's important to Katie. However, I can't let her see that. I don't want her to think that her ability to perform has anything to do with my love for her. Like dust particles, those sinister lies are also floating around every home.

I want to say something else, something wise and tender that will reassure her, calm her anxiety, and wipe away her doubt about her upcoming performance. But what can I say to convince my daughter of her gifts, grace, and beauty?

Nothing. Not at this point, anyway. So I say exactly that—nothing—and exit the room.

I tell myself this is my parenting win for the day because I didn't provoke her any further.

———

I once coached a kid in baseball who was a lovable goofball. A happy-go-lucky twelve-year-old, Bobby was always quick to smile and laugh. But there was always a stream of anxiety flowing just beneath the surface of his round, freckled face. Bobby was older than most of the other kids on the team, but he hadn't played much baseball. What little talent he possessed had never been developed, and he was struggling. He could throw and catch okay, but with a bat in his hands, Bobby could fall out of a boat and never hit water. Whenever he stepped into the batter's box, the poor kid was a bundle of nerves—stiff and twitchy, feet shuffling all over the place. Bobby's age and physical maturity helped him overcome some of his awkwardness, but not enough to earn him much game time. Ever the optimist, I had the crazy idea that if I could help Bobby with his swing—just correct a few fundamental flaws—the kid might start hitting the ball, gain some confidence, and earn more play time.

One day I pulled Bobby aside to work with him in the batting cage. I started by talking to him about his grip on the bat, planning to address one small thing at a time. Once that was corrected, he stood at the plate and I took my position behind the pitching screen.

"Don't do that," I heard one of the other coaches, Jim, whisper behind me. I turned to face him. "Don't mess with Bobby's swing. His dad's kind of a control freak. He sees you changing Bobby's swing and you'll hear about it." Jim must have read my incredulous expression. "In this case, let Dad handle his own kid."

I couldn't believe what I was hearing. "Does he like seeing his kid strike out?" I asked low enough so Bobby wouldn't hear.

Jim shrugged as if to say, *Do what you want, but I warned you.*

I looked across the field and found Bobby's dad leaning against the outfield fence, peering at us. Suddenly it all made sense. I realized that every time Bobby stepped into the batter's box, he wasn't looking for fastballs; he could only think about his dad's expectations and critical gaze from the fence line. I believe father and son loved and cared for each other as well as they could (like the rest of us), but the disconnect between two disparate souls came into focus. I started to realize that Bobby didn't care so much about baseball. Not really. He enjoyed being around his friends, but I think he was only in uniform to please his dad. All kids crave that, and that desire can become pretty warped and damaging if we're not careful. Bobby wasn't much of an athlete, and I'm sure he felt like a disappointment to his dad. I can't imagine what the rides home from the baseball field must have felt like for the poor kid. Not that Bobby's dad was cruel—I never saw that—but when you think you're a failure in someone else's eyes, even well-intentioned counsel can feel like an assault.

I didn't want to interfere and cause trouble for Bobby, so I took Jim's advice and gave up on helping the kid develop his own, natural swing. That decision still haunts me. The window of opportunity to help someone remains open for just a brief moment.

After the season ended, the years stacked up. I never saw Bobby again. The next thing I heard about the young man was from a news report. Bobby had murdered his dad and was somewhere on the run.

In Ephesians 6:4, we're told to "not provoke your children to anger by the way you treat them" (NLT). Colossians 3:21 offers a similar warning: "do not aggravate your children, or they will become discouraged" (NLT). As a dad, I'm left scratching my head. My kids are often angry at me for one reason or another. My "Good morning, JoJo" is usually met with a growl and a scowl as Katie zombie-walks toward the coffeepot each morning. How can you be a parent of any teenager and not "provoke" or "aggravate" them? It comes with the territory. Those little nuclear warheads of raging hormones are usually provoked and aggravated before I even enter the room.

Don't provoke them.

Don't provoke them.

Okay, I won't do that. That seems an easy enough parenting tip. However, isn't that part of my job as a parent? Am I not supposed to engage in uncomfortable moments to spur the growth and development of my children? Kids are malleable, and they need to be shaped, right? I've seen too many self-centered brats who have never had their egos challenged. As a teacher, I've seen the fallout from parents who were too afraid to "provoke" their children. I once taught at a high school where a large number of our students were well-to-do children of privilege. We had a saying for these kids: "How many ____s (insert name) does it take to screw in a lightbulb? Just one. She stands there and holds it while the world revolves around her."

The Message translates Colossians 3:21 this way: "Parents, don't come down too hard on your children or you'll crush their spirits."*

Oh, good glory.

You don't get through life without having your spirit crushed a thousand times over. Shouldn't we be preparing our kids for that while they're still young and the cost is relatively small? Doesn't that take some provocation and aggravation? Every powerful military throughout history has followed the same type of soldier training: constantly tear them down in order to build them back up and make them stronger. And isn't that our goal—growing strong kids?

But, friends, we're not developing living, breathing weapons. Or are we?

When Ben was still in high school, he came to me early one morning and handed me a paper. "Dad, will you sign this?" I studied the blank form and tried to decipher all of the blank lines and empty spaces. At the bottom was a line for a parent's signature.

"What is this?" I asked.

"It's a stupid thing we have to do for health class," he grumbled. "We're supposed to keep a food diary for a week. Nutrition and stuff. It's due today."

"Dude"—I sighed heavily—"there's nothing on here. What does my signature prove?"

"It's stupid," he repeated. "I'll just make stuff up and write it down in homeroom."

"So you're admitting that you didn't do this, and you're asking me to lie about it?"

---

*Eugene H. Peterson, *The Message*. Bible Gateway, www.biblegateway.com.

"Dad, it's stupid."

I shrugged, opened my desk drawer, pulled out a black Sharpie pen, and then went to work on the bottom of Ben's blank form. After signing my name, I handed him the paper. Ben read what I had written in permanent marker above my elegant autograph:

Ben did not complete this assignment.

He glared at me, crumpled the paper, and then stormed out of the house.

I probably should've handled that better. I'm pretty sure I'd provoked and aggravated my son at the worst possible time. He went off to school enraged at me—which I'd anticipated. However, looking back I now realize how exhausted, frustrated, and alone Ben probably felt. He was taking all honors and Advanced Placement classes. He had baseball practice every day after school and was usually doing homework and studying until the early morning hours. He was also wrestling with all of the normal teen challenges of relationships, identity, self-confidence, social pressures . . .

On top of all that, Laura and I had been urging Ben to start thinking about colleges, which always threw him into a tailspin. He refused to even discuss the subject. In short, the young man felt like he was juggling chain saws. My script at the bottom of his health form surely felt like I'd only tossed him another one. I don't regret refusing to sign my name to a lie, but if I could do it over, I'd definitely take a different approach. The way I handled it was far from loving. Eugene Peterson's translation of Ephesians 6:4 reads: "Fathers, don't exasperate your children by coming down too hard on them. Take them by the hand and lead them in the way of the Master" (*The Message*). In this instance, I failed. I made my point, but I didn't lead my son in the way of the Master. I only demonstrated a petty display of unreasonable passive aggression that drove my son away. I engaged Ben in a teachable moment, but without wisdom, tenderness, or strength.

I provoked him.

———————

We've given Danny a choice for his sophomore year of high school. He can participate in marching band again (which he complained about all last year), join the cross-country team, play football or baseball, join the theater—anything!—but he's not going to sit around and do nothing. Danny is the kid who needs a structured activity. Otherwise he ends up sitting around doing not much of anything and becomes a miserable, depressed cur. While Ben and Katie usually take on too much, Danny complains about anything that "wastes his time."

Last night we were discussing the issue after dinner, and Danny became agitated.

"I just don't like being told I have to do something," he whined. He turned his accusing glare toward me. "Dad, you know I love to ride my bike. But if you say, 'Danny, why don't you go out and ride your bike?' it just makes me not want to do something I really want to do!"

The boy often drives me nuts, but on this subject, I understand. I really do.

When I was in junior high, I was second-chair trumpet in the band. I'd spend hours not only practicing our assigned music, but also figuring out the melodies to some of my favorite pop and rock songs. Mom saw my talent and interest and encouraged me as best she knew how. Each day I'd hear the same thing: "Did you play your horn today?" Our band teacher had recommended we practice at home at least thirty minutes each day. Mom took this as gospel.

At first, it wasn't that big a deal, because the answer was always yes. However, by my eighth-grade year, life was happening. I was struggling socially, figuring out the mystery of girls, trying to find my place in a weird world, and being bullied by a gang from the rough side of town. But I felt like Mom didn't care about any of that.

"Did you play your horn today?"

Every. Single. Day. After a while, it started to feel like an ice pick though my ear.

Did it provoke me?

Heck yes, it did. In fact, I'm growing angry sitting here writing about it.

"Did you play your horn today?"

That question felt so nagging, uncaring, and out of touch with all the other things I was going through that I had to find some way to make it stop. So I quit the band, packed away my trumpet, and never played it again. Some years later I sold it for $40 in a yard sale, thinking being rid of that thing would provide some kind of revenge or vindication. It brought neither. I should have known.

Had my mother provoked me? Even though she'd never meant it, she had.

I now find myself dealing with Danny, trying to walk the tightrope between encouraging dedication and avoiding provocation. I want him to experience the satisfaction and success that can only come from hard work, but I don't want to be the overbearing taskmaster that kills his passion. But how do I find the balance?

Studying those verses mentioned above, I came across theologian Charles Ellicott's commentary for the Ephesians verse. That's where I found the key to unlock this mystery. In scriptural terms, we provoke our children when we arbitrarily rule over them without sympathy.

Are you an unsympathetic parent?

None of us wants to be or intends to be, but we are exactly that from time to time. It's part of our brokenness. It's impossible to always be empathetic toward our kids, because even in the closest parent-child relationships, kids struggle with stuff they don't even recognize or understand. How can we possibly know all that's swirling around in their souls?

When Paul tells us to not provoke our kids, he's telling us to be loving and strong, but to be tender at the same time.

A dear friend was having a hard time with his preteen son. Zack is an athletic, competitive kid who reminds me a lot of my Katie. They're both tormented by the not-good-enough demon.

"He's killing me," my friend said to me one day about his son. "He could have three hits, seven RBIs, and turn ten double plays, but God help us if he makes one mistake on the field! He won't let it go. I try to remind Zack of all the things he did right, but that only makes it worse. It's almost like he wants me to be as mad at him as he is at himself, and the fact that I'm not just sets him off like some psycho."

I'd been through the same thing with my kids when they were younger.

"I'd advise you say nothing," I said to my friend. "You're trying to pull Zack out of a storm, but you're only getting sucked into the tornado. Stop responding. Let him feel bad about a play he didn't make. If you try to argue with him, you're really just telling him that he has no right to feel how he feels, and that's not fair."

A few weeks later I saw my buddy and he told me that he'd taken my advice. "Things are actually getting better. He has his emotional spell, I let him go, and then we get on with our day."

I'm not patting myself on the back here for getting this right. I screwed up in this department for years until finally figuring it out with Ben after some baseball meltdowns.

Too often, we provoke our kids to anger, frustration, and despondency because the true motives behind our words and actions aren't sympathetic, but actually quite selfish. I can't count the times Ben would be in the throes of self-cannibalization over some mistake that had "lost the game" for his team. Out of what I thought were love and encouragement for my son, I would fall into some crazy argument, like a lawyer before a judge pleading my case and presenting the evidence that would acquit the boy of all guilt. I now realize I was only invalidating my son's emotions. I wasn't being sympathetic toward him. I just wanted him to get over it so I could feel better. Being around someone who's deep in misery is . . . well, miserable. But sometimes our kids need that. They need the space and freedom to wrestle with their disappointments, frustrations, and fears.

> Too often, we provoke our kids to anger, frustration, and despondency because the true motives behind our words and actions aren't sympathetic, but actually quite selfish.

> They need the space and freedom to wrestle with their disappointments, frustrations, and fears.

To try to talk them out of it isn't encouraging or loving; it's only provoking. That's exactly why I left Katie alone with her cup of coffee this morning. She was upset, frustrated, and worried. I can't fix that for her. And I'm not going to invalidate her feelings by arguing with her about how beautiful and talented a dancer she is. I will, however, tell her I love her every chance I get; and when the time is right, I'll remind her that she is important to me not because of anything she does, but simply because of who she is.

I often find myself thinking of Bobby these days.

The world is not kind to our kids. There is an unseen war being waged against their hearts, driving them to either rage or discouragement. We have to be cognizant of that and constantly take counteractive measures. Realize that whenever you engage your kid, you're also tapping into their wounds, doubts, fears, hopes, joys, disappointments, and a tapestry of truth and lies that are swirling around inside of them. Even when we approach our kids with the best of intentions, we risk provoking some tender, broken places. We have to be sympathetic to places we can't even identify. I urge you to seek out those places. Don't drill your kids with questions about their struggles. Heck, sometimes they don't even know what's eating at them. However, prayerfully and empathetically search for understanding so you know how best to navigate the rocks and waterfalls. When it comes to your kid, you have to know where the chinks in the armor are, what de-

> When it comes to your kid, you have to know where the chinks in the armor are, what demons they're wrestling with, and what larger challenges are hidden beneath the surface.

mons they're wrestling with, and what larger challenges are hidden beneath the surface.

Years ago, I had a buddy arrange to have his son play on my baseball team. Pete would do anything we asked of him, and he tried like crazy to make his dad proud. Unfortunately, he just didn't have much talent when it came to sports. But that didn't stop him from trying his best and doing it with a smile. That's why I was a little shocked when his dad came to me about three weeks into the season and handed me Pete's uniform.

"I've never let my kids quit anything," he said with some shame, "but I had a long talk with Pete. I was beginning to suspect he really wasn't having much fun, and I realized something. He'd never wanted to play baseball. The only reason he signed up was because he thought I wanted him to. He knows how much I love the game."

I wanted to hug the guy. He stepped out of his own shoes and walked around in his son's for just a little bit, and it made all the difference. Now, years later, I often come across Pete—he's an amazing artist and musician—and I think back to that day when his dad handed me that uniform.

The key to not provoking your kid is to explore with love and wisdom what's going on in his heart. Sometimes the waters are too murky and you simply won't be able to see into the depths. That's okay. Just love them and try to understand them. Sometimes that means trying to connect with them, and sometimes it means giving them some space and grace.

I often wonder what finally provoked Bobby into a despondent rage that I simply can't comprehend. Or perhaps don't want to, terrified that it's something floating around all of our homes, looking for a place to land. Like dust in the air.

CHAPTER 8

Come Out and Play

*Play is an expression of God's presence in
the world; one clear sign of God's absence in
society is the absence of playfulness and laughter.*
—Mike Yaconelli

Want to save your kid's life?
Try this:

Put on a silly hat (if you don't have one, make one out of paper). Go find your kid, step in front of him, and in the most theatrical performance you can muster, sing your favorite song. When you're finished, bow and walk away without saying a word.

We try so hard to usher our kids into adulthood. The result? We surrender some of life's best magic. But what if you took regular breaks from growing your kids up and, instead, let them draw you back into childhood?

As Bob Dylan sings, "I was so much older then, I'm younger than that now."

Indeed.

If Danny remembers only four words from his childhood, I fear they will be, *What were you thinking?* I'd probably asked him that question hundreds of times before he reached the age of ten. From there it grew exponentially.

A collection of logs, sticks, and trash bags strung together

with rope and duct tape on the hillside like a squatters' camp—
What were you thinking?

Power saws, wrenches, and screwdrivers strewn over the garage floor, along with the abandoned parts of his Power Wheels truck he'd outgrown. He'd cut it apart to make some cannibalized Frankenstein go-cart—*What were you thinking?*

After this discovery, I was sitting on the patio looking at my son in disbelief that he'd done something so foolish. Again. It was a hot summer day. I'd just finished cutting the grass and was talking with Laura. Danny was standing in front of me, waiting patiently for his lecture so he could move on to his next adventure. (You'll recall this story from chapter 2, but it's worth revisiting because it reveals something essential to recapturing your playful heart—playfulness sometimes defies logic.)

"Son," I said, "what were you thinking?"

He huffed in exasperation. Brow furrowed. Head tilted to one side and palms up in the universal sign of *why can't you understand?*

"Dad, I had a plan," he said. "It just didn't work out. Sometimes you try things that don't work out."

Laura was smirking at me, trying her very best not to laugh. *Point to Danny*, her eyes mocked me.

"Danny." I looked back at my son, but couldn't find the words. He'd sucker punched me. "Get out of here." I shooed him with a dismissive wave and away he scampered. Laura broke out in laughter, no doubt thinking of my many Clark Griswold moments. However, I couldn't laugh. Danny's words hit me somewhere deep.

I was often frustrated with my son because of his constant drive for taking something mundane and creating risk and adventure. He always started with a plan, and although he never knew how it would turn out, that never dissuaded him from forging ahead. Me, on the other hand . . . I'd grown up. I'd learned to control my universe, nail down as much as possible, make my world safe and predictable, and avoid risk whenever possible.

My son's innocent declaration was both right and wrong. I still had plans and sometimes they didn't work out, but they were small, petty plans I could control: a minor plumbing project, maybe a bathroom remodel, repair the tractor, etc. However, I'd quit taking real risks. I didn't cross a bridge unless I knew what to expect on the other side.

I'd managed to reduce my life to a routine of safe predictability, and Danny's words were a wake-up call that hit me like that catchphrase from Stephen King's *Rita Hayworth and Shawshank Redemption*:

"Get busy living or get busy dying."

My friend Steve and I had a regrettably awesome idea: "Let's have the most unforgettable Fourth of July fireworks display *EVER!*"

We pooled our resources and headed across the river to smuggle boxes of explosives back into West Virginia. Rockets. Missiles. Screamers. Repeaters. Roman candles. Dozens of exploding mortars (those are the big ones, kids).

As family and friends filled our yard, we anxiously awaited the cover of darkness so we could light up the night sky. It was going to be . . . *glorious!*

Unfortunately, communication along the front line suffered a setback, resulting in a "slight weapons malfunction." To cut to the chase, a random spark ignited some misplaced mortars, and our backyard became a war zone.

Within sixty seconds, nearly $500 worth of fireworks came roaring to life and attacked in all directions. The rockets' red glare. The bombs burst in the air . . . and on my house . . . and next to screaming people running for cover. At one point I saw my wife's cousin, just home from Iraq and still in uniform, running through the yard, tossing children over his shoulder and extracting them from the battlefield. People were diving in the pool as my wife screamed, "Get under the water! Stay down!"

You know that final scene from *Caddyshack* when Carl blows up the entire golf course? That was child's play compared to our epic disaster.

———

About a year later, we're standing on the deck of a US Navy aircraft carrier. Fireworks rain down over the Pacific Ocean. Breathtaking. Majestic. Actually, those words don't come close to this beauty as lights and colors erupt into existence and then float down to kiss their own reflections on the water. And there, in the midst of this stunning display, stands fifteen-year-old Ben with a disinterested, bored-to-death expression.

"Dude!" I growl, giving him a hard elbow. "Really?" I gesture emphatically at the explosions as if to say, *This! You melancholy punk! Do you not see THIS?!*

"It's all right," he mutters with a shrug, "but it's just not that exciting if you're not running for your life."

Truth.

———

There is something deep within us that craves adventure and exploration. Our souls long for it like our lungs burn for oxygen.

Meanwhile, an opposite force pushes back, an accusing spirit that taunts us: *Gain control. Limit risk. Don't be vulnerable.*

Consider how much effort goes into trying to control your world and make it safe. I'll admit, I was once a control freak. But I now realize my attempt to limit risk didn't make my world any more predictable or pain-free; it only left me on the sidelines of life, watching the adventure from afar, growing more bored (and anxious) by the minute as some spark within me fought for breath.

The heart is a wild, mysterious landscape that was never meant to be tamed. If you demand control and strive to avoid risk, all you really accomplish is a divorce from your own soul (and the life you're meant to have). "Security," Helen Keller stated, "is mostly a superstition. Life is either a daring adventure or nothing."

> The heart is a wild, mysterious landscape that was never meant to be tamed.

And the blind shall see . . .

Think back to the Genesis story and the fall of mankind. Evil enters the story and makes a convincing sales pitch. Consider what Satan was dangling in front of the world's original playful parents.

It wasn't an apple. Along with planting a mistrust of God, the offer was control.

You can have all the answers. And with all the answers, you gain control. With control, you remove vulnerability and risk. Then you can make your world predictable and safe.

In that context, we see how original sin (turning away from God) came with a twisted desire to make our lives . . . well, boring.

However, boredom doesn't mean that unpredictability, danger, and risk are banished from your world. Life remains uncontrollable. Boredom only suggests that you've stepped out of life's arena. You've unplugged. If you're bored or detached (with yourself, the world, or your relationships) it's likely you've quit taking risks. I'm guessing your date night consists of renting movies and not salsa lessons. Meanwhile, some deep anxiety smolders in your soul. Your heart cries out for adventure . . . for life.

One of my friends in ministry had a social media meltdown a few years back. Through his cryptic Facebook post, I could hear his frustration beneath the words, "I've decided that from now on, I'm going to start treating kids like kids and adults like adults!"

Think how much effort goes into forcing our kids to "grow up" (whatever that actually means). I often tiptoe around adults hoping to avoid conflict. Meanwhile, I'll rip into my kids for being childlike.

There's a great scene in the movie *Hook*. Robin Williams stars as an all-grown-up Peter Pan. The original lost boy is now married with kids, has a house, a mortgage, and a high-anxiety, soul-sucking, white-collar job, and he has completely forgotten who he really is. To our horror, we're confronted by a driven control freak whose name should be synonymous with risk, adventure, and play. Aboard an airplane on a family trip, adult Peter (who is terrified of flying) is berating his son for bouncing a ball that goes astray and pops open an overhead compartment.

"Would you stop acting so childish?" Peter barks at his son, Jack.

"But," Jack replies with a playful grin, "I *am* a child."

Anthropologist Garry Chick, PhD, notes that postmodern adults still play, but our ability to be *playful* "has been replaced by aggressiveness and the feeling that more needs to be crammed into less time."* We don't let ourselves get lost in the adventure of true, spontaneous play. Even our "leisure" activities become tainted by our overscheduled, control-seeking sickness. Meanwhile, our souls are crying out for risk and adventure, a journey to where the outcome can't be predicted.

In her book *The Art of Risk*, Kayt Sukel reveals how the brain changes over time. As we age, we become more controlling and less risky. However, Sukel says the very risk-taking we associate with childhood comes with a beautiful benefit: learning and growth. Our society tells kids to grow up by planning for security and control, but science tells us that true growth and development come from risk and adventure. Meanwhile, most parents are telling their kids, *Here, let me teach you how to build a stagnant existence*, when we should be inviting them into playful adventures, telling them, *Here, let me show you how to play!*

There's a psychological reality to Jesus's urging us to become like children again. We've stopped taking risks and we've forgotten how to play, and we need both of those things to unlock the mysteries of who we really are and what we were made for. "Risk taking," says psychologist Thomas Crowley, is "important for the species and the individual."† All human development and advancement have come from the playful art of taking risks, with some imaginative dreamer thinking, *What if . . . ?*

---

*Hara Estroff Marano, "The Power of Play," *Psychology Today* (July 1, 1999), https://www.psychologytoday.com/us/articles/199907/the-power-play.
†Florence Williams, "This Is Your Brain on Adventure," *Outside* (March 19, 2009), https://www.outsideonline.com/1896581/your-brain-adventure.

And though we all have some predispositions toward either taking chances or playing it safe, having either an attitude of adventure or a spirit of fear and dullness can be taught and nurtured. One of the best ways we can do that for ourselves and our children is through our play.

————————

Jesus tells us that we'll never see paradise unless we become like children again. Our response to that has become a slavish addiction to work, control, and growing up. Meanwhile, something inside of us either slowly withers on the vine or shows up in some warped, dangerous ways. Think of the middle-aged woman who starts sneaking off to have an affair, or the man who abandons his family to run off and find some foolish adventure. Both of these reveal the buried hearts of children, forced to grow up and quit playing, and now they're crying out for release.

Working with teenagers in addiction recovery, I once took them some coloring pages to drive home the point I wanted to make during our discussion. What I quickly realized, however, is that once they started coloring, they (every single one of them) slipped into another universe. They had no interest in one another, me, their problems, the discussion—nothing but coloring their pictures. These are fourteen-to-nineteen-year-olds. With coloring books and crayons, they didn't look like world-hardened young people locked up in a rehab facility. They looked like kids lost in the heart of play. As they shared their pictures, explaining them and revealing funny, imaginative stories, they became like children again and I saw a spark of life burning in each of them. They were rediscovering something precious that had been stolen from them—a child's ability to play—and it melted my heart.

My friend Alex (who's worked daily with these types of kids for decades) said, "Most of them had to grow up so fast and learn to survive, they missed out on some of the simple pleasures of childhood." Like the healthy risks that come with simple play. So their risks became truly dangerous ones.

I spent the next few weeks coloring with these kids. I had a few points to make, but mostly I just let them play and be childlike, and it was probably more life-giving than anything I could have offered them.

We are designed for adventure. There's something in our soul that cries out for it. Look at creation. As John Eldredge writes, "creation is unapologetically wild."* God made a risky, unpredictable world and then set Adam and Eve in the midst of it and said, *Go for it!* Look throughout the Bible of what a walk with God is really like. It's never safe and predictable. It's about incredible journeys, battles, storms at sea, shipwrecks, jailbreaks. We are made to walk with God—even if we forget this in our minds, our souls never forget—and that walk reveals the essence of playfulness, where we find the joy of risk and adventure, where the heart of a child comes alive.

Can you remember the first time you went down a tall slide? Your first dance? First bike ride? The first time you skied? Your first kiss? Do you remember how your heart came alive? It was part of the adventure, and there was something at stake. You had to take some risks.

That's core to who and what we are.

Mike Yaconelli shares the story about pulling his kid out of school one day without warning. He walks into the office, asks the secretary to call down his son and bring his stuff. He'll be

---

*John Eldredge, *Wild at Heart* (Nashville, TN: Thomas Nelson, 2011).

leaving for the day. His son, surprised and confused, asks what's going on as they walk out together. Mike hushes the boy and tells him to just get in the car that's waiting out front . . . with the boat hitched up to the back.

Mike made it a point to have spontaneous play dates with his kids because he knew that play—and playfulness—is critical for life. If mankind spent half the effort in pursuit of play as we spend toward control, can you imagine what a paradise we could create?

Thy kingdom come, thy will be done on Earth as it is in Heaven . . .

Dad, I had a plan. It just didn't work out.

Friends, I'm not talking about being irresponsible and foolish or taking risks just for the sake of danger. I'm talking about being playful.

———

One of Webster's definitions for "play" is "recreational activity for pleasure, esp. the impulsive activity of children."

What's the last impulsive thing you did?

Children do spontaneous stuff all the time. Sure, some of it might be silly, but play reveals the essence of the life God wants us to have. In our effort to teach our kids to be responsible, make good decisions, and play it safe, we might drive playfulness from their vocabulary, but not their hearts. The soul yearns for play and the benefits that come with it: creativity, flexibility, health, wellness, and longevity. Something about play gives us drive while shielding us from its sinister stepsibling—drivenness—and the damaging consequences that come along for the ride.

Temple University studied incoming first graders, comparing those who'd received early reading instruction to those who had a less structured background of simple play. As expected, the first group performed better . . . but by the end of the year that reversed. Brian Sutton-Smith, PhD, notes that kids who are allowed and encouraged to be playful develop better memories, stronger cognition, and become . . . well, happier. Those kids from the other group, Sutton-Smith found, "were more depressed. The opposite of play is not work. It's depression."*

I think of those young people who have turned to drugs and alcohol and wonder, how much of that risky behavior is actually self-medication for the soul's cry for good old-fashioned healthy play?

I will warn you, if you're not living some kind of adventure and inviting your kids up into that world of play, they will go off seeking it in other places, and that may not turn out well. Never stop playing with your kids. Play for no other reason than the joy of play itself, and that joyous activity will strengthen and grow you, your child, and your relationship.

> Never stop playing with your kids. Play for no other reason than the joy of play itself, and that joyous activity will strengthen and grow you, your child, and your relationship.

St. Irenaeus is often credited with having said, "The glory of God is man fully alive."† So, what makes you come

---

*Hara Estroff Marano, "The Power of Play," *Psychology Today* (July 1, 1999), https://www.psychologytoday.com/us/articles/199907/the-power-play.
†This is a common quote in Christian circles. However, some scholars argue that the quote is either misattributed or mistranslated from St. Irenaeus's writings, warning of the quote's potential misuse to encourage any attempt of self-fulfillment apart from God.

alive? You might have to go back into your childhood and think about what you played, why you loved it, and then ask yourself, *Why that?*

I love fishing and camping. My kids' enthusiasm for such play varies from being on board to "Thanks, but no thanks." That's okay. I fish, camp, and hike because I love those things and have since I was a boy. I'd abandoned them for many years of my life, but I'm recapturing those joys. Sometimes Laura and the kids join me. Sometimes they don't. But they see me at play, and that can be as important as playing with them.

A friend often laments the disconnection between him and his son. "He doesn't talk to me," my buddy has said more times than I can count. He's a great father. Loving and supportive and always involved. However, I now suspect that most of what they did together as father and son had more to do with Dad's interests (athletics) than the boy's notion of adventure and play.

Just the other day he was telling me about his son going to South America to scuba dive. The young man has also taken up camping, bird-watching, rock-climbing, and skydiving.

"Dude," I said, "that's so awesome! Why don't you join him in some of that? How cool would that be?"

He smiled from behind his desk. "My idea of camping is no room service."

My point here is twofold. There are some adventures your kid may be wired for that aren't meant to be part of your journey. Same with you and your adventures, and that's okay. We play because it's good for our souls, so encourage your kids to do their own thing. However, children always need their parents' counsel, and play is one of the ways we can teach them and nurture our relationships.

Think about what you do with your friends, the ones who

share your deepest heartaches and joys. Isn't there usually some type of play involved? Maybe it's fishing, golf, baking, or exercising. Whatever it is, it's through play that we often water and grow our relationships. And it's the most risky, adventurous play that forges the deepest bonds. The best kinds of play are something akin to stepping into battle. Any soldier will tell you, a spiritual bond is forged between hearts that share trenches.

Brian McQuinn and Harvey Whitehouse once asked soldiers about how connected they felt to certain groups.* Forty-five percent of the "front-line fighters" felt a stronger bond with their fellow soldiers than with their own families. Adventurous play delivers the same benefits. Play allows us to test ourselves in different scenarios, with relatively safe challenges, and invites us to take some risks and unravel some of the mysteries of the heart. In short, it takes us and our kids closer to God and his desires for us.

———

There's a great scene in the movie *Never Cry Wolf* where a crazy pilot (Rosie) is flying a nerdy scientist (Tyler) into the arctic wild. Soaring over frozen mountaintops in a rickety prop plane, Rosie shares a crucial secret to life: "We're all of us prospectors up here, eh, Tyler? Scratchin' for that . . . that one crack in the ground. Never have to scratch again. I'll let you in on a little secret, Tyler. The gold's not in the ground. The gold's not anywhere up here. The real gold is south of sixty—sitting in living rooms, stuck facing the boob tube, bored to death. Bored to death, Tyler!"

---

*Harvey Whitehouse, "Libyan bands of brothers show how deeply humans bond in adversity," *The Conversation*, November 12, 2014, http://theconversation.com/libyan-bands-of-brothers-show-how-deeply-humans-bond-in-adversity-34105.

At that, the propeller sputters to a stop and the plane begins to fall toward the mountains.

Rosie screams, "Aaaaaaahhhh!"

"What's wrong?" Tyler pleads.

Rosie takes a deep breath, then turns his gaze to his passenger. "Boredom, Tyler. Boredom. That's what's wrong. And how do you beat boredom, Tyler? Adventure. Adventure, Tyler."

With that, Rosie climbs out of the plane with a wrench, a wild playfulness burning in his eyes.

––––––––––––

One day I was in the kitchen fuming as I rearranged the dishes in the dishwasher. Again!

Cups go here! Spoons up—forks down! Oh my—just look at this! You can fit three more bowls over here! Why can't they figure this out?

As I slammed dishes around the dishwasher, my insane rage growing, I happened to look up and see my three children watching me from the kitchen table.

My God. What had I become?

I'd surrendered so much of my life in an effort to get everything right, secure and protect what's mine, and arrange my world with total order, leaving no room for chaos. Or a bowl out of place. Or a spontaneous mess. Mike Yaconelli says we find God in the mess. I'd lost sight of that. And for a brief moment I saw myself through my kids' eyes: a stressed-out, driven man whose sanitized version of play came through the self-medication of a bottle, and whose greatest adventure was my mastery of dishwasher loading.

Play is about testing your limits, seeing what you're made of, but within the amusement park of joy. If we don't actively pursue play for ourselves and our children, psychologists agree: we kick open the door to drivenness, anxiety, depression, social dissonance, and a host of soul-crushing side effects . . . and that is not the life God wants for you or your child.

Adventurous play is also critical for the stability of your marriage. Terri Orbuch, PhD, says "few factors undermine a relationship more than boredom."* How often have you heard women lament the loss of passion (an emotional adventure) while men complain their women are trying to tame them? I hear it all the time. Meanwhile, we quit playing, stop living any sort of adventure, and turn to self-medication to numb ourselves to some loss we can't name. God made us in his image, and we are designed for adventure and play, but we work so hard at training our kids to grow up and stop playing. Our kids watch us make our lives as dull and lifeless as possible, and then we wonder why they want nothing to do with us.

> *Play is not an escape; it is the way to release the life-smothering grip of busyness, stress, and anxiety. Playfulness is a modern expression of hope, a celebration of the flickering light of the gospel that plays with the dark by pouncing on the surrounding darkness like a cat toying with a mouse.*
> —Mike Yaconelli, *Dangerous Wonder*

If you want your kids to know God, let them see his passion, his willingness to take some risks, and his playfulness in you. They were created for a lifetime of stepping out of the boat. Walk it with them.

---

*Anna Miller, "Can This Marriage Be Saved?," *American Psychological Association* 44, no. 4 (April 2013), https://www.apa.org/monitor/2013/04/marriage.aspx.

Dad, I had a plan. It just didn't work out. Sometimes you try things that don't work out.

Through my kids, I'm learning to play more and plan less.

We've recently taken up backpacking into the wild. It's an adventure, for sure, and I feel young again doing it. To be honest, I'm learning as I go, never sure how it's going to turn out. On our first trip, we made every rookie mistake you can imagine—carried too much gear, tried to hike too many miles, couldn't get a fire started. But something in me was tested and reawakened, and I found a renewed passion to share with my family.

On our last trip, I decided to try sleeping in a hammock. Laura and the boys were in the tent (Katie wanted no part of this adventure). It was a swell plan. Then the coyotes started circling. For hours they yipped and screamed all around us, coming within twenty yards of my hammock. Finally, they moved deeper into the valley. I was just beginning to doze off when I heard the heavy footfalls of something much bigger than a coyote or even a buck. Something in me knew it was a bear. We'd brought a can of bear spray, but I didn't have it with me, so there I hung, wrapped in my hammock like a defenseless people burrito. My heart pounded in my throat as I lay as still as possible, trying to control my breathing.

Maybe it's not a bear. Perhaps just my imagination serving up old childhood fears as I teeter on the boundary of sleep.

Then my trekking pole hit the ground. It had been leaning against the tree I was hanging in. In a moment of madness, I cleared my throat loud enough to sound like a growl and spun around in my hammock, turning on my flashlight. As I did, I saw the silhouette of a huge black bear disappear into the trees. Without thinking, I sprang from my hammock and raced over to the tent, waking up Laura and the boys as I struggled to open the zippered entrance.

"There's a bear out here!" I hissed. "I'm coming in!"

As I tore open the flap, Danny looked at me, drunk with sleep, and said, "Dad, what are you doing?"

In the back of my mind, I heard the voice of a playful child: *I had a plan. It just didn't work out.*

Laura and the boys still laugh at me about that night. No doubt the story will develop over time and grow into legend, thanks to our willingness to do something spontaneous, silly, and playful.

Johan Huizinga, the Catholic scholar, says the best play leaves us "standing quite consciously outside ordinary life as being *not serious*, but at the same time absorbing the player intensely and utterly." In other words, when we are able to lose ourselves in play, we find ourselves. The authentic self—the *X*, the treasure—is unearthed.

At the time, my run-in with that bear felt serious and not at all like play. Every time I tell the story, the bear gets bigger and closer to my hammock, and I always point out that "I almost died."

Laura laughs at that. "You didn't almost die. You saw a bear!"

Ben and Danny agree with her. Still, I like my playful, risky, adventurous version of the story.

As a youth pastor who inspired millions to rediscover life through childlike faith, Mike Yaconelli knew the importance of playfulness, laughter, and adventure. He often said that if he dropped dead at any moment, he hoped to have just enough air in his lungs to whisper with his dying breath, "What a ride!"

O my God, please let that be so. For me and my children.

PART 3

THE HARD STUFF

When Ben and Katie were little, they wrote an illustrated book about me.

Before you give me that sentimental, *Aw, how sweet!*, let me offer some details.

Danny was sporting stitches in his busted chin. Ben and Katie (who'd been sentenced for the crime—unjustly, they still argue) had been grounded to their rooms. While doing hard time, they passed their manuscript back and forth through the air vent as they collaborated. The main characters were a skeletal walnut tree in our backyard and yours truly (drawn as a nerdy ogre). In their tale of retribution, I was constantly under attack as the tree launched poisonous black walnuts at me.

In truth, I probably deserved it. My attempts to discipline my kids have often missed the mark.

I've read hundreds of comments about the X-Plan. Of those, a predictable concern arises from the no-questions-asked part: "You mean you're not going to punish your kid if she's not where she's supposed to be? If there are no consequences, she won't learn from it!" However, as Sarah Kupferschmidt (Board Certified Behavior Analyst) points out, this "is not the time to get into a discussion about his/her whereabouts and/or punish him/her. This will lead to them not bothering to use the XPlan."*

Few things seem to cause as much anxiety among parents as the concept of discipline. And why wouldn't it? It's hard! And it's one of the things that trips up every parent. This is likely because "discipline" is often twisted up with warped notions about *punishment* and *control*.

Providing our kids with discipline is a sacred responsibility. However, we've got to view it within the proper context and motive. It's not about controlling behavior. Good discipline is about guiding kids with strong but tender wisdom. Mess this up, and you'll suffer the fallout (black walnuts to the head are a delight in comparison!). Get it right, and you'll see the emergence of your child's courageous, loving heart. Either way, you can never control the painful heartbreaks that will come against you and your kids. Sometimes evil assaults us, and no amount of structure can fully insulate us or our kids.

> Good discipline is about guiding kids with strong but tender wisdom.

Parenthood is a hard sort of blessing. Let's get real about the hard stuff that can take us and our kids off course.

*Sarah Kupferschmidt, MA, BCBA, "Giving Your Teenager a Way Out: Teach Them The XPlan," *Behavioral Science in the 21st Century*, March 5, 2017, http://bsci21.org/giving-your-teenager-a-way-out-teach-them-the-xplan/.

QUESTIONS TO X-PLORE

1 When you were a teen, what was your parents' discipline like? Did you ever feel they were heavy-handed and controlling? Looking back, do you wish they'd guided you with more strength and wisdom in some cases?

2 How do you think your parents defined "sin" when you were young? How did their expectations, rules, and discipline reflect that definition? Were they ever hypocrites? What's your definition of "sin," and how does that show up in your parenting?

3 As a teen, did you feel your parents taught you to act like a Christian, or follow Christ? Is there a difference? Was there a spiritual component to their parenting? Do you think they recognized how evil assaulted your young heart? Do you recognize those attacks?

4 Consider some of the strongest people you know, the ones who left lasting imprints on your heart. How would you describe them? Were they Christ-like? What behaviors and attitudes did they model?

5 What's the worst thing you can imagine ever happening to one of your kids? If that happens, is your heart strong enough to endure it? How did your parents handle heartbreak?

6 How will your kids answer these questions in thirty years?

CHAPTER 9

Spare the Rod

Her sandy blond hair is pulled back into a ponytail, highlighting a round face and crystal blue eyes you could drown in. Even at four years old, she somehow knows about holding it in and keeping it together, but the quiver in her tiny jaw tells me she's close to breaking. The stuffed animals around her room stare in frozen suspense.

Daddy's girl.

I never understood the weight of those words until Katie Jo came along. I love my sons, but—wow!—this one stole my heart. I know that's cliché, but when it comes to my Katie Jo, it's the truth. She is forever "my baby girl."

This time, though, my baby girl has disobeyed us (a rarity for her). I'm on my knees, hands on her tiny shoulders as I pontificate about expectations and disappointment. She lets me finish, then looks into me with her anime eyes. Much like Wonder Woman's lasso, Katie Jo's eyes have superhero power, and I'm already melting.

Those gems open wide, glistening with tears, and she asks in a soft, morning rasp, "I'm not your baby girl anymore?"

RED ALERT! SYSTEM FAILURE! DEFENSES DOWN!

She had me. Those eyes!

I'll admit, many times my attempts to discipline my kids have sent horrible messages. And sometimes I've lived out a twisted version of Browning's sonnet (*How do I hate thee? Let me count the ways.*) by not engaging my kids in difficult, teachable moments.

We often fail to discipline our kids because it's just plain hard. It welcomes pain (sometimes physical, always psychological and emotional), and we're terrified of risking something we cherish—our relationship with that child.

> We often fail to discipline our kids because it's just plain hard.

Folks, let me be blunt. If you think your child is (or will become) your best friend, then you need some actual friends. Don't pin that on your kid. Children need a parent who's willing to guide them, not a buddy. Through my years in education and ministry, I've seen the tragic fallout from situations where a parent's underlying motivation is to be adored by their child. Hey, I get it. We all want our kids to love us. However, the best parents seem to agree on one thing: you have to love your kids enough to not care if they like you.

> The best parents seem to agree on one thing: you have to love your kids enough to not care if they like you.

I'm not your baby girl anymore?

But how could I ever punish my delicate Katie Jo? It would literally hurt me more than it would her (another parenting euphemism that lingers only because of the rock-solid truth). For a brief moment, I almost caved. Over ten years later, I can still feel the inner struggle. It killed me, but discipline her, I did. I had to. I'm her father. The job comes with sacred responsibilities.

When we talk about children, one of the most common scriptural references I hear is "spare the rod and spoil the child" (which isn't from the Bible, but a Samuel Butler poem). We throw that line around about the kid who gets away with murder (sometimes literally). Here in Appalachia, a long-standing parenting quip goes something like, "That kid just needs her little butt busted!" Meanwhile, I have friends and family working in social services who cringe at those words, having seen the horrors of physical abuse.

When it comes to discipline, how do we navigate these waters filled with so many hidden rocks? How do we correct our little hooligans while not damaging something fragile inside of them?

Here's what the Bible actually says:

> *Whoever spares the rod hates their children, but the one who loves their children is careful to discipline them.*
> —Proverbs 13:24 (NIV)

Do you hate your kid? No? Then don't spare the rod.

But what does that mean?

I've seen endless debates about whether or not this verse encourages physical punishment. There are millions of awesome parents who spank and millions who don't. We rarely spanked our kids, but when we did, there were rules: never spank when angry and only after a calm discussion. The few times that spanking seemed appropriate, I had a format: (1) age-appropriate talk about the situation; (2) the spanking; (3) a strong hug when I tell them, "I love you" (not "I'm sorry" . . . although I always was).

If you're against spanking, kudos. Each parent, child, and situation is unique. In many cases, spanking is not only inappropriate, but lazy and heartless. Think of a pony pulling a cart. The pony stops and refuses to budge. The driver's natural instinct is to get out the whip and drive the beast. But what if the pony is ill? Is something jammed in his hoof? A fractured leg? Do you continue to beat him to make him go? You do if you're either ignorant or cruel—and I suspect you're neither of these. It's worth asking what's causing the problem instead of just punishing what might be a symptom. Sometimes "bad" behavior is a cry for help.

Right now, Danny is in our doghouse. His recent grades were bad. For some time, Laura and I wrestled with how to cross this minefield. Danny's older siblings are academic superstars. However, *book-learnin'* (as we say around here) isn't exactly in Danny's wheelhouse. He has other gifts, and we can't expect him to be like Ben or Katie. However, we still have expectations for him. Danny struggles with the notion that he's "not that smart" (his words), so we have to tread lightly. We don't want to wound him where he already feels weak. But we've been warning him about his grades.

As a toddler, Danny's speech was developmentally delayed. That set him back quite a bit. Throw in attention deficit disorder and anxiety issues, and the boy has his fair share of obstacles.

How do we discipline him for bad grades while encouraging him to work a little harder to experience more success?

We decided to take away his cell phone and we put the ball in his court.*

"Danny, here's the grade point average we expect from you. Show us your grades every Friday. If they're good, you get your phone until the next Friday. If not, the phone stays with us. If you need help, it's up to you to ask for it."

"But, Dad," he said, "I don't know when I need help! I think I understand stuff, but then I turn something in and get half of it wrong."

"Well, son, that's something we'll have to figure out together. Phone, please."

We live on a hill away from town, so Danny is somewhat isolated from his friends. His phone is his social lifeline. However, it's also a constant distraction. Taking away the phone has helped him realize how much time he wastes and how the constant notifications from friends were throwing him off course. I taught under a principal who used to say, "There's a fine line between a rut and a groove." We're trying to help Danny find his groove.

When it comes to discipline, you should always question your motive. What is it you're really after? Don't consider just the desired outcome, but ask yourself *why* that even matters. It's quite a wake-up call to realize that many of our parenting struggles come from us projecting ourselves into the lives of our kids. We punish them for not being what we want them to be instead of helping them live out their unique design. Too

---

*Katie laughed at this. "How's he going to text an 'X' now? Find a pay phone and just scream, 'Eeeexxxxx!'?" Our kids are tough critics.

often, parents use punishment for no other reason than to exert their will and demonstrate their power. *I'll show you who's in charge around here!* is a great credo for the control freak whose kids become either timid mice or lying snakes. Don't be that mom or dad.

> Too often, parents use punishment for no other reason than to exert their will and demonstrate their power.

Sometimes we parent with good intent but hidden motives.

Were we upset about Danny's grades because after two straight-A students, the kid struggling to make a B average tarnished our parenting image? Was Danny's crime merely his failure to be like his siblings? In this case, no. We don't really care about the grades. We're immensely proud of our son, even if he fails every class. But it's our job to teach life lessons about things like effort, perseverance, and overcoming hardships.

We didn't spare the rod, but we didn't beat him into compliance, either. The key to understanding "the rod" is that it's not about punishment. It's about guidance. When we talk about *sparing the rod*, we'd do well to remember two things: first, kids need discipline, but second—and more important—consider handing that big stick to Jesus. What would he do with it?

Jesus refers to himself as the good shepherd. Think of Psalm 23:4: "Your rod and your staff protect and comfort me" (NLT). How does a shepherd use a rod/staff? Imagine Jesus with that staff, thrashing his sheep until their snowy coats are blood-soaked. Is that hard to fathom? It should be. Effective discipline has two unified aims: keep our kids safe while strengthening who they are. If you cling to those criteria, your kids will know your heart for them. If your discipline delivers strength and security, then your kids will know Psalm 23 comfort.

Loving discipline offers strong but gentle guidance. Think of our shepherd. If a wolf shows up, his crook becomes a weapon to defend the vulnerable flock. Most of the time, however, the shepherd uses the staff to guide the sheep, nudging that wayward rebel along to keep him safe. We've discussed parenting out of weakness and how that damages our kids. Likewise, your own healing, wholeness, and strength will determine the effectiveness of your discipline. Think of parenting skills as a muscle group. You're not born with the ability to lift five hundred pounds. With some nourishment and exercise, though, you'll be surprised at the weight you can carry when it comes to shepherding your kids. It takes constant effort and is always inconvenient and costly, but your kids are worth it.

Once when our three were little, I was at home rushing around trying to tackle my lengthy to-do list. I'd planned just enough time for a grocery trip so I could have dinner ready when Laura got home from work (yeah, ladies, I'm a keeper). Every parent knows the adventure of herding three small kids through the grocery store jungle—you just want to get the flock out of there!

We survived, made it home and put away all of the groceries, and then I started making dinner. I was chopping up stuff I could throw together when I heard a small voice behind me.

"Daddy?" I turned to find six-year-old Katie Jo. Her hands were hidden behind her back. "I have to tell you something." With excruciating hesitance, she produced the thing in her hands—a small toy, the junk you find in every check-out lane in America, just high enough for a kid to see . . . and grab.

"Danny stole this."

Discipline . . . punishment . . . guidance.

I closed my eyes, took a deep breath, and huffed it out. I didn't have time for this.

"Okay," I said. "Get your brothers. Let's go."

A spanking or time-out would have been much more convenient for me, but neither would have been appropriate. We climbed into my truck and headed back to the store—about a thirty-minute drive. How did I discipline him? Danny was going to have to go back into the store, ask for the manager, hand her the stolen item, confess, and apologize. He was about four years old at this time. I knew what a challenge it would be for him. Diagnosed with apraxia,* Danny didn't utter a word until he was three. Even after a couple years of speech therapy, talking was like chewing rocks for the poor kid.

As we drove, I could hear him whispering from his booster seat behind me, rehearsing his lines. Over and over he tried to form the words, "Can I . . . see . . . the man-nah-jew? . . . I t-took this . . . I'm s-sah-wee." Hearing my son struggle, I was overcome with emotion. Irritated that he'd put us in this situation, I was still rooting for him. But something deeper was stirring in me as I heard the fear and shame in my son's awkward, hesitant voice.

When I was a boy, our home was rather dysfunctional at times. I recall many of the stupid ways I reacted and rebelled against my world (I have great empathy for kids who end up in

---

*Children with apraxia, a neurological and motor condition, struggle to find and form words. Early on, we had to use basic sign language to communicate with Danny.

trouble). As I sat listening to my son trying to get the words right, I was hearing another kid—me as a boy, who once had to confess to breaking in and vandalizing the school. In a meeting with the principal, the police, and my parents, I was sentenced for my crime: the principal made me pick up trash around the schoolyard for the rest of the year while my friends played at recess. I was publicly humiliated day after day, but after that meeting, Mom and Dad never said another word about it. I wish they had. At the time, I suspected they were too ashamed of me to even give voice to their disgust. As I drove back to the store, hearing Danny wrestle with his confession brought all of my twisted childhood emotions back to life. I didn't want my son to feel the isolating shame I'd felt. But I had to engage this teachable moment with my son. An unseen war raged inside of me, and the part of me that wanted to turn the truck around and go home was gaining ground. Going through with this was going to be hard on all of us. Danny knew he'd done wrong. Wasn't that enough?

If you hate your child, spare the rod.

Guiding our kids through life is both inconvenient and uncomfortable. But we have to love them enough to carry through with it.

Danny completed his task with honor. I put my hand on his shoulder, and we walked out of the store with our heads high.

"Son, I'm proud of you," I said.

————

As a teacher, I learned early on that discipline stands best on three legs: be firm, fair, and consistent. I have a relative who is neither firm nor consistent, and his kids are a mess. I refer to him as the bobby-cop dad. Think of the old caricature of the British police officer armed only with a whistle: "STOP! Or else I'll say 'STOP' again!"

If you say something, it should have some weight to it, and you'd better follow through with it. Be firm and consistent. As Barbara Coloroso puts it, "children are counting on us to provide two things: consistency and structure."* If you don't give your kid a structure to support their growth, we all pay for it later.

Bobby-cop dad works full-time and is just trying to survive each day. He's usually too distracted or exhausted to deal with his kids. For his own survival, he takes the path of least resistance and always spares the rod. When his kids were younger and got out of line, he relied on two tactics: ignore them or (when that became impossible) blow up and yell empty threats. My uncle once commented, "If those kids end up close to normal, it will be a miracle." He was prophetic, but we're still holding out for the miracle.

———

Another parenting extreme is the debater: the parent who thinks every incident requires a full dissertation and several rounds of verbal sparring. As our kids become older, their psychological development allows for more discussion (as we usher them into adolescence, we should invite more frank, open talks). However, this isn't effective or appropriate when they're little. We have a friend who is at his wits' end with his daughter. The kid can be a handful and needs constant correction. Unfortunately, Dad's

———

*Quoted by Steven Baumbarger, "Inner Disipline Theory Barbara Coloroso" (September 15, 2016), https://prezi.com/pkgogeuswsuj/inner-disipline-theory-barbara-coloroso/.

an explainer, a debater . . . and the child knows it. She realizes if she can keep the volleys going (she's a master of "But . . ." and "Well, what if . . ."), Dad will wear down as she escalates the negotiations. The frustration soon lights up Dad's face like warning lights in an industrial explosion. The little lady's ability to keep Dad talking is how she wrestles the rod away from her father and takes control. She may not get want she wants, but if she can keep Dad debating until he's been shoved into an emotional corner, then the kid wins the power struggle. I've seen this girl hold her entire family as emotional hostages in a war that's all about control. The result? They've all learned to tiptoe around her . . . but she's really the victim.

Adults look at this kid and say, "She just needs a spanking!" She might not be that way if Dad would talk less and discipline more. Unfortunately, this is part of his wiring. He's from a long line of debaters. As a boy, he had to survive a father who was a know-it-all, an emotional bully with a special talent for verbal sparring. Now a grown man, Dad's been conditioned to believe that the best orator wins the day—to use words to control others. Meanwhile, his daughter is adrift in a sea of words.

The girl struggles socially. Having learned to demand her own way, she remains oblivious to others—and their needs and desires—and lacks the slightest amount of empathy. When others refuse her will—debate time! Her peers avoid and exclude her, and my heart breaks for the kid. Once behaviors become habit, they are hard to unlearn. But Dad keeps talking (or totally disengages after throwing up his hands, which is becoming more common). As parents, we should constantly evaluate what behaviors we're actually teaching and reinforcing in our kids. Sometimes our misguided attempts at discipline do more harm than good.

One sunny August morning we were visiting Laura's family at their farm. After breakfast, we hitched the wagon to the tractor for a ride up the hillside to church. Ben was a toddler at the time. Fascinated by anything with big wheels ("Big trucks!" he called them), Ben wanted to ride on the tractor. We tried to explain there wasn't room, it was unsafe, and he would love riding on the wagon with us. But Ben wanted to ride on the tractor. So we explained everything again, but with enhanced descriptions and rationale. But Ben wanted to ride on the tractor. On and on it went. Laura's cousin, a veteran of the parenting wars, was observing this preschool courtroom drama from the shade of the barn. Finally, she approached, a knowing grin playing about her lips, and whispered to me, "Sometimes they don't need an explanation." She winked. "Your final word can be enough."

Sage advice.

We let a lot slide when our kids are little because they're so darn cute and entertaining. I'll admit we've laughed at some of the inappropriate things our kids have said and done. (Danny learning the *F*-word comes to mind.) However, we must try to remember this: when your kid does something that draws a laugh, ask yourself if it will still be cute coming from a thirteen-, twenty-five-, or fifty-year-old. That helps put things into perspective. If left unchecked, some cute, entertaining, and seemingly innocent behaviors can grow into something monstrous. Just the other day, Laura and I marveled at a little girl throwing a fit at a baseball game. The poor mother was walking the tightrope between blowing up and breaking down as the child raged.

"Our kids never did that," Laura said.

"Because we made them toe the line early," I replied.

Strong discipline on the front side allows a ton more freedom down the road. Too many parents get that backward and try to cage the monster they've grown. I was just talking with a mom whose kids always ran the show. When they were little, they told Mom and Dad what, when, and where they would eat; what they would and wouldn't do; where they would go and wouldn't. Now in their teens, these kids have crashed into a world that doesn't cater to their every whim, and they're not handling it well. The kids' social confusion and anxiety are now showing up in severe behavior problems, and their parents are now trying to stuff a couple of genies back into a bottle.

> Strong discipline on the front side allows a ton more freedom down the road.

"My son disappeared for a couple of days," one father told me. "Just cussed me out, got in the car, and drove off. But," he said, holding up a defiant finger, "he doesn't know I put a GPS tracker in the car." That last part seemed to give him some satisfaction in his masterful handling of a sixteen-year-old kid.

"Instead of a tracker," I said, "have you considered taking away the keys to the car?"

"Oh"—he looked at me as if I'd suggested stapling the kid's ear to the wall—"I can't. He'd never let me do that."

Strong parenting demands you step up early and confront the uncomfortable. Weak parenting arises when we fail to act, either out of ignorance, ego, or comfort-seeking self-preservation.

Discipline is the epitome of self-sacrificing love.

In 2 Samuel, we see some lousy parenting from an unlikely character. A firstborn son rapes his sister. The girl is then cast out as damaged goods, forced to live out her days in desolation. The father becomes enraged when he finds out about it, but he does nothing. Not long after, another brother kills the first to avenge his sister.

Can you say, *dysfunctional*?

Friends, we're not talking about a lazy moron of a father here. This is David: the shepherd boy who became king, the slayer of giants. But when it came to guiding his children, David was weak. If raising strong kids was a challenge for *that* guy, we should revere it as the grueling job it is. Discipline is a lot tougher than killing giants and ruling a kingdom. It can't be an afterthought, and you have to keep working at it.

Be firm and consistent, but also be fair.

Know, however, that "fair" and "same" are not synonyms. My kids have scoffed at how we treat them differently. Of course we do—they're different people. They have unique needs and abilities and face distinct challenges. If we treated them exactly the same, that wouldn't be fair. Katie lives for ballet. There have been times we've taken that away from her as punishment. However, if we disciplined Danny by grounding him from band practice, that would be unfair. Danny—a homebody—would love to miss practice. Treating them the same is not only unfair, it's unwise. Too often parents pick some disciplinary program and bow to it like a graven image. This is as lazy as not having any discipline at all. You just wind up hiding behind a formula instead of parenting out of wisdom and strength—and that comes with staying on your feet, juking and jiving, and always preparing to fight for (not with) your kid.

Guiding our kids is a holy task that's been entrusted to us.

They desperately need us to never *spare the rod*. But we've got to remember that discipline is more about guidance and less about punishment. You can punish a cheese thief with a mousetrap, but the little bugger isn't going to grow from the experience. You may have demonstrated your power, but you've done no favors for the mouse.

Whoever spares the rod hates their children, but the one who loves their children is careful to discipline them.

Too many people think discipline is all about punishment. It's not. Punishment should be one of the least-used tools in your parenting arsenal. B. F. Skinner saw punishment as a heavy-handed weapon of control. "The pattern is familiar," he writes. "If a man does not behave as you wish, knock him down; if a child misbehaves, spank him; if the people of a country misbehave, bomb them."* While punishment can be effective, use it selectively (it has loads of potential side effects, none of them good).

We spanked Ben more than our other two combined (he was our first, and we were learning—*sorry, Ben*). Unfortunately, he learned more from his punishment than we intended. After a while, we realized that Ben was becoming the kid who would lash out physically: bashing a kid in the head with his sippy cup; shoving his cousin into a cactus; abusing his little brother. I have a friend who says, "People do what they know." Ben learned to establish control in moments of frustration through physical violence. That's what he knew, because that's what we taught him.

Again, punishment (any kind of penalty for some offense) can be used to help discipline (guide) your kids, but think

*B. F. Skinner, *Science and Human Behavior* (New York: Macmillan, 1953).

about the potential side effects. In punishing your kids, have you taught them to use violence for control? To be vengeful? To be passive-aggressive? Deceptive? How to argue? How to withhold love? Use silence as a weapon? The list goes on.

While you're teaching them obedience, they're learning other lessons, too. Besides, punishment is often unnecessary. Life is a wonderful teacher and usually delivers its own consequences. Plus, there are better ways to deal with kids. One of my psychology professors would preach, "If you want to grow a child, you'd better be watering the green spots." Amen.

Not sparing the rod is about providing structure for your kids' growth. At times, they may despise you for it, but you're not after their friendship. If you're firm, fair, and consistent, they'll thank you for it.

Meanwhile, cut yourself a little slack. Nobody gets this right all the time. (David, God's own man, choked in this arena.)

We all do the best we can as we stumble along, trying to map out this parenting journey. I'm exhausted by the parent shaming we often see on social media, because there's not a parent out there who hasn't damaged their kid somehow. I know I have. We're all likely to become topics in future therapy sessions.

I don't intend to shame any parent—I don't have the luxury to do so. Those I've mentioned are just illustrations, urging you to consider your own disciplinary skills. As I said, every parent, kid, and situation is different. Do the best you can. Be willing to admit when you're

> Do the best you can.
> Be willing to admit
> when you're wrong,
> where you're weak,
> and then adapt.

wrong, where you're weak, and then adapt. I'm horrified at some of my parenting faux pas (and more mistakes linger on my horizon), but I'll keep guiding my kids as best I can.

I try my best not to spare the rod.

Why would I? I don't hate my kids.

CHAPTER 10

When Discipline Invites Sin

Don't drink, don't smoke . . . What do you do?
—Adam Ant, "Goody Two Shoes"

Confession time.

I fear my attempts to guide my kids toward a Christian lifestyle have—in some cases—either confused them, distracted them, or actually driven them away from Christ.

I had a high school history teacher who was a Vietnam vet. He once informed us, "Just so you know, I did tours in 'Nam. Tick me off and I might pull a gun and kill every one of you. And I'd get away with it, too. Just shrug and say, 'Sorry. Flashback.'"

We laughed, but it was an uneasy moment of humor. Part of me believed that guy might actually snap and kill us. That's probably why he never had discipline problems in his classroom. I can't recall a single lesson he taught us, but I do remember often wondering . . . *Will this be the day?*

Most teachers don't have the luxury of a convincing *stay in line or I'll kill you* method of classroom management. That's why kids suffer the beginning of every school year listening to hours of rules recitals: when they can speak, when they can't, when pencil sharpening is permitted, how to staple papers, where to sit, how to sit, when to breathe . . .

Ahhhh, the glorious worship of soul-stifling rules.

Ever consider why young children are so excited to start school they can barely sit still, but after being in the system for a few years, they learn to despise the whole factory? I think that's what life in general feels like for most of us. We waste the best years of our youth longing to *grow up*, but when we get there . . . ? Well? Be honest. Is your life the dream you thought it might be, or is it one of compromise, resignation, marginalization, and surrender? Do you feel truly free to live an unfettered life? If not, could that have something to do with the life-smothering regulations that keep you in line? (Whatever "in line" actually means seems to depend on who's holding the rule book, by the way.)

Ponder that, but for now let's step back into the classroom.

I can usually spot weak teachers just by their classroom rules. If you're not a strong educator, your only hope is a litany of guidelines and prescribed punishments. Some are such control freaks, they feel like a crippled Moses handing out stone tablets to kids too weak to even lift them. *This ought to slow them down!* There's an old axiom that requires teachers to set the tone early. Establish control or suffer a *Children of the Corn* revolt before Thanksgiving. Other than a fractured few, kids don't learn much from the totalitarian teacher beyond fear, disdain, and deceit. And when a kid's in real trouble and needs help? It's rarely the rule-worshipping taskmaster they go to. When you're drowning, the last thing you need is a judgmental lifeguard who will admonish you for violating the swimmer's code.

———

One of the coolest teachers I ever worked with had one rule. Just one.

"There are two words you may never use in my class," she told her students each year. "I don't want to hear the words 'Shut up!' in here. That's it. That's my rule. Everything else we can talk about as we go along."

She then briefly explained the rationale behind her solitary rule: She had grown up in a dysfunctional and somewhat abusive home where she often heard "Shut up!" This was a beautiful moment of transparency. No heavy-handedness. Just authenticity and vulnerability as a strong, loving woman revealed her heart to the kids who were going to walk alongside her for the next year. She then went on to affirm that each of them had value, had something worth saying, and she wanted them all to feel safe in sharing their thoughts and opinions. Their ideas might be challenged and discussed, but never devalued or silenced. She invited those kids to risk stepping out in order to unveil who they really were. Her students loved her for that, and I watched kids thrive under her loving leadership in an atmosphere of encouragement and empathy.

Jesus's disciples walked intimately with him, and when he left them, they continued on the path he'd set for them.

Disciple.

You don't have to be a linguistics expert to recognize that word in "discipline." Clearly, disciples must practice discipline if they hope to walk with Christ. But what if our perverted concept of discipline actually threatens our walk with Jesus?

Merriam-Webster defines "discipline" as . . .

1. Punishment

2. Instruction

3. A field of study

4. Training that corrects, molds, or perfects the mental faculties or moral character

5. Control gained by enforcing obedience or order; orderly or prescribed conduct or pattern of behavior; self-control

6. A rule or system of rules governing conduct or activity

I look at those definitions and see only the faintest glimpse of discipleship. Sure, the longer I travel with Jesus, the more he restores me and guides me, but I don't feel any burden of control; nor is my life dictated by an authoritative, socially prescribed litmus test of morality. However, that's not the case for many who come to the church in need of healing. Some people spend their whole lives in church but fail to ever experience Jesus. Too often they're handed a rule book (just like on that first day of school) and simply told how to behave. A life-giving relationship is reduced to a grace-robbing code of conduct.

Pastor Kyle Idleman shares a story about a man whose "prodigal daughter" had gone off the rails. The father, distraught and worried for his child, knew the score. "We raised her in church," he said, "but we didn't raise her in Christ."

Idleman writes:

> *Do you hear what he is saying? She was raised to look right on the outside but was not taught to give attention to the*

inside. Like some of you, she had been taught to keep all the
rules and say the right prayers, but somehow missed that
those things come from a personal and genuine relationship
with Jesus.*

Religious observances, dedicated church attendance, and behavior modification are not the same as a relationship with Jesus. Parents need to wrestle with that sobering challenge.

It's not enough to raise your kids in church. They need to learn to walk in freedom with Christ. And they need to learn it from you. While I'm at it, I'll just step across the line and throw down the gauntlet: if you're not raising your kids in Christ, raising them in church might actually be doing more harm than good. Jesus heals the broken. Religious posturing just does further damage.

> It's not enough to raise your kids in church. They need to learn to walk in freedom with Christ. And they need to learn it from you.

Let's be honest. Sometimes it's less messy and more convenient to just worship the rules. Prop up the Ten Commandments, add a few sprinkles of Old Testament social structure, give an obligatory nod to Jesus and forgiveness, and then be on our way. I wonder how many Christians are truly interested in Jesus's mission to heal a broken world by changing hearts with love instead of law. But that opens you up for too much risk . . .

---

*Kyle Idleman, *Not a Fan: Becoming a Completely Committed Follower of Jesus* (Grand Rapids, MI: Zondervan, 2016).

like staring down a roomful of teenagers and telling them that outside of saying "Shut up!" they're free to grow. Some parents are too afraid to even take that kind of risk with their own kids. Structure. Order. Control. Corral the horses, chain up the dogs, and cage the lions . . . and if one breaks free, then it's easy to tell the saints from the sinners. Right?

I wasted too many years shackled and drawn by religion without ever experiencing Jesus, and I wouldn't wish that dullness on my worst enemy. Too often people consider a walk with God as a slavish, whip-cracking, soul-smothering march through the desert. Wander for forty years, hungry and thirsty . . .

But if you follow all the rules, you might earn a golden ticket to the great beyond.

I really don't think that was Jesus's point.

But disciples surely need someone to discipline them, right?

If we peel back the layers of the word "disciple," we find something worthwhile. A disciple is a committed learner, someone who possesses a "willing, listening, and obedient heart."* A disciple is never held in place by a crippling set of rules. She feels free to follow, completely out of desire and not fear of punishment. My teacher friend with her one rule walked through each school year with far more disciples than those teachers who had pages of commandments.

Discipleship requires the freedom to not follow. Otherwise, it's just slavery dressed up in nice clothes on Sunday morning.

I realize some of you are scratching your heads, thinking, *This contradicts that earlier stuff about not sparing the rod.* In-

---

*"2. Understanding the Meaning of the Term 'Disciple,'" Bible.org, https://bible.org /seriespage/2-understanding-meaning-term-disciple.

deed, we all need structure in our lives. Our kids certainly need to be socialized and taught what's acceptable and what isn't. I'll confess: it drives me nuts to see some brat running wild, leaving behind a path of destruction while his parents somehow remain oblivious to the madness. However, when it comes to unleashing hearts and setting captives free, we need fewer disciplinarians and more disciples—people who model Christ's freedom and passion rather than morality guards aching for social control. Ultimately, I want my kids to be disciples whose growth isn't stunted by the misguided heavy-handedness of rule worshippers.

Do you really want your kid to walk with Christ, or are you more concerned about what your pew neighbors think? Ultimately, what's your motive behind teaching your kids not to sin?

This is where the path gets steep and slippery.

One of my favorite stories is Jesus's interaction with the adulterous woman and that bloodthirsty crowd that wants to punish her for her lifestyle. As the mob spews its venom at the naked, bruised, cowering woman, Jesus calmly squats down and draws in the sand (how playful and free, by the way; unaffected by the law-enforcement death squad). He invites the one without sin to throw the first stone. Unwilling to perjure themselves with pride, the morality police slink off in defeat. Jesus then tells the woman, "Go and sin no more."

Confused, the woman asks him, "Specifically, what do you mean by that?"

Jesus then disappears into the temple and returns with armloads of scrolls that spell out everything the woman can and can't do, when she can do them and when she can't, what she can no longer eat or wear, who she can talk to and what she can say (depending on the day and her geography).

In this beautiful moment of healing and compassion, Jesus unloads the scrolls onto this woman, who's lucky she's not stone-dead. She takes the bundle into her arms but drops three of them. She struggles to pick those up and fumbles some more. Meanwhile, Jesus drifts away on a cloud—his irritation over the sacred scrolls being mishandled is burning in his narrow expression. He says something from the distance, and she strains to make out the words.

"Study those rules . . . I'll be back later to juuuuudge yoooouuuuuuu . . ."

Okay, theologians. You got me. I clearly fictionalized that last part. But a lot of Christians live out their faith as if that's what really happened. Of course it didn't. Not even close. But what are we to make of "Go and sin no more"?

I can't count the times I've watched kids grow up in loving Christian homes where they are smothered by well-intentioned parents trying to protect them from the world. *Don't do this. Don't do that. And don't even think about . . .*

I recently watched a friend's kid go off to college. It came as no surprise to learn the young lady was struggling through her first year. For the first time ever, she was hours away from her helicopter parents. One of the girl's friends confided in me: "She's a mess. She's doing everything she was ever told not to do. And way more."

Her parents' hovering presence had always kept this kid in line. She never had the freedom to screw up and learn from it when the stakes were low. Through her teen years, this girl's every step was orchestrated by puppeteer parents who were overly concerned with one thing: how their daughter was perceived by others. Tragic. They're all prisoners of morality and public opinion. Until the daughter was paroled and she went off to college, that is. Then she went wild.

> *Forbid us something, and that thing we desire.*
> —Geoffrey Chaucer, *The Canterbury Tales*

> *There are three ways to get something done: do it yourself, hire someone, or forbid your kids to do it.*
> —Mona Crane[*]

Too often, our kids regard faith as little more than behavior control: just another disciplinary system, the control of forbidden desires to escape some cosmic punishment. However, clinical social worker Devra Renner points out the problem with parenting through a system of *Don't do that.*

"'Don't,'" says Renner, "doesn't tell them where to go. It doesn't move you forward. It tells you to stop."[†]

Jesus came to move us forward and lead us to freedom. He didn't come to just tell us to stop. Our kids need to know that. Following Christ is not about worshipping some moral code. It's about having a unique healing experience with God. It's a messy, irrational jump through mud puddles with the one who restores our hearts with joy, adventure, love, and passion. That's

---

[*]Stephanie A. Sarkis, PhD, "14 Quotes on the Forbidden," *Psychology Today*, January 26, 2012, https://www.psychologytoday.com/us/blog/here-there-and-everywhere/201201/14-quotes-the-forbidden.

[†]Kelly Wallace, "Kids behaving badly: When old rules of discipline no longer apply," CNN.com, Updated February 7, 2017, https://www.cnn.com/2013/11/05/living/parents-kids-behaving-badly-discipline-rules/index.html.

the Christian life I want my kids to know. If they find even a glimmer of that, I don't have to worry too much about telling them what not to do.

––––––––

The biggest problem is how our notion of sin has been hijacked. When Jesus poured out his compassion on the adulterous woman, he didn't give her a litany of rules to follow. Not unlike that teacher I mentioned earlier, he gave her one simple rule: "Go and sin no more."

Sin.

If I ask a room full of people to make a list of sins (and I have before), I can expect both the obvious and some head-scratching stuff: *Murder. Theft. Lying. Yelling in the halls. Not tithing. Dressing inappropriately. Speeding. Judging others. Not judging others. Cheating on my taxes. Standing for the national anthem. Not standing for the national anthem . . .* I've had some entertaining discussions with folks over our concepts of sin.

Laura grew up in a family of nondrinkers. She now laughs about it, telling me she once believed drinking to be a sin. If you drank, you were a sinner and an alcoholic. Period. Not surprisingly, seeing family friends occasionally have some wine with dinner confused her.

Alcoholic sinners . . . but they go to church with us?

Little wonder so many children grow up with the unholy capacity to determine who's worthy and who's not, believing that God's grace is up to us and not him, as if he were little more than a cosmic scorekeeper.

Granted, there are many reasons to avoid alcohol, but to tag drinking as a sin is just silly. I've even seen a handful of people go so far as to deny Jesus's first public miracle of turning water into wine. They argue (with no historical basis) that wine in those days was really just grape juice. Well, anybody could gather some grapes and squeeze out some juice. But what I can't do is take barrels of water, circumvent the whole fermentation process, and present you with hundreds of gallons of alcohol. That's why it's a miracle. If you think drinking should be avoided for health and social reasons, I'll not disagree with you. But don't label drinking as a sin and misrepresent Scripture to argue that opinion.

Drinking alcohol is not a sin. But it can be.

Sex is not a sin. But it can be.

Going to church is certainly not a sin. But even that can be.

Sin has more to do with motive than morality. Until parents get that straight, they'll never be able to point their kids toward Jesus and their own authenticity.

———

One afternoon Danny and I were in the backyard with our bows, target practicing. Danny had some decent groupings (arrows landing close together), but they were missing the bull's-eye by more than a foot. We adjusted the sights on his bow by the tiniest fraction, which caused him to turn his body so slightly that the casual observer would never be able to tell a difference. His next arrow group annihilated the center target.

He had been missing the mark, so I adjusted his sights and turned him back toward his target. He had been sinning, and I helped him repent.

The word "sin" comes from an old archery term that literally means "to miss the mark." Archers know that your body needs to be properly aligned to your target. The slightest turn away will cause your arrow to fly wide. You will miss the mark. If you're turned too much, you could lose an arrow . . . or worse, accidentally kill someone (how's that for a sin?). You'll miss the mark if you're turned away, but turning back realigns you with the target. Turning away and turning back. Sin and repentance. The Christian life is about where you're pointed. What's your target? What's your motive?

When Jesus offers that woman his one guideline—"Go and sin no more"—he's not telling her to stop breaking the rules. Rather, he's pointing her to freedom by reorienting her direction. Jesus's counsel to "sin no more" simply means *Don't turn away from God.* He could have easily said, *Quit screwing around, dress with some dignity, get a respectable job, and stop wearing all that trashy makeup* . . . but he didn't. In the brevity of those five words—*go and sin no more*—he said so much more: *You're forgiven. You are loved. You matter. I want you to have so much more life than you think you deserve. Just don't turn away from the one who wants to set you free.* Jesus spoke deep into her heart to ignite a desire—a motive—for a life worth living.

———

Writing about the Ten Commandments, G. K. Chesterton* offers this:

> *The truth is, of course, that the curtness of the Ten Commandments is an evidence, not of the gloom and narrowness of a religion, but, on the contrary, of its liberality and humanity. It is shorter to state the things forbidden than*

*The American Chesterton Society, "Quotations of G. K. Chesterton," https://chesterton.org/quotations-of-g-k-chesterton/.

*the things permitted; precisely because most things are per-
mitted, and only a few things are forbidden.*

Only a few things are forbidden? Tell that to the morality police.

Too many kids are being raised in the church, but not in Christ. Little wonder church attendance is in a free fall and young people are leaving the church in droves. They grow to see the hypocrisy of a religion that talks about an abundant life, but in their parents they see drab, bitter, judgmental life sentences behind pasted-on, phony masks they don in public. Young people are tired of being told what a Christian should look like instead of being invited into a life-changing relationship with Jesus. In short, they've come to see Christianity as little more than a political tool used for control. As Brennan Manning says,

*The greatest single cause of atheism in the world today is
Christians: who acknowledge Jesus with their lips, walk
out the door, and deny Him by their lifestyle. That is what
an unbelieving world simply finds unbelievable.**

The helicopter parents I mentioned earlier taught their daughter to avoid many *forbidden sins* so she would look like a chaste young lady. Meanwhile, they not only modeled but demanded their daughter constantly break one of the big ten: *Thou shalt not worship other gods.* In every aspect of this girl's life, she was taught to contort herself into a soul-sucking struggle of chasing approval and applause. They made sure their daughter was in church every time the doors were open, but they also trained

---

*Some readers will recognize this Manning quote as the introduction to the song "What if I Stumble?" from the *Jesus Freak* album by DC Talk.

this girl to worship a fickle, false god: the opinions of others. Once she hit college, she was a peer pressure pushover; forbidden fruit ripe for the picking. Rules couldn't contain her anymore, so the girl's well-groomed desire for approval took over and led her into some pretty dark places.

I'm guilty of this parenting misstep myself. All parents are, to some degree. Instead of teaching my kids to only take that question—*Who am I?*—to God, I have often encouraged them to go out into a broken world to seek validation and approval. In short, I had bad motives.

Whatever guidelines you set for your children, start asking yourself, *Why do I want to see that in my child?* If there's even a hint of concern for what others might think of your kid or your family, you need to stop right there, get knee-bound, and ask Jesus to help you unpack that

> **The opinion of others is probably the most dangerous god we teach our kids to worship.**

mess. The opinion of others is probably the most dangerous god we teach our kids to worship.

Our kids have to know that sin isn't about a particular set of behaviors. Sin is turning away from our life source. How many times each day do our kids see us sin? How often do they see us hurt, angry, or bored, and watch us go to something other than God for comfort or escape? Do they see you worshipping at the gym or yoga studio? The bottle? The television remote? The cell phone or iPad? Friends, anything we turn to for life instead of turning to God models a sinful life, and our kids are watching.

My daughter called me out on this just last night.

"Dad, you're always on your phone!" she mocked.

"Yeah," I argued, "but it's work. I'm a writer. I have to keep growing my presence on social media to promote my stuff."

See how slippery the landscape of sin really is?

Your sin is anything you turn to for validation and pain relief instead of turning to God. For some people this is alcohol and drugs. For others, it might be the arms of a lover. Or a career and social status. I've known poor souls whose greatest sin is church busyness—pouring themselves into every possible activity, but not with a full, glad heart; rather out of some screwy sense of guilt, obligation, or need for recognition.

Motive. It's all about motive. I can't say that enough.

When it comes to your sins, how do your kids see you turning away from God and putting other gods before him? I encourage you to explore this. They learn far more from what we model than from anything we say to them.

A few years ago, we had an invasion of weeds overtake our brick patio. I purchased some weed control that guaranteed total eradication. *KILLS THE ROOTS*, the label promised. The day before heading out of town, I sprayed every weed I could find. A few days later, we returned home and the weeds were gone. That was a curiosity. Normally the yellowing weeds would hang around for a while before finally giving up the ghost to be carried off by the wind (a process that usually took weeks, not days).

I shrugged it off and went on with my life. About a week later, I found dozens of weeds sprouting up between the bricks. They were returning with a vengeance. I soon realized what had happened. While house-sitting for us, my mother-in-law had tried to clean up our home. In her loving, well-meaning way, she'd gone out and pulled all of those weeds. She's an awesome mother-in-law, and I love her caring, selfless heart. However, in her attempt to beautify our patio, she'd denied my cure the chance to work. She'd pulled the weeds (the visible part), but the roots remained. If your discipline doesn't get to the root of the problem, you'll spend your whole life constantly pulling weeds.

We run this risk in our faith walk by thinking we can remove ugliness from our lives without turning to Jesus to get to the root of it all. For several years, my sin was alcohol. If I was hurting, feeling down or anxious, I grabbed a bottle. Instead of turning to God in my desperation, I turned away from him and chose a false god to comfort me. All along, I knew I could stop drinking. Quitting really wasn't a problem. But until I asked Jesus to reveal why I felt the need to drink, I would never invite his healing into some pretty dark places.

I was self-medicating something broken inside when I needed my Father's loving discipline.

What I'm encouraging you to do is not only ask Jesus to reveal where and how you're turning away from his healing, but invite him to reveal why you keep going to those false lovers. It's not enough to set rules for yourself: *I must stop _____ (fill in the blank)*. You need to get to the root of your brokenness. Until you do, the weeds will just keep growing back. What's your motive? You'll continue to sin in ways you don't even realize, even while doing things that look acceptable or even holy to the religious crowd. You'll continue to turn away from God while you labor to keep your patio nice and neat so the neighbors won't talk. And your kids will come to recognize the unbelievable hypocrisy of it all.

In short, they'll lose faith in you.

Our kids need to know that we follow Jesus because we

want what he offers—healing, strength, love, passion . . . *LIFE!* Our kids need to see true discipleship in us.

> Our kids need to know that we follow Jesus because we want what he offers—healing, strength, love, passion . . . *LIFE!*

I once talked with a Major League Baseball groundskeeper about weed control. He said the best way to prevent weeds is to avoid bare patches. If your lawn is healthy and full of thick grass, weeds just aren't a problem. If you think of sin in those terms, sin won't take root in your kid's life if it's rich and full.*

Don't tie your kids' hands just to keep them out of the cookie jar and then wonder why they can't feed themselves when they're older. Try giving them more life and fewer rules. Point them toward Christ. Invite them into that life of freedom, joy, and adventure. When they experience the real Jesus, they'll want nothing else and they'll follow him forever. Like the disciples.

Parents usually come to rely on heavy discipline and helicopter parenting for one of two reasons (or some dangerous blend of the two):

1. An unhealthy need to control our kids' growth and direction. This is just foolish, and it reveals sin at its worst—the vain ethos that we have it all figured out. We've got to leave plenty of room for God to operate and allow our kids the chance to participate in the wildness of his X-Plan.

---

*Mind you, busy and overscheduled aren't the same as rich and full; our insistence on keeping our kids in year-round activities is killing us and them, in this parent's humble opinion.

2. We're desperate to keep our kids safe from harm so we lock them in a box of overprotection, never letting them experience the natural risks and potential heartbreaks of growing up.

Both can be devastating to kids. The first will break them in ways you can never predict. Think of it like trying to squeeze an egg into a bottle. You push hard enough and eventually the shell cracks and you're left with a mess. The second will weaken and cripple them both socially and psychologically. If you find yourself desperate to control your kid's path and protect her every step, let me warn you: both reveal more about your insecurities (your brokenness) than anything about your child. If you don't deal with the hidden motives behind keeping your child on a leash or under a blanket, it won't end well for either of you.

Your sin isn't what you do. It's *why* you do what you do. Why are you turning away from God? Let Jesus get to the root of that. Only then can we model for our kids how to live with authentic strength . . . like true disciples traveling a long, winding road.

CHAPTER 11

Voices . . . I Hear Voices

How could anyone have such a cold and scary voice inside of them? Such a traitor to the cause?
—Stephen King, *The Girl Who Loved Tom Gordon*

Laura and I became better parents when we realized our family is haunted. Sometimes, though, we still find ourselves trying to ignore the voices, convince ourselves they're not real, or pretend they are our own. And when that happens, our whole family suffers.

The rain is pounding on the roof of our tiny camper like the boots of an invading army. I'm looking at Laura, feeling defeated and disheartened. Again.

"I know it's not what you said," she whispers to me in her uniquely challenging, but loving way, "but what you said isn't what he heard. It hit him in a place where he's already feeling insecure."

Once again! I'm the bad guy. I'm sick and tired of taking the fall for someone else's issues. It's so freaking exhausting! I don't even know why I try anymore. I can't win. Everything I do and say blows up in my face. I might as well just give up. Take the Hippocratic Oath of parenting—do no harm—along with the hypnotic oath—disengage. Make sure they're clothed and fed and just stay out of the way.

The rain has trapped the five of us in what now feels like a prison cell. I look across the camper to Ben's bed (a mere ten feet away) and see the soles of his shoes. I also see the hurt and rage steaming off his stiffened body. I look at my seventeen-year-old Katie Jo sitting beside me and she shrugs, wide-eyed, as if to say, *I have no idea what just happened, but that escalated quickly.*

And it did, too.

One minute we're all hunkered around the hobbit-size dinette playing games, trying to make the best of our rained-out camping weekend, and the next thing I know my twenty-year-old son takes an innocent stab of sarcasm, plunges it into his own throat, and bleeds out all over me before storming off and collapsing onto the bed, prompting Laura's loving admonition.

The frustrating thing? I know she's right. What I said had no lethal intent. It was a playful barb, not unlike any other witticism we poke at each other on any given day. But this one caught Ben off guard and landed like a sucker punch, causing him to lash out at me like a wounded animal.

He's just being a baby. He's always been emotional. He lost the game, and you know he hates to lose. That's his problem and you know it. When he wins, he's an insufferable, gloating jerk. When he loses, he's a hundred times worse. Maybe teach him a real lesson and refuse to ever play anything with him again. And when he begs you to play some yard game, you can tell him why—because he's a baby who can't handle winning or losing and you won't play games with babies. That will teach him.

I look at the bottoms of Ben's shoes sticking out from the bed and find myself thinking back to when we had to put shoes on his toddler feet just to keep his socks in place. He had pudgy ankles and small feet, and socks just rolled off him like a snake shedding skin. We didn't even call his footwear "shoes." We came to identify them by their function: "sock-holders." My son. Nearly a man. Still learning to walk. Feeling under assault and beaten down at every turn. Just like his dad so often feels. And listening to whispering voices that come from someplace cruel and unholy. The voices of accusation, diminishment, and isolation.

What did I say?

We just finished a couple of fast-paced games, ones that require you to think on your feet and react. Ben lost.

"I stink at these games," he admitted, throwing up his hands but smiling, accepting his defeat with as much grace as he could muster. "I hate anything where you have to use your brain that fast—I just can't do it."

Sometimes my brain works with painful speed, outpacing my heart and judgment. Or maybe that's just my mouth.

"Then you're going to hate teaching," I laughed.

At that point, our tiny, ultralight camper was sent reeling by unexpected winds from the simmering storm. With no warning, we were sucked up into a deadly emotional tornado. Everything about my son's countenance changed. His body stiffened. Eyes narrowed. He dropped his cards onto the table, stood up, and glared at me.

"Sometimes you're just a jerk," he said before storming off to his less-than-secluded bed a few steps away. (His words actually weren't that kind, but I won't repeat the quote here.)

[W]hat you said isn't what he heard. It hit him in a place where he's already feeling insecure.

Ben has been wrestling with his life's journey. He recently decided to change his major from physical therapy to education. He loves history. He's also discovered a passion for working with young people. He has a rare gift of being able to connect with kids and guide them with wisdom and care. At the age of twenty, he is already being recruited by high school coaches because they see his natural gifts as a teacher and coach. He just finished up as an instructor at a Cincinnati Reds youth camp. Meanwhile, I've been advising my son on following his heart and his talents, but also thinking about practical stuff like income potential, the ability to support a family, desired lifestyle, etc. You can't always follow your heart and live a life of leisure, I warned him. You can support a family on a teacher's salary, but you won't be able to afford a lot of luxuries.

He listened. He understood. He thought about it a long time and finally decided to go for it, even though he knows it's a risky change of course that, as a junior in college, comes with a host of unknown challenges. In the midst of that particular storm, I know my son is wrestling with doubts and insecurities. If he weren't, I'd be worried for him.

Then came my chiding, playful remark: " . . . you're going to hate teaching."

I meant it as a joke. But to Ben it came as an attack.

Somewhere between my mouth and his heart, my words became twisted into a damaging assault: *You're not smart enough to be a good teacher. You will fail. Your own father doesn't even believe in you!*

Friends, I did not say that. I do not think that. But as the storm clouds pounded down on our family, huddled together in our flooded campground lifeboat, evil assaulted my relationship with my son, driving a wedge between us. Emotionally,

Ben and I retreated to our corners, licked our perceived wounds, and plotted the punches we would throw in the next round.

We hardly spoke to each other for the next forty-eight hours. Even though I knew in my heart what was happening, I was too angry and confused to see my way through the fog. I knew what I needed to do, but I just couldn't drop my defenses, allow myself to become vulnerable, and go after my son's heart. I was wrestling with my own accusations.

You suck as a father. You're a judgmental jerk, and you've wounded your children beyond repair. Everything about you is phony, and they see through all of your nonsense. They don't love you. They don't respect you. Don't trust you. At best, your children tolerate you. Why even try? What's the point?

Friends, this is how evil works.

This is how the thief robs us of life.

———

Living in a town that leads the nation in overdose deaths and babies born into addiction, we often talk about "functioning addicts"—the people who are actively using drugs but are still able to hide it as they continue to go about their lives like everyone else, blending in, doing their jobs, and functioning as if nothing's amiss.

In my opinion, the functioning alcoholic and the functioning drug addict are the most dangerous people of all. These are the people you come to accept and trust, never suspecting they could make a chemically induced mistake at any moment that might cost you or a loved one dearly.

The deadliest weapon that pins down the functioning addict and puts everyone around them at risk is always the same: denial. There's nothing quite as harmful as the refusal to recognize and admit the truth.

The refusal to admit the truth is also running amok in many of our churches.

A friend once asked a group of lifelong church members a simple question: *Who really believes that Satan exists?* With heads down and eyes closed, he asked for a show of hands. Hardly any hands went up. Throughout my years, I've found this to be an alarming dilemma—the claim to believe the Gospel, but the refusal to acknowledge the presence of evil and its threat against our hearts.

I asked a friend in ministry why evil is so rarely addressed from the pulpit. His reply: because people don't want to hear about it. They want inspiring stories of hope and grace, and a good morality tale.

The functioning addict and the functioning alcoholic deny they have a problem, and they ignore the damage being done to themselves and those around them. Much the same with what I call the *functioning atheist*. Sadly, we live in a world dominated by a Christian faith that is overrun with functioning atheists. These are the people you sit beside every Sunday and Wednesday in church. They know the words to say and the moves to make. They've embraced the socially acceptable song and dance of the religious folk. But when it comes to the nitty-gritty, down-and-dirty parts of good vs. evil and spiritual warfare . . . *well* . . .

While everything in Scripture teaches us how to navigate a spiritual reality, the functioning atheist refuses to believe. If pressed, they'll confess their belief in God (like that's a big deal—

Satan also believes in God); however, the functioning atheist treats the Bible as little more than a morality manual with the occasional cameo appearance by that wish-granting genie in the sky. The functioning atheist has an unhealthy addiction to self-realization and self-control while denying the spiritual dangers around them. But they know enough of the songs and verses to look like a Christian.

If that sounds like a harsh challenge, it is. Because we are living in a world at war, and your kids need your protection and guidance, not just physically, but spiritually. X-Plan parenting requires it.

> Because we are living in a world at war, and your kids need your protection and guidance, not just physically, but spiritually. X-Plan parenting requires it.

Revelation 12 reveals the spiritual war being waged between good and evil. Guys and gals, hear me: *This is not metaphor or fairy tale.* It's our history, the story we're living in (whether or not we want to admit it). John tells us how Satan and his army rebelled against God, but they were beaten back and cast down from Heaven. Evil then retreated to a new stronghold—Earth. I agree with C. S. Lewis, who writes, "Enemy-occupied territory—that's what this world is."* It's not enough to say that evil lurks around us. The greater truth might be that your life is often tainted by anxiety, frustration, and sadness because you're digging for scraps in the dumpsters of the enemy's camp. But there's more to the story:

---

*C. S. Lewis, *Mere Christianity* (New York: HarperSanFrancisco, 1980).

Christianity is the story of how the rightful king has landed, you might say landed in disguise, and is calling us all to take part in a great campaign of sabotage.
—C. S. Lewis, *Mere Christianity*

Jesus spotlights evil's presence when he predicts his own spiritual assault. He warns his disciples that the ruler of this world (Satan, not the government or religious leaders) is coming for him (John 14:30). Paul also advises us of Satan's attacks, urging us to "stand firm against all strategies of the devil" while reminding us that we are not fighting "flesh-and-blood enemies, but against evil rulers and authorities of the unseen world, against mighty powers in this dark world, and against evil spirits" (Ephesians 6:11–12, NLT). Peter tells us that Satan is constantly on the prowl around us, looking to destroy us (1 Peter 5:8). Revelation 12:17 leaves us with this sobering warning: after Satan failed to destroy Jesus, he vowed to wage war against the children of God—us!

And our kids.

At the core of our faith is the spiritual understanding of a war being waged. If you read the stories of Jesus and the words of the apostles, you find that becoming attuned to the spiritual forces of good and evil isn't some hocus-pocus, wishy-washy, supernatural afterthought. It's a given. A must. Functioning in a spiritual reality isn't a suggestion; it's part of the deal. It's the universally accepted way of life for the Christ follower. Over and over again, we're told to resist the spiritual assaults of evil that come against our hearts and the hearts of our loved ones. We are called to actively participate in these spiritual realms.

Now, I know a few of you might be hearing voices right now, prompting you toward disbelief. *This stuff is wacky! Non-*

sense! But stay with me. Silence those voices and open your heart only to God. If you do, you'll first begin to feel, and then see glimpses of spiritual truths. Knowledge is most often first revealed at the level of the soul, so give yours some space to move (and be moved).

Scripture couldn't be any clearer about the spiritual battles around us: an ongoing epic war in which evil has pledged to destroy you and your children. Meanwhile we sit in church among functioning atheists who refuse to believe this truth, leaving us to wander across blood-soaked battlefields with decorative, bejeweled blindfolds. We want a comfortable, pretty religion that shields our eyes from the spiritual carnage around us.

At the risk of going off track here, I should tap the brakes.

It would be foolish and a little crazy to suggest that every bad thing in life is the handiwork of evil. I'm not convinced that Satan gave my cousin a brain tumor or caused my friend to lose her job. Nor do I suspect that it's part of God's epic battle plan to provide convenient parking spots for the faithful. C. S. Lewis also writes:

> *There are two equal and opposite errors into which our race can fall about the devils. One is to disbelieve in their existence. The other is to believe, and to feel an excessive and unhealthy interest in them.*
>
> —*The Screwtape Letters*

With that being said, let's not go nuts on the subject. There's not always a pitchfork-wielding devil out to wreak havoc and create mayhem like that guy in the insurance commercials. Sometimes in life, stuff just happens and there's no great cosmic purpose to it. However, I think the con man Kint from *The Usual Suspects* said it best: "The greatest trick the devil ever pulled was convincing the world he didn't exist."

If we don't recognize the spiritual assaults against our children, we'll never be able to counter the attacks and reclaim sacred territory. Until we learn to recognize it, evil will continue to rob us of all we're meant to have.

In John 10:10, Jesus makes a bold offer: "I have come to not only give you life, but also that you may have it to the full." That's paraphrased, but all translations carry the same meaning. Some translations use the word "abundantly" instead of "to the full." I was discussing this verse with a friend who studied divinity and then somehow ended up in law school. He proposed that this verse merely suggests the offer of eternal life.

"I'm not disagreeing," I said, "but I don't believe the *eternal life clock* lies dormant and only starts ticking after you're dead."

Jesus offers an abundant life not just in the great hereafter, but also in the great right-here-and-now. A life with Jesus—one of adventure, passion, and joy—is waiting right now in this very moment . . . *IF* we're willing to live with authenticity. That's part of Jesus's beautiful promise. However, a key part of that verse too often gets ignored. The first part warns: "The thief comes to kill, steal, and destroy."

Jesus, God in flesh, the man who looked evil in the face, entered depths of darkness we can't begin to imagine, and then came walking back out with the keys to our freedom . . . he tells us that someone is out to steal our very lives. Why else would Jesus offer a life worth living only after telling you about the thief who wants to mug you?

Friends, a life worth living has a two-part offer: seek and

embrace that abundant life we're promised, and fight for your heart (and your children's hearts) in these spiritual arenas.

The voices are urging you to dismiss this, right?

Of course they are.

We've talked a lot about our brokenness, those fractured places within us where we feel damaged, wounded, unsure, and afraid. Think of these places as shards of a busted mirror. Pieces of the whole. We are made to reflect the image of our creator, but alas, we are broken. All of us. As promised, Jesus has come to heal the brokenhearted, bind up the fractured pieces of the busted-up soul, and restore us to our full glory. This is a beautiful gift of grace, but it's also a lifelong, ongoing healing process. With every busted shard left lying around, we present evil the opportunity to reflect something dark, harmful, and destructive toward the people we love. Though we can learn to resist it, we can never fully avoid it.

I once heard Christian author John Eldredge present our dilemma: evil doesn't cause every bad event in our lives—it's a dangerous world and bad stuff happens. However, Satan is always waiting in the wings (ready to feed you lines that *sound* like your own voice) to put his diabolical spin on things, twisting the truth (and your heart) into a tight-fisted knot of hurt, anger, betrayal, accusation, and judgment. Hebrews 3:15 urges us to not harden our hearts to the voice of our Father, but that's exactly what happens when we listen to that other voice and allow evil to whisper through those fragments of our broken souls.

As I witnessed the spiritual assault against my son during our camping trip, I was reminded once again that what is actually said or done against us isn't always the thing that wounds us, but the dark whispers that hijack the message and plunge it deep into our souls, like broken glass thrust into our most tender places.

Earlier I mentioned my mother demonstrating her love through baking, yet how she simultaneously tried to help my sister lose weight by hiding fresh pies and cakes around the house. The aim was love. However, evil twisted a loving intention and offered my sister another message: *Love will be withheld from you, hidden and locked away because you are not worthy. You're fat and ugly. Your own mother is disgusted by you and ashamed of you.*

Again, this couldn't be more untrue, but evil always finds a way to reflect its blackened heart through our brokenness.

We all have a running inner dialogue. Think about the times you have entire conversations with yourself (or what may seem like parts of yourself). Psychologists have studied and theorized about this inner dialogue for decades. As we come to understand more about the human psyche, we are realizing that people don't just consider their reality in terms of the inner "self" (the *me* part) and the external *others*. Rather, the self and others all mingle in the inner realm. How many times have you walked away from some confrontation only to continue that debate in your mind for days, weeks, or even years?

Put simply, we let others take up residence in our hearts and minds. Psychologists refer to this as the dialogical self, the reality that you're not alone inside of your own skin, and those characters are carrying on dialogue all the time.

Of course there are voices in our heads that don't come

from us. Scripture also warns us of these *others* who, through our brokenness, gain access to our hearts and minds. Why else would we be told to guard our hearts *above all else?** "Above all else" should give you a clue, as in *This is really important, gang! Drop all the other stuff right now. Whatever it is, it can wait. The most important thing is your heart, and if you're an open door to the enemy's whispers . . .*

How often are you hurt or enraged by perceived slights from others? Insulted or embarrassed by something you've said or done that was completely misinterpreted by someone else?

Friends, it bears repeating: not every thought that comes into your head is your own; nor is every thought or interpretation of some interaction a reflection of truth and love.

The thief comes to kill, steal, and destroy.

He does it to us. And he does it to our kids.

I'm guessing you locked your doors last night because there's a chance that someone might try to come in while you're asleep and rob or harm your family. There's less than a 2 percent chance we might be burglarized, and yet we guard our homes with locks and guns. Meanwhile, Jesus tells us, "There is a thief who's coming to rob and destroy your heart," but because we've become functioning atheists, we do nothing to defend ourselves or our families from these spiritual attacks (even though there's a 100 percent chance they'll occur).

Just like the functioning addict puts himself, his family, and his friends in harm's way, the functioning atheist does the same by denying that we have an enemy who will steal life from us if we let him.

---

*Proverbs 4:23, New International Version.

To be honest, I probably waited too long to go after Ben's heart following our camping run-in. I'd like to tell you I'd paused out of wisdom and judicious timing. However, that's not the case. For a few days I was still reeling from the hurtful things he'd said to me. I was also ashamed because I realized how my words had hurt him. The biggest obstacle, though, was my fear. I was afraid of confronting the uncomfortable; risking emotional vulnerability and possibly stirring up a bigger, uglier conflict; possibly driving my son even farther away.

What finally moved me into action? My inner dialogue. That dialogical self and my prayerful decision about the voices I would permit to speak and the ones I had to silence.

"I will choose to listen and believe the voice of truth."*

The voices that bring fear, anger, and discouragement are not from God. Remember the intent of evil: to poison your relationships; plant seeds of mistrust and loathing as we hide from each other and destroy ourselves; and ultimately, divide and conquer.

As Ben's father, I knew I had to fight to restore what was broken. To do that I had to start listening to the voice of truth, the one that was urging me: *He's hurt. He's worried about his future. Thinks you're angry and disappointed with him. You have to go after his heart. Rescue and restore him. Speak truth. Speak love. Encourage him.*

Meanwhile, the other voice was still whispering: *Ben knows you're mad because you should be mad. Have you forgotten the awful, hurtful things he said to you . . . and about you?! You must*

---

*"Voice of Truth" by Casting Crowns.

*discipline him with tough love. If you give in, you'll look weak . . .
and you are weak. You're a weak, impotent father, and your kids
will all struggle in life because you've never been tough enough on
them. You suck as a father. You know it and Ben knows it.*

When you hear whispers in your soul, you have to ask
yourself one simple question: Does the message bring life, or
does it rob you of life? If the voice of your "other" threatens
your capacity for love and joy, you can be sure it's from the
thief.

I quickly realized I had to fight off the thief and lock him
out of my house.

I went looking for Ben and found him in the garage.

Father, heal and restore my heart . . .

———

Ben is standing in the garage, facing the work bench. He hears
the door open and looks to find me standing there with a slight
grin.

"What?" he asks.

I say nothing. But my grin blossoms into a smile. I love my
son, and the sight of him brings me joy.

"What do you want?" he demands.

I step forward and playfully open my arms, going in for the
bear hug.

"Don't touch me," Ben says as he turns away, trying not to
smile. His body goes rigid, and I notice how broad the young
man's shoulders are becoming. I put my hands on his shoulders
and give them a squeeze.

"I'm sorry for what I said the other day. I was trying to
crack a joke, and it missed the mark completely. It wasn't funny.
I know it hurt your feelings, and I'm really sorry for that."

"It didn't hurt my feelings," he lies.

The enemy—the thief—will dupe you into burying your own feelings as he stokes your ego and vengeful pride, telling you to be strong, to not acknowledge pain and hurt. Deny and lie. Deny and lie. You have to fight this at the level of the heart by speaking with love and truth.

"Yes, it did. And I'm sorry. I realize why my words were hurtful and I was wrong for what I said and how I've handled it these past couple of days. I love you and I'm very proud of you."

I pat his shoulders and walk back into the house.

My apology didn't heal Ben's wounds. However, it was a step toward redemption, and as parents, that's sometimes all we can do.

I wish I had the infinite wisdom to know how to forever keep the thief out of my house. However, he keeps finding his way in. That's why Peter tells us to stay alert and keep watch. That's why Proverbs urges us to guard our hearts. One of the greatest gifts we can give our children is to recognize the ways in which the thief comes to rob us and them of life. As we learn to resist his attacks and deny him access, we become stronger. We find ourselves moving deeper into the presence of the one who wants to heal us and bring us life. Abundant life. A life lived to the full. When we as parents learn the nuances of that journey, we are better positioned to fight for our children's hearts and nurture their authentic strength. We'll learn to recognize where and how they have fallen under the spell of the accuser, when they're being assaulted and robbed of life. It will be some time before our kids are old enough and wise enough to even understand what's coming against their hearts. That's why we must be ready to move in for the rescue when we get that "X" message. Too often parents go to battle against their children when they should be stepping in to defend them and go to spiritual war on their behalf.

As our children grow, we can begin to reveal more of our faith and those spiritual realities to them. Until then, we have to fight some spiritual battles for them as we protect them from the thief who comes only to kill, steal, and destroy.

CHAPTER 12

The Fuel Gauge of a Strong Heart

''ve been horrified to realize how I've punched holes in my kids' souls, like jamming a rusty screwdriver through the gas tank, draining them of precious fuel they desperately need for this journey.

Friends, there's one clear way to gauge your parenting attempts and how they're affecting your child's heart.

Twelve-year-old Charlie Parker reminded me of this.

Charlie had just played the game of his life. In a tournament that had started with over forty teams, it was now down to eight, and Charlie's team was among that elite group. The unsuspected superstar of the game, Charlie (normally that "utility" guy who does nothing flashy but gets the job done) had been a man among boys on this night. He'd hit, fielded, and pitched with such skill and grace that it seemed he'd been putting on a clinic for the other boys.

I hope they were all watching.

After the game, the coach assembled our boys outside of the fence where they were all sprawled out in a weedy dirt patch, soaking in their victory. Coach congratulated them on their win, pointing out some keys to the victory (watering the green spots). He then turned his attention to Charlie, who was sitting in the middle of the group.

"And Charlie," Coach said. "You pitched a great game." The boys all applauded. "And I don't think there's any question who deserves this game ball." With that, Coach flipped a baseball toward Charlie, now blushing with a sincere *Aw, shucks!* expression smeared across his face. The applause of his teammates grew even louder as that ball spun through the cool night air and landed in the bare hand of a kid who did nothing but work hard and encourage his teammates every chance he got. It was a beautiful moment for a kid who couldn't have been more deserving. And then the unthinkable happened.

"No," Charlie said as he waggled his game ball in front of his face the way a southern gospel preacher might shake his Bible to drive home his point. "I appreciate it, but I don't deserve this." Charlie shifted his body slightly to the left and nodded toward some of the boys behind him. "When the game was on the line, that kid saved my hide." Charlie then flipped the ball over his shoulder to one of his nine-year-old teammates. A huge grin spread across that kid's face before the ball even made it to him. That Little League rookie who only got the mandatory play time each game, the kid the coaches tried to hide in right field (thinking it was where a rookie's mistakes might least likely hurt a championship run), looked up and caught his second ball of the night. The first had been a high fly ball that would have tied the game had the youngster not caught it for the victory-clinching final out.

I was stunned.

In a society of every man for himself, a twelve-year-old kid reminded this sinner what a Christian is supposed to look like: someone who's not in it for their own trophies and praise, but one who uses what he's been given to bless and lift up those around him.

At twelve years old, Charlie was already a better man than me.

————

One of the greatest gifts I've ever received came with a desperate wake-up call.

Years ago, a teacher who'd had all three of my kids as students said to me, "Your kids always cared about their classmates in ways not many kids—or even adults—ever do. They have hearts for other people, and that gives me hope for the world. Good job, Dad."

With that she patted me on the shoulder. I thanked her for the kind words . . . and wanted to crawl into a hole.

It's the greatest compliment I could ever be given as a parent. The ability to care for others requires more strength than just about anything else in this crazy world. It demands a superhuman mix of empathy, peace, awareness, mindfulness, plus the ability to read people and decipher unspoken messages of the heart. I say again, authentic strength. The stronger the person, the greater is their ability to love rather than denigrate (or worse—ignore with indifference). Weak, broken people use their skill sets to wound others with their words and actions. I'm pointing in a mirror here. When I am petty and snarky, I'm merely lashing out with the tentacles of some wounded creature chained to the walls of my heart. In the depths of my depravity, I can unleash a verbal lashing that might come off as sharp humor, but is intended to cut and wound in ways that might come close to my own pain. I am the king of one-liners, dropping wit bombs from the protection of my own emotional distance.

Once, my brother and I had a falling out that left us in-communicado. During the period of our cold war, he went through a divorce and remarried. At a community tailgate party before a football game, my brother found the guts to track me down and confront me.

"Hey," he said with an uncomfortable hesitance. "How've you been?"

"All right," I replied coldly, letting the icy silence choke him so I wouldn't have to. After a couple of strained moments, he tried again.

"I got married," he said.

"I heard," I replied, nodding with a squint-eyed expression I hoped resembled Clint Eastwood before a shoot-out.

"We're having a party to celebrate." He laughed nervously. "Figured we'd use tailgating as our reception and kill two birds with one stone."

"Good idea," I said. I was trying to look in control, but inside I was a wreck—my heart was pounding out of my chest. I was so angry with my brother for a number of reasons, but I also missed him, cared about him, and wanted desperately to step down off my high horse and meet him where he was. I just couldn't.

The next words that came from my brother's lips floated like an easy, underhanded lob to a home-run hitter, and I had to swing at it.

"You want to meet her?" he asked.

A major frustration with our biological father has been his multiple marriages. Once, when my brother's third marriage was on the rocks, I'd said to him before storming out of a bar: "You've spent your whole life despising the very thing you're becoming." And now, here in this public place, with my closest friends around, he found the audacity to ask if I wanted to meet his fourth wife? Was he serious?

I took a deep breath, cocked my cap slightly to one side, and just stared at him for what seemed an excruciating five minutes. It was probably only five seconds, but that moment between us lingered forever as I battled with my thoughts and emotions.

You want to meet her? Meet her? Is he totally out of his skull? Does he have a clue about what he's—

Finally, I drew and fired.

"You know what, brother?" I said with deliberate precision. "I think I'll just hold off and meet the next one."

Boom! Drop the mic! Thank you and good night!

We didn't speak for almost another year.

————

Once, in a moment of beautiful candor, Laura said this to me: "Honey, I know you think you're being witty and funny with your hip-shot sarcastic comments. And people who really know you . . . well, they know your heart. But everyone else? They don't think you're funny. To a lot of people, you just seem like a jerk."*

She wasn't being cruel. She wasn't joking around with me, either. She said this with the sincerity and concern of a doctor telling me I have cancer, and it pierced my armor when I least expected it. Although it felt like a kick to the gut, I love Laura for moments like these—those cold-water comments that bring into focus my brokenness, those fractured places in dire need of healing, my ungodliness that cripples and robs me of the

———

*My sometimes salty love can be brutally honest with me. "Jerk" is a more gentle word than the one she used.

strength to extend grace, forgiveness, acceptance, and love to others. Even to my own brother.

When the kids' teacher offered me her humbling compliment, I was trampled by a bull rush of emotions. Of course I was proud of my kids. However, her blessing also terrified me. I thought at once of Laura's words. I was reminded of what an uncaring, judgmental critic I could be in my worst moments. Somehow, by the grace of God, I hadn't poisoned my kids with my own jaded cynicism (or so I prayed).

When I say their teacher's words came as a gift—it brought into focus the treasure, the loving heart that God had placed inside each one of my children; it reminded me of how the world is slanted against that kind of spirit and will actively work to weaken, twist, or break it; it was the voice of our Father speaking through another, instructing me, *Protect and nurture these loving hearts I have entrusted into your care.*

But had I been protecting and nurturing those hearts? I was reminded once again how broken parents end up damaging their children, and how much more healing my heart required if I could ever hope to be the father God wants me to be.

Protect and nurture these loving hearts I have entrusted into your care.

But could I really do that? Hadn't I survived all of the assaults against my soul because I'd been able to harden my heart and protect it with my intellect? Did I really even want my kids to become bleeding hearts in a world of soul-sucking vampires? Isn't that like chaining sheep to the fence posts and ringing the dinner bell for the wolves? Shouldn't I be teaching them to build really tall fences for protection?

Those are questions that often rise up in this desperately sinful, weak man.

I realized at once, without the restoration of my own heart, I would never be able to help my children walk with passion and strength through a broken world, where the hope of redemption is on life support, longing for the healing power of authentic love to appear.

Friends, this world needs our kids to be unbroken enough to love like Jesus.

––––––––––

We learn a lot from our parents, and most of the lessons are unspoken.

I can't recall my parents ever preaching at us about extending kindness to others. They probably did, but I don't remember it. However, I can't count the number of times I saw Dad hand money to some stranger in need (and though we were pretty well off by West Virginia standards, we didn't have a lot of money to spare; most of my clothes were hand-me-downs, and soup beans were on the menu at least once a week, only to reappear a few days later as chili). I also remember seeing Dad every Sunday morning standing in his bedroom, top dresser drawer pulled open, arranging a wad of cash (which seemed impressively large to small eyes) that he would later slip into the church offering plate. He always wrapped a one-dollar bill on the outside, but I knew there were plenty of tens and twenties underneath. That lump of cash delivered a lesson I would continue to learn throughout my life—what's on the outside is just wrapping for the world to see. You can show the world whatever you like, but the real value of a thing lies beneath the surface. It's the heart that matters. Mom and Dad would go out of their way to help others. They never failed to reach out to friends and family who were in trouble. They loaned out money, sometimes knowing it would never be repaid.

I also watched others take advantage of my parents' kindness, something that soured my heart against the thorns of ignorance and altruism.

My mother (the youngest of nineteen children from a dirt-poor West Virginia family) lived in poverty for most of her young life. Her father was a country preacher who worked as a door-to-door salesman through the week just to put food on the table. Each winter, Christmas came to the Hodge family in joyous but modest strains. My mother and her siblings would rise on Christmas morning and race to their gifts. Beneath the skeleton limbs of a misshapen tree, they would find a collection of brown paper sacks with their names written on them.

Each child would rip into their bag and find two gifts: a piece of fruit and something that had been handmade just for them. The boys might get a wooden popgun. The girls would delight at a new hair bow or maybe even a dress painstakingly stitched by my grandmother.

When you're poor, the smallest thing can seem like Heaven.

However, when you've never known the sting of poverty, it's easy to dismiss your fellow man and blame the poor for their own condition. It's nothing to stand at the top of the ladder and look down on others with disdain and ridicule. My mother and her siblings knew what that felt like. While all children have an incredible capacity to love and accept others, too often they are soured by attitudes of cruelty. The Hodge kids surely felt the sting of judgment from schoolmates born into families of advantage and opportunity.

Let's face it, folks. Many of us were born standing on third base and act like we hit a triple. We look down on those worse off than we and dismiss them for their lack of effort and laziness. I can't imagine what my mother must have endured under the assault of the beautiful people waltzing through the school halls with their splendid clothing, shiny shoes, unblemished skin, and perfectly arranged hair. Mom rarely spoke about those times, but I can easily fill in the blanks. I know how despicable and condescending ignorant jerks can be—I've been one more times than I care to admit.

It's no surprise that my mother's own wounds would lead her to open her heart to others in need. She'd been there, felt the immense sting of poverty and the lack of care from those with the ability, yet refusal to help. As a result, I saw my parents' tremendous love and care for others on a regular basis. However, I also saw something else: a paranoid jealousy and bitterness toward anyone who might consider themselves to be superior in any way. Mom often used the word "uppity" to describe such folk, and there was little tolerance for these people and their uppity ways.

I once came home to find Dad building a large wooden fence along the edge of our property. Mom stood on the porch supervising.

"Now she won't be able to gawk at me," Mom said with satisfaction.

Mom was convinced that our neighbor spent all of her free time spying and judging us through her kitchen window. Granted, the lady was at that window a lot, but since her kids and I were friends, I knew something that Mom didn't: their kitchen sink was beneath that window. Hardly anyone had dishwashers back then, so a lot of time was spent at the kitchen sink.

My brother and I were quickly drafted to help with the

project. After several days, we had the holes dug out, posts set, and concrete poured. Everything went as planned, and Mom was delighted that she'd soon be protected from the assault of our neighbor's uppity "gawking." However, as the fence panels started to go up, Mom realized something awful: it was too short. The top of the fence barely came to the bottom of our neighbor's kitchen window. Mom was devastated. My brother and I laughed like hyenas at the comedic futility of it all . . . until we found ourselves back at work, that is. Before our tears of laughter dried, we were building a fence addition Dad had quickly devised to appease Mom. After framing up several feet of latticework and nailing it to the top of the fence panels, Mom's fence was finally just high enough that she could sit (not stand) on the back porch and be shielded from all that awful "gawking."

I still look back on this and laugh at the silliness of it all. But it also makes me a little sad. Mom's own poverty had made her such a loving, caring woman to anyone in need, but it was also used by sinister forces to twist her heart into knots of ridicule. I now realize that if our neighbor was standing at her window, it wasn't my mother (the grown woman with a hardworking, successful man and three bright, healthy children) who felt someone's eyes crawling all over her. It was a poor little girl from Wayne County, West Virginia, who felt like she was being ridiculed and mocked by the rich girl next door.

Sadly, that kind of sickness—if left untreated—becomes hereditary.

———

In 2 Corinthians 13:11, Paul urges us to "Encourage each other. Live in harmony and peace" (NLT). When I think of people who need encouragement, my mind races to those beneath me, the unfortunate ones who are struggling socially, financially, maybe even physically. It's something ingrained in my heritage. I love to cheer for the underdog, the loser, the outcast. I'm a Cleveland Browns fan, and a twisted part of me hopes they never find a way to become successful. Maybe I don't want other people climbing on my bandwagon after all of my suffering as a lifelong fan. Something about supporting a loser provides me with a kind of sanctimonious power, feeding an unhealthy Jesus complex that poisons many Christians (whether they realize it or not).

One of my closest friends once said to me, "You're certainly no respecter of persons. I'll give you that. And I mean that as a sincere compliment."

He knew me well enough to know I didn't bow down to the landed gentry, the aristocracy, or even the nouveaux riches in our community. He'd many times seen me laugh with and embrace the dispossessed while standing up against the audacity of the blue bloods who were accustomed to showing up and having their way simply because of tradition and their last name. Serving on boards and committees together, my friend knew I would never give preferential treatment to someone based on who they were or the position they held. He knew I would treat the housekeeper with as much love and respect as I would the CEO. However, he was wrong. Dead wrong.

In my bitterness, something inside of me raged against anyone I perceived to have (in my mind) always had it easy. I took a sick delight in watching the haughty fall; and if I could plant some obstacles to trip them up and bring them down to size, then even better. I was doing the Lord's work and doing them a favor by helping them to become poor and humble just like me. How I hated the silver-spoon types who'd never known an ounce of struggle.

Not a respecter of persons? Indeed. I was a loather of persons, and I saw the world through a kaleidoscope of evil. If you were successful, it was because you inherited it, stole it from someone, or sold your soul to get it. But I saw you for the fake you really were, and in my heart I longed for you to be exposed and humiliated. I didn't treat everyone the same. I actually went out of my way to tear down the proud and talented and level the playing field. My attitude of justice was less about lifting others up and more about hamstringing those on top I deemed unworthy.

My God. How sick and twisted is that?

Sadly, that kind of sickness—if left untreated—becomes hereditary.

And it did. I started to recognize that same type of disdain toward others in my children. It was subtle. At first I would catch a snide comment here and there, but before long I realized my kids sometimes took fiendish delight when the social upper crusts stumbled. One of my kids watched a classmate start to fall apart psychologically and socially. But instead of compassion for the kid (whose parents are rather "uppity"), my child only showed bitterness toward the boy, who'd been caught cheating and in possession of drugs, yet escaped punishment because "Daddy got him out of it . . . just like always."

For a split moment I saw myself in my own child, and I realized what I'd been teaching all of them. While I specifically told them to love like Jesus and extend grace and compassion to everyone, they also grew up hearing Daddy's rants over social issues, politics, education, and economics . . . (you name it). For years, they'd heard the bitterness in my voice toward others I not only disagreed with, but had come to despise. I'd been teaching them to separate people into categories of right and wrong, smart and dumb, worthy and unworthy. I was turning my kids into hard-hearted cynics just like their old man. The funny part is how I believed I was beyond all of that nonsense, that Jesus had healed enough of my brokenness, that I could easily love anyone whether or not I thought they deserved it. If I was bitter toward another, it was justified; they'd earned it. But seeing even a hint of animosity and judgment in my own kids told me that I still had a long way to go. I had to get better—and *be* better—so I could *do* better as a father.

Trust me. You don't want your kids hiding behind a ridiculously tall fence, bitter about who does and who doesn't get the game ball. But I'll wager that's exactly what you're teaching them through some of your own brokenness.

When we talk about others in terms of black or white, gay or straight, rich or poor, liberal or conservative, Republican or Democrat, the only thing you're defining is your own brokenness. You're teaching your kids to put up some tall fences, sort people to one side or the other, and reduce all of humanity to the cruel imprisonment of labels. In other words, you're teaching them to care about certain people while not only denying love to others, but despising them because of some label. In short, you're teaching them to be more *un*-Christ-like than any atheist ever could. You're chipping away at the soul of God's X-Plan.

If we hope to ever unleash the power of Heaven, we have to teach our kids to love with open hearts. Think of the scandalous stuff Jesus said that landed him on the cross: *Love others. Love your neighbor. Love your enemy. Forgive over and over and over. Feed my sheep.* We have to demonstrate that kind of altruism and empathy, because no matter what we tell them on the way to church, they're watching us and listening throughout the rest of the week.

Now, I'm not suggesting we teach our kids to become responsible for every broken person they encounter. We don't want our kids to become doormats to the world. However, if we try to practice loving others from a place of authenticity, like Jesus, our kids will see how we do it. While I'm hesitant to give actual "steps to success" (when we have them, we often stop relying on God for his guidance), I'll offer a few tips to practice loving like Jesus:

> If we try to practice loving others from a place of authenticity, like Jesus, our kids will see how we do it.

1. Jesus extended grace to everyone. He even blessed those who were killing him with a prayer on their behalf: "Father, forgive them . . ." If our kids don't see us speaking love and kindness toward others (and not just in public, but in the sanctity of our homes), the world's bitterness will poison their hearts. It's just that simple. Stop categorizing people. Take labels out of your vocabulary and teach your children to learn people for who they really are.

2. Catch and release. Be prepared to catch someone—anyone—when they fall. Ask Jesus to help strengthen your own heart so you can love even those you suspect might not deserve it. However, also be prepared to release them. Don't let others become your responsibility.

That's unhealthy, and you don't want your kids to learn to become abused victims in codependent relationships. Think of the people Jesus blessed and healed. He didn't catch them and hold on. He caught them and then released them to God.

3. You have to care for your own soul so you'll have the strength to love others. Taking time and space for soul care isn't selfish—it's required! You can't fill others if your tank is empty. Jesus was always going off on his own for prayer and communion. If he—the son of God—needed that, think how much more we need it. Our kids need to see us practice that so they learn to care for their own souls.

4. Set boundaries. You can't completely surrender yourself to emotional vampires who feed on empathy. There are many broken souls out there who will latch on to your kindness, demanding more and more of your heart, but offer nothing in return. These soul suckers will leave you empty, dry, exhausted to the point where your heart is twisted, wrung out, and you're left so battered, ill-used, and embittered that you lose your ability to love and care for anyone else.

An elderly woman at our church once shocked me with her admission. Several months after 9/11, she said to our group, "I pray for Bin Laden every single day. I feel bad for him." She waited just long enough for a few gasps and grumbles to dissipate, and then she continued, "His heart must be so broken and bitter, and that must hurt something awful. So

I pray that he might know Jesus. I pray he might find some peace and joy."

Ah, the empathy of a bleeding heart.

Can you imagine a world full of people like that?

If we nurture our kids' authentic strength, their loving hearts will shine through and they'll build that world . . . instead of fences.

If you get that "X" in the middle of the night, you rescue your kid, and she doesn't show concern for those who might be left in a bad situation, take notice.

Empathy is the fuel gauge of X-Plan parenting.

CHAPTER 13

There Will Be Pain

I'm just pain covered with skin.
—John Steinbeck, *The Grapes of Wrath*

I'm going to give you an awful gift. Read this aloud:

No matter how strong my relationship with my child, no matter how much healing I've experienced, no matter how closely we walk with God, no matter how wisely I discipline, guide, and strengthen them, no matter how much of Christ's love they shine into the world . . . my children may experience rape, disease, or tragic death, and I have to find some kind of peace with that terrible confession.

I was recently reminded of this truth.

One minute we're sitting around playing music and laughing, and then all of a sudden we find ourselves in darkness. The lights are still on, but the air is sucked from the room, leaving us all breathless. It's as though a stranger just burst in and threw a grenade in the middle of the room. We can only wait for it to blow up in our faces.

"Have you ever lost like we have?" Terry's wife is glaring at me. The joy that had been in Shelly's eyes only a moment ago is gone, ripped away by memory, anguish, and accusation. I look into her face. Her vacant, burning stare. Half-furrowed brow caught between stoicism and rage. The corners of her mouth drawn tight. An ever-so-slight quiver in her chin betrays the truth of her broken heart. It's been nearly four years since their teenage son's body was found, and I know that even though she's looking at me, I'm not the target of her challenge. I know her heart. Though I'm usually expecting it, I'm not prepared for her guttural loathing of God to come charging at me in this moment. Maybe that's for the best.

For a frozen moment, I can only look at my friend.

Have I lost?

A part of me wants to rip off my metaphorical fig leaf and show my scars, let her know that she hasn't cornered the market on pain. Some part of me wants to tell my story and let her feel my wounds (and there are many, running the gamut of mistakes, disappointments, betrayal, abandonment, abuse, and even murder). I believe in the power of transparency and authenticity. I know that openly sharing our scars can bring us into Holy Communion, a painful but necessary step toward healing. However, I can't go charging into this fragile moment. Instead, I hold space and soon find my soul reaching out with a simple prayer: *Father, what does she need to hear from you right now? Please don't let me get in the way.*

He answers before my mind even registers the words my heart is speaking.

This is not the time to dive in with what would feel like the sinful challenge of who's been hurt the most. Shelly can barely keep her head above water. Telling a drowning person about the times you were pulled under isn't always helpful. She's been lost, drifting in a sea of pain for years, and this is the first time she's admitted it to me with this much raw honesty. I have to honor that.

"No," I say in a half whisper. "I've never experienced loss like you."

That much is true. All of my children will be sleeping in their beds this night. Though I've watched several friends endure the horror, I can't imagine the soul-raping anguish of an empty bed, clothes that will never be worn again, laughter that is stolen from our ears forever.

Without another thought, my heart takes the lead. I unstrap my guitar and lean it against the sofa. I cross the room to where she sits like a gargoyle statue, an abandoned relic atop some medieval castle, frozen in time, far away from anyone's touch.

"I'm so sorry," I say as I put my arms around her. "I'm so incredibly sorry."

I have a brief urge to say something else, maybe tell her it's not God's fault her son is dead. I want to share how God's heart is breaking over her family's torment. I don't. There have been a precious few times when I've been dialed in so perfectly to our Father's voice, and right now I'm following his lead.

You don't need to fight for me, he's telling me. *Fight for her.*

I happen to glance across the room at Terry, who is silently watching all of this through jagged-glass eyes. He is one of my best friends, and I know he's grown weary waiting for their broken hearts to heal. He gives a brief nod before looking down at his trembling hands.

This house is filled with pain.

Gabriel says to Mary, "You are favored. The Lord is with you."

That sounds like a good thing. I can almost hear the game show announcer:

"All right, Johnny! Let's tell her what she's won!"

What follows leads me to question the angel's proclamation. In this case, here's what being favored by God means for Mary:

Your fiancé will think you've betrayed him, slept around, and gotten yourself knocked up. He'll probably break off the engagement. You'll likely become an unwed teenage mother (if you don't get stoned to death when folks see your belly swell). But if all that works out, you'll still get to spend your pregnancy on the road. Your pregnant "glow" will be hidden beneath road dust and grime. You'll give birth in a cave, surrounded by the filth of animal excrement and disease-carrying insects and vermin. Your joyous years of early motherhood will be on the run as a refugee. You'll have to endure your son being treated as a loony troublemaker, even by his own family. And one day you'll get to stand by and watch your child be unjustly charged, publicly scorned, and then brutally beaten to the point of death. Finally, you'll get the special honor of standing among strangers who jeer at your child as nails are driven through his limbs and he is strung up on public display like a treacherous criminal. You'll get to look into his swollen, bloodied face, remembering the tiny infant you brought into the world and nursed at your breast, as he gasps for his final breaths.

Indeed, there will be pain.

If there is a greater warning for parenthood, I've not seen it. Indeed, there will be pain.

———

"It might be a problem with the monitor," the nurse said, trying to reassure us as the machine screamed out a warning about our unborn son's disappearing heartbeat. I looked at Laura, saw the fear and immense pain in her eyes, and all I could do was squeeze her hand. I was helpless and felt like I was going to vomit. We'd done everything right. Read all the books. Gone to birthing classes. Healthy lifestyle. Vitamins. Regular doctor appointments.

Please, God, let her be right. Let it just be a problem with the monitor.

It wasn't. We were losing our son.

The nurse looked at her coworker, who correctly interpreted the unspoken question.

"Dr. Paul is on her way," she said.

In a brief moment that felt like an eternity in Hell—my wife in tremendous pain and that cursed monitor screaming out, *Your son is dying*—the two nurses had another silent exchange that was more alarming than shrieks of terror. The second nurse turned and left the room. She barely made it past the doorway when I heard her yell down the hall:

"Doctor! We need you!"

A man we'd never seen before entered the room. After a blur of activity, he looked at us and said, "We have to get this baby out now."

All I could do was put my head against Laura, trying to breathe with her just like we'd been taught in birthing class. The nurses were scurrying around the room as the stranger in the white coat barked out instructions.

"Give it a good push, honey," he said to Laura. "Ready? NOW!"

Laura's breathless scream tore at my soul.

"The cord's wrapped," the doctor said to the nurse with urgency. "Let's go for suction."

"She hasn't had any pain meds," one of the nurses informed the doctor. He shot her an angry glare, to which she quickly added, "There wasn't time. She dilated too fast."

That wasn't true. The nurses had dropped the ball, but this wasn't the time to argue about blame.

The next ten minutes were among the most awful in my life. The birth of our first child was supposed to be a beautiful moment of joy, not one of excruciating horror. As I breathed with Laura like a lunatic—*ahee-ahee-ahee-ahee*—I was preparing myself for the birth and death of my son all at once.

Laura's not going to survive this, either.

I shoved that voice away with all the strength I could muster.

After the suction didn't work, the doctor went to forceps to try and extract Ben from inside my wife, who was feeling every shard of pain.

"This baby has to come out now!" the doctor barked. He looked at Laura with a calm sympathy. "Honey, hang with me. We're going to do this."

Laura nodded. "Ahee-ahee-ahee-ahee!"

The next thing I knew, this man I'd never seen before had both of his hands inside of my wife and one foot on the table, pulling with such force that I could see the veins exploding from his forearms.

At that point, I saw myself walking out of the hospital alone, leaving behind the bodies of my dead wife and child.

Surely our Father wouldn't permit that.

Please, God! I prayed in desperation. *Please!*

———

"Oh," Terry says to me with piercing eyes, "I've not lost my faith. I completely believe in God. I just think he's nothing but cruel, and I don't want anything to do with him."

This is from a man who'd once dedicated his life to ministry.

The death of Terry's son changed everything. It wasn't just

the loss of his child, however. The lashes from well-meaning Christians also did some damage through misguided phrases like "God has a plan" and "God's in control" and "It's in God's hands." People say these things with hopes of kindness, but these sentiments tend to deliver a special kind of cruelty. In this case, it would have been just as kind to tell Terry and Shelly, *God wanted your kid dead; he could have prevented it—he's in control, you know—but he probably planned it for some great cosmic purpose. Thanks for your sacrifice, brother and sister. So let's all give thanks, sing a round of Kumbaya, dig into this casserole, and then get on with our lives. . . . Praise Jesus! Call if you need anything. . . . We know you won't, because God's in control.*

And Jesus wept.

Terry came to Christianity through a hard-line (although neatly packaged) hellfire-and-brimstone brand of faith. Follow the rules and avoid being smacked down by that angry god (and yes, I used a little *g* there on purpose) who's just aching for a reason to unleash his wrath and toss you into the flaming pit if you displease him. This is the god Terry was shown. An all-powerful deity who sits in judgment, demanding your worship, your fealty, and your best behavior. Anything short of that comes with a swift dose of cosmic punishment. When Terry's son died, he was sure God had planned it, caused it, or—somehow even worse—stood by with indifference and let it happen.

I had once written an article that struck a chord with Terry.

"'The opposite of love is not hate, it's indifference,'" he quoted Elie Wiesel back to me. "That's powerful, man. I'd never considered that. I used to think God hated me for some reason and was punishing me, but maybe that's not the case.

Maybe he's just indifferent, that ultimately he really doesn't give a f***."

I cringed inside, hating that my article had been used to drive a wedge even deeper between my friend and the source of his healing. I didn't know what to say. I was surprised when the Bible story of Daniel sprang to mind.

Struggling and in need of rescue, Daniel finds himself on the edge of torment. Desperate, he reaches out to God. Our Father, however, seems to have gone off-line and (in what must have seemed like holy indifference) forsakes Daniel to his suffering. Or has he?

Daniel prays for weeks, surely feeling abandoned by God's disinterest, but then . . . an angel finally shows up.

"Sorry, man," the angel says to Daniel. *"I sort of got held up."*

Daniel learns that God hadn't ignored him or abandoned him. In fact, God had dispatched an angel at the first whisper of Daniel's prayer. However, the angel had fallen under attack and wound up locked in combat against dark forces for weeks. Evil had blocked his way.

With this story playing in my mind, I looked at my friend and thought, *Surely angels sent to care for his family are still being blocked by forces I can't comprehend.*

I resisted the urge to change Terry's mind with some self-righteous theological debate. I simply smiled at my friend, told him I disagreed, and hugged him. "I love you, man," I said, praying that he might hear God's voice and not mine.

I can't take away my friend's pain. But I can love him and try to hold off the enemy as best I can until Terry's angel breaks free and shows up to rescue his family.

The old Scottish preacher George MacDonald once suggested that it's better to not know God at all than to have learned him wrong. I fear Terry learned God wrong, swallowing the lie of bitter fruit . . . that life is a series of rewards and punishments dispensed by the whims of a distant, supernatural monarch. I look at my friend and see that, long ago, he learned our Father wrong. He thought an alliance with an all-powerful deity would protect his family, never realizing that such an alliance would actually put them in evil's crosshairs.

Author and counselor John Eldredge often links our heart's joys and passions to our relationship with God. Every good thing we're meant to have comes from our intimate fellowship with our Father. However, "it would be a cruel thing," he writes, "to tell someone to follow her dreams without also warning her what hell will come against her."*

No one had ever warned Terry, so when devastation hit, it must have been God's will . . . or indifference. Either way, the notion keeps delivering a crushing blow to Terry's spirit. The loss of his son was horrific. But sometimes it's not tragedy that ultimately takes us out. Sure, it might hurt like an amputation, but the real damage is done through the messages that follow, those sinister lies that torture and torment us and keep us from healing even when it's available.

———

"Is Laura okay?" my brother, Tom, asked from the other end of the phone. I was standing in the hospital corridor, watching through the nursery window as the nurse bathed my newborn son. I couldn't hear him through the thick glass, but his contorted body and red, pinched-up face told me he was screaming. The nurse looked up at me and gently patted my son's head. She

---

*John Eldredge, *Waking the Dead* (Nashville, TN: Thomas Nelson, 2003).

mouthed the words, *His head hurts*, and gave me a basset hound expression. I appreciated the unnecessary acknowledgment. I knew his head hurt. It was smashed up like a piece of rotten fruit. The top of his scalp bunched up in a horrific pile of loose flesh that moved between the nurse's fingers as she washed him. The doctor had assured me that Ben would be okay, but looking at my infant son in this moment, I wasn't so sure he would ever be normal.

"Brother?" Tom asked. "You still there?"

"Yeah," I finally replied. "I'm here. Sorry. She's in a lot of pain, but she's going to be okay. We're all okay."

"Awesome," he said. "We'll be driving up tomorrow. Can we bring anything? What do you need?"

I was looking at my son's radically deformed head, traumatized from Dr. Strong Arms and his torture devices. Ben's mangled noggin looked like something from a horror movie.

"Hats," I said to my brother. "Bring lots and lots of hats."

———

As awful as that birth experience had been, it still seems like a walk in the park compared to the sleepless nights spent worrying about our kids. There have been so many gut-wrenching moments that I sometimes wonder why anyone would invite such pain into their lives. Of course I often remind myself how lucky I am that all three of my kids are healthy and—more important—here! I could write for hours about friends who have suffered unspeakable pains of parenthood. Terry's son. Another friend whose child died in a horrific car crash. My all-American, middle-class buddy and his wife—pillars of the community, always involved in youth sports and events . . . who had to bury their kid after a heroin overdose. Another friend's daughter was murdered by her own father. And my buddy—a 9/11 responder whose deep, loving soul warms up any room—who watched a brain tumor ravage his baby boy with no mercy.

I could continue, but I won't, mostly because my tears flow too freely for my friends who have suffered such loss . . . and suffer still. And it only compounds the mystery when I remind myself that these are all good parents who made the right choices for themselves and their kids.

Father, if we get it right, why must there still be pain?

His reply?

Life is complicated.

Life is complicated.

John the Baptist carried out his life's mission of preparing the way for Jesus. It landed him in prison with a beheading on the horizon. Was he distressed? Confused? Feeling betrayed and abandoned? He had to be wrestling with all of those things. To quiet his own soul, John reached out to his cousin, asking, *"Are you really the Messiah?"* Perhaps John was thinking the truth would set him free. Literally.

Mike Yaconelli summarizes Jesus's response in a way that feels like a throat punch:

> *"Hey, John. You are exactly right. The blind are seeing, the lame are walking, the lepers are cured, the deaf can now hear, the dead are raised, and the poor are hearing the good news." Jesus was saying, in effect, "Yes, I am the Messiah. Yes, I am healing the sick and raising the dead. And, no, I am not getting you out of prison. Life is complicated, John."*

---

*Mike Yaconelli, *Dangerous Wonder* (Colorado Springs, CO: NavPress, 2003).

If you stop for just a few minutes and consider Jesus's life, not as God in flesh, but as a man, you see a landscape marked by pain. Born on the run as a refugee. The mockery he must have endured from his own family. The majority of followers lost interest and turned away from him. And then there's the temptation in the wilderness.

That whole scene is easier to imagine if I think of him as Jesus the Christ, God Almighty disguised in a skin suit. However, what was Jesus, the man, experiencing? He was hungry. Thirsty. Alone. In the presence of evil more foul and cruel than anything Stephen King could dream up. Follow that up with his crucifixion. I can't imagine the feelings of betrayal and abandonment that Jesus must have been wrestling with—perhaps not unlike what Terry and Shelly are still experiencing. But let this be an eye-opening lesson for us as parents: for reasons we may never fully understand, God doesn't always protect us or our children from the natural dangers of a risky world. Nor will he always come charging to the rescue when evil assaults us. However, he will never abandon us. Ever. We are the ones who turn away, usually under the spell of evil's lies . . .

> Don't make agreements with darkness. It will only taint your heart and rob you of life and the strength you'll need to live it.

God doesn't care . . . he allowed this . . . he MADE it happen.

Friends, don't make agreements with darkness. It will only taint your heart and rob you of life and the strength you'll need to live it.

We know God was with Jesus throughout his suffering

and torment. We know that during his temptation in the wilderness, angels were sent to care for him and strengthen him. Still, God didn't swoop down and extract him from the trenches of war.

It's a dangerous world full of pain and mystery. My wife's cousin was killed by a shark. My cousin died just this morning from a brain tumor. Where was God in either situation? For the sake of my own heart and the hearts of my children, I have to remind myself that sometimes bad things just happen . . . and sometimes evil wins the day. But whether it's evil or simply random tragedy that breaks our hearts, it only has the last say if we deny our own healing, give in to the darkness, and turn away from our Father. Our kids can't see that kind of surrender in us.

How do we tell that new mommy and daddy holding that tiny, swaddled bundle of Heaven, *There will be pain so deep that you'll feel like your soul is being torn out of you?* It's just not enough to tell them to (as the old hymn says) *trust and obey . . . oh, there's no other way.* I'm hesitant to lay it on the line because I don't want to seem fatalistic or discouraging, but the closer you get in your walk with God, the more evil will come against you and your children. I've seen it. And I've lived it. However, the flip side of that coin is that your walk with God is the only thing that will prepare you to defend your heart and the hearts of your loved ones against those assaults. You have an enemy. And even when he's not at work, it's still a dangerous and unpredictable world. Satan doesn't have to ignite the bombs that blow up in our faces. The thief comes to rob, steal, kill, and destroy, but he usually does that through his lies. Terry lost his son. That was a tragedy. However, the thief convinced my friends that God allowed it. I'm not so sure evil stole their boy, but I know evil has stolen their hearts by driving them away from the one who loves them and wants to heal their pain.

Ben's head actually did return to normal shape and size. However, many things in our lives will never return to "normal" (at least not until the renewal of all things).

I can't arrange for myself a world without pain. I can't save my children from the heartaches they must endure. There are just too many forces at work, both in the physical and spiritual realms.

We've been given a life of abundant beauty and overflowing joy. Such joy often comes into the world with ten tiny fingers and ten stubby little toes. However, with that gift comes a special invitation into the depths of anguish.

In Genesis 3:16, Eve is told, "In pain you will bring forth children" (NASB). We usually think of this in terms of the pains of childbirth, but I think it's more than that. It's possible that the births of Eve's sons were no less painful and horrific than Ben's (she didn't have the luxury of a clean hospital and modern medicine). However, that physical pain came and went in the blink of an eye. How could that possibly compare to the agony of her child being murdered by his own brother? That grief must surely have eclipsed any labor pain.

Elizabeth Stone says that having a child is "forever to have your heart go walking around outside your body."*

---

*Tom Krazit, "The Backstory Of Steve Jobs' Quote About Parenthood," Gigaom.com,

No kidding.

In pain you will bring forth children.

One of my favorite quotes comes from Rocky Balboa:

The world ain't all sunshine and rainbows. It's a very mean and nasty place and I don't care how tough you are, it will beat you to your knees and keep you there permanently if you let it. [. . .] But it ain't about how hard you hit. It's about how hard you can get hit and keep moving forward.

That's authentic strength.

No matter how much you get right, no matter how strong and prepared you think you are, you're going to get hit. Hard. And so will your kids. Just keep reaching for the one who wants to help you up off the mat. Be ready to fight for your heart and the hearts of your children.

Ultimately, the X-Plan was meant to be one small tool to help with that job.

> No matter how much you get right, no matter how strong and prepared you think you are, you're going to get hit. Hard. And so will your kids. Just keep reaching for the one who wants to help you up off the mat. Be ready to fight for your heart and the hearts of your children.

October 11, 2011, https://gigaom.com/2011/10/11/419-the-long-backstory-of-steve-jobs-quote-about-parenthood/.

PART 4

THE BIG *X* OF INTENTIONAL MOMENTS

I have a confession: as of this writing, the X-Plan "emergency" text has never been used in our family. A part of me bristles at that. How can I preach about something I've never experienced? I can't tell you about the time Ben, Katie, or Danny texted us that dreaded letter and how Laura and I sprang into action like superheroes.

However . . .

I can tell you about our larger X-Plan—the anthology of intentional moments that converge to tell a larger story, the tale of a journey to discover our kids' true hearts—their strength and authenticity—over time. Sometimes we've gotten it right. Sometimes we've royally screwed up. However, we can't cling to a few particular victories or failures. We reserve the right to step back from individual memories and see the larger story being told.

We deserve that grace.

So do you.

The heart of the X-Plan isn't found in the one instance when you did or didn't respond to your kid's cry for help. Instead, it's all of the intentional moments spread out over the years where you have walked alongside your child to cultivate her beautiful, peculiar, authentic heart.

The X-Plan is about the relationship you forge with your child along the journey. It's about walking with Jesus and learning to see the epic story God is telling in your family.

QUESTIONS TO X-PLORE

1 Looking back on your life, can you recall times when you were striving for a particular outcome, but God was moving in another direction? How did that feel at the time? And now? As a parent, have you ever experienced a tug-of-war with God over your kid? Have you endured sleepless nights worrying about your kid, only to later realize that God had it covered all along?

2 Which of these prayers were your parents more likely to pray? If you could choose, which one would you have wanted them to pray? Why? What's the difference? What's each prayer mean for the child? For the parent?

• *Father, please bless my children and their efforts.*
• *Father, please awaken us to how you've already blessed our kids.*

3 Can you recall times when your parents simply struck out? What about the times you've crashed and burned (sometimes even in spite of your best efforts)? Do those failures linger and haunt you? Do they still define your life in some way? How do you think God sees those events (and you)?

4 Do you think your parents ever felt isolated and alone? How closely did they walk with God? Did they have close friends with whom they could be honest and vulnerable? In either case, how do you think it affected their ability to love and nurture the person you were becoming?

5 How will your kids answer these questions in thirty years?

CHAPTER 14

Seeing Through God's Eyes

*G*od's *not at work in my kids' lives.*
         God doesn't speak.
    I know what's best for my kids.

Ah, the sinful trinity behind my most misguided parenting efforts . . .

We're sitting around the dinner table and Ben is telling his girl-friend about his horrific childhood:

"The boomerang. I'm still traumatized by that whole experience.

"I was about six years old. Dad took me to Toys 'R' Us as a reward for something—I don't remember what. He let me pick out a new toy, anything I wanted, and I chose a Nerf boomerang. It was so cool. Bright orange. Three blades. It looked like a medieval weapon, and my imagination kicked into high gear. The picture on the box showed some kid flinging that beautiful twirling claw through the air, and I could almost see the adventures in store for me. My life was never going to be the same.

"We left the store and Dad took me straight to the park,

where I'd have plenty of space. I was so excited, I could hardly even speak. We walked to an open field on a hillside and Dad stopped. He surveyed the landscape, the battlefield where my adventures were waiting for me, where my new life would soon begin. Satisfied with the location, Dad held out his hand and asked for my beloved prize. In a moment of insane obedience, I handed him my boomerang, never suspecting the worst.

" 'Here, son. Let me show you how to do it.'

"Dad then coiled up and unraveled like a busted spring, launching my new toy into the pale blue sky. It was majestic as it shot out of his hand, those three legs spinning into a solid orange blur as it sailed . . . and sailed . . . and kept sailing. Straight as an arrow. Not even the slightest turn. Finally, it lost momentum and fell from the sky, landing on top of the park amphitheater.

"My heart sank. I was going to be sick. I just stood there in horrified disbelief. My boomerang. Gone. I never even got to throw it.

"Trying to make it up to me, Dad took me back to the store and let me pick out a replacement toy, but he wouldn't let me get another boomerang.

" 'Waste of money,' he grumbled. 'Those things don't even work!'

"I ended up picking out some stupid Superman action figure—its head popped up and spun around and the Man of Steel suddenly turned into a bad guy, an evil Superman or something ridiculous. Actually, though, now that I look back on it, that replacement toy was perfectly symbolic. It reminded me of Dad—my hero one minute, and my evil nemesis the next. I was so mad at him . . . and I hated that Superman toy. I

never played with it. I chucked it into the bottom of my toy
box along with all the other broken pieces of my sad, shattered
childhood.

"My heart was set on that boomerang. But because Dad
didn't know how to handle it, I was robbed of what would've
been the best gift ever, and my world was crushed.

"That was the worst day of my life."

We all laugh. All I can do is shrug. Guilty as charged. But,
come on. The worst day of his life? All over a toy boomerang
that I'm still convinced suffered from a serious design flaw? A
three-legged boomerang?

"The worst day of your life?" I challenge him. "Really,
Ben?"

He nods at me from the far end of the table, his eyes wide,
like someone trying too hard to appear serious, as if this is now
an unscheduled counseling session and he's just daring me to
dig deeper and risk unearthing more skeletons.

"Obviously," he says. "I'm still talking about it, so it clearly
haunts me. You scarred me for life, Dad. Didn't even let me
throw it one single time. Just took control and snatched all my
hopes and dreams right out of my hands and then threw them
away, never to be seen again."

We all laugh again at Ben's melodramatic flair, but somewhere behind his retelling of the boomerang saga lurks a greater
truth, something I suspect we've been misinterpreting all of
these years, an unheard message, an unlearned lesson.

Later that night, before I fall asleep, I find myself still pon-
dering that event from so long ago. That blasted boomerang.
I'd all but forgotten about it. Honestly, I don't recall Ben being
that upset. Had I truly broken his heart that day? Had he hidden his emotions from me behind his stoic façade, the boy try-

ing to look like a man? Or had I simply shielded myself from the truth out of self-preservation, the sinful denial of my own shame, guilt, and failures as a father? In my egoistic desire to be my son's Superman, had evil reared its ugly head from somewhere deep inside of me?

Or was Ben just yanking my chain with this whole story, blowing it all out of proportion just for a good laugh? He's witnessed true devastation and heartbreak, and I know the fateful flight of a toy boomerang doesn't come close to his worst day ever.

But something in his eyes when he told that story . . .

Father, I pray before drifting off to sleep, *what is it you want me to see? I know there's something here for me, something you're trying to tell me, but what is it? Speak to me, Father. I'm listening. Help me see with your eyes. What have I been missing? Show me how you're moving so I'm not fighting against you.*

It's never something so simple as a Nerf boomerang, that's for sure. Sometimes the most trivial things can become weapons of destruction if we don't stop, look, and listen.

————

When I was a boy, I used to go water-skiing with a friend's family. One day my buddy Steve was shredding from side to side, hitting the crest of the boat's wake, and launching himself into the air. After touchdown, he'd cut back for another pass to the opposite side of the boat. Graceful and poetic. Back and forth. Not just walking on water, but running and jumping with wild abandon. Steve swung around for one more jump, but everything changed. The ski stopped dead as if it had hit a wall. Steve instinctively tossed the rope, but the thrust of his momentum slammed him face-first into the water. I went numb as my friend crashed against the liquid pavement, skidded across the surface, and then disappeared beneath the water. The impact had been so loud we all heard it above the motor's roar.

"Charles!" Steve's mom cried out, but Steve's dad was already spinning the boat around in a tight circle. Steve was motionless, kept afloat by his life vest and now bobbing up and down in the river's uncaring waves.

"Steve!" Charlie called out to his son as the boat came alongside him. A slight, high-pitched quiver betrayed the fear in his deep, barrel-chested voice. It was the first time I'd ever recognized a grown man struggling against his own terror. Charlie killed the engine and reached over the side for my friend.

At first all I heard were the waves slapping against the boat's hull, but then came the muffled sob of a young boy.

Steve lifted his face to his father. The waters of the Ohio River camouflaged his tears, but not enough that Steve could ever deny them. Why would he anyway? His face was already dynamite red and swelling. It looked like he'd been hit by a truck, which wasn't too far from the truth.

After Charlie pulled Steve back into the boat, he drove around to retrieve the ski that was drifting away in the current. Steve's big brother pulled the ski from the water. He flipped it over and revealed the culprit: a small piece of driftwood, no more than a few inches thick and less than a foot long, was stuck to the bottom of Steve's ski. It had been floating just beneath the water's surface, so small it had gone unnoticed, but just big enough to be deadly (like so many other things in life). Any bigger and we might have seen it coming; any smaller and it wouldn't have been a threat. The fin on the bottom of Steve's ski had somehow managed to find the unsuspected danger and bite into it.

We were all too shaken to ski any more that day, but it wasn't long before we were back on the water. Steve recovered quickly, but he skied with more caution and hesitation for some time.

I was thankful that Steve was okay, but only now do I look back on that as a parent and realize how badly it could have ended. It's no stretch to imagine that Steve could have been paralyzed or even killed. And all because of some driftwood that nobody had noticed, lying in wait in just the right spot. Steve paid the price for what we all failed to see.

It's often those small, unseen things that hit us the hardest. The difficulty of parenthood is learning to recognize the potential hazards, the flotsam and jetsam of life, while not becoming so hyperfocused that we lose sight of the big picture. We can't drive ourselves crazy trying to sort out all the details and forget to live with a healthy amount of joyous abandon.

> We can't drive ourselves crazy trying to sort out all the details and forget to live with a healthy amount of joyous abandon.

I hadn't thought of this story in years, but I found this movie reel playing in my head the day after Ben shared his boomerang story.

Was that just mental randomness, or did those two tales—Ben's boomerang and Steve's driftwood—have something in common that God was trying to show me?

I don't think I forever crippled Ben's soul by accidentally throwing his toy onto the amphitheater roof. However, could there be a small piece of driftwood floating around out there, just beneath the surface, a dangerous obstacle to my son's path?

Leanne Payne writes, if we don't "practice the Presence of God, we will practice the presence of another."*

I believe our Father speaks to us and reveals himself constantly. It's up to us to work on our hearing and vision. Our families rely on us for this, whether or not they even realize it.

Father, show me . . .

————

Laura says nothing, but the tender admonishment in her eyes slaps me in the face: *You're not making this any more pleasant.*

I'm not saying anything, either, but that's my MO. Like a submarine, I run silent, run deep when trouble hits. I'm well aware how my rigid silence can paint a room with my anger and frustration. I'm not proud of it, but I'm aware. But what else can I do? If only the babysitter hadn't canceled! This was supposed to be a quiet anniversary dinner, a respite from a life that was grinding both Laura and me to bits, and we both needed a breather and a chance to reconnect.

"Owwww, Ben!" four-year-old Katie cries out, drawing even more stares from around the restaurant.

"Ben, why would you do that?" Laura asks our six-year-old. I have no idea what he's done, but it's always something.

Meanwhile, two-year-old Danny is screaming at us. Still not able to communicate except with finger-pointing and caveman grunts, his frustration comes out in screeches and howls as the muscles in his face contort into a mask of bloody rage.

————

*Leanne Payne, *The Healing Presence: Curing the Soul Through Union with Christ* (Ada, MI: Baker Books, 1995).

This is why some animals eat their young, I suspect.

The past year had been hard. Laura and I had taken some terrifying leaps and more than our share of lumps. We'd made the mistake of buying a house we couldn't afford, and we found ourselves living the ugly side of the American Dream— we were house poor. Gluttons for punishment, we'd also opened a new business that was struggling. Surviving on loans, both of us working sixty-plus hours a week while trying to raise three active kids, our marriage had quickly devolved into an uneasy partnership of scheduling, daily after-hours business meetings, arguments over staff, inventory, regulations, taxes, and finances. As if that weren't enough, my family had recently gone through a heartbreaking trauma that had left us all fractured and distant—my parents, my brother, and my sister . . . none of us were speaking to one another any more than we absolutely had to. And the cherry on top? Murder. A man had been killed on the doorstep of our property— a random argument that ignited and ended with a gunshot to the head. As the property manager, I'd won the terrible honor of cleaning up the remains of a man I'd known. This I'd never considered before: when the authorities take the body after a murder, what's left behind is left behind. There are some things you can never *unsee*, never *unfeel*, and although with time comes the grace to endure, that sort of healing is far in the distance for me. Here, on this night, our wedding anniversary, that murder is still fresh in my mind and chewing away at my soul.

I look around the table at the chaos of my family.

God, how I needed this night. How Laura and I both needed it! I'm going down here, Father.

Normally, something like a canceled babysitter would be an

inconvenience. On this night, however, it came as another fierce lash to a man chained to a whipping post.

"Let's go," I growl at Laura as she tries to orchestrate the storm that is our children. We pay the check, collect our spawn, and make our way to the exit.

And then the real fun begins.

The snow is coming down in thick cotton balls. The ground is already covered with a fresh two-inch coating.

"Great," Laura sighs.

Neither of us had expected snow. Life is so insane for us right now, checking the weather forecast is way down on the priority list.

"We can make it if we hurry," I lie in an unconvincing voice. Our house sits on top of a steep, twisting, narrow road. There's no way our minivan will make it up our hill, and the snow is piling up by the minute. Still, desperation and determination often hang out together, and I'm not going to have another moment of this night stolen from me. I'm going to make it home. We're going to put these brats in bed, and if nothing else, Laura and I will have a bottle of wine while we both resist the terrible habit of talking about work while we pretend for just a couple of hours that everything's going to be okay.

Two hours later, after trying and dangerously failing to make it up our hill, we're sitting in our minivan watching cars slide off the road. Every now and then I start the engine so we don't freeze to death.

"Honey," Laura whispers, "please. We're low on gas. The road crews might not treat the road until morning. Let's go stay with my dad."

I don't want to—that's like admitting defeat—but I finally

surrender to her logic. In the middle of the night I drive my family to my father-in-law's house.

"We're not staying long," I insist. "Just let the kids warm up and give the crews a chance to treat the roads." I sit down on the couch and within minutes I'm passed out from exhaustion.

I'm not sure why I wake up, but I come alive with a start, as if shaken by some unseen hand. I look at my watch—two a.m.—and nudge Laura, asleep beside me on the couch.

"Let's go," I hiss.

"Hon—"

"We're going now!" I cut her off. "Get the kids."

Thankfully the roads have been treated and we finally make it home. We carry the kids to bed and, for the first time in what feels like forever, Laura and I are alone together. At three a.m., I turn out the lights, slide beneath the covers, and kiss my wife. Maybe something of this night can be salvaged.

As if reading lines from a television sitcom, right on cue, Laura wrinkles her nose and asks, "Do you smell something?"

Indeed, I do smell something, but until she mentioned it, I'd allowed myself to ignore it. I lift my nose into the air and draw in a slow, deliberate whiff. I catch the faint but distinct smell of electrical burn.

"Are you *KIDDING ME*?" I scream as I throw back the covers and launch myself out of bed. "What now?"

I start pacing the room as I sniff at the air like a maniacal hound dog. Catching a trace of the source, I follow my nose to the wall behind our bed. I start running my hands over the wall like a blind man reading a giant braille sign. Then I feel it.

The electrical outlet behind my nightstand is hot enough to burn my fingers. Without a word, I rush to the garage, flip some breaker switches, and grab my tool bag. In the soft glow of my flashlight, I see Laura sitting up in bed as I drop to my knees and go to work. I remove the outlet cover and yank the outlet from the wall.

On the backside of the outlet, I find that one of the wires had somehow come loose and created an arc of deadly electricity. The wood stud inside the wall is black and smoldering.

Overcome with something I can't understand, I nearly break down in tears.

A tremendous piece of parenting advice is tucked away in the book of Acts.

The high priest and religious officials have sent the temple guards to arrest Peter and those stubborn, noncompliant, upstart apostles. Again. For reasons the council simply can't fathom, these troublemakers just won't shut up about Jesus. At their wits' end with the Jesus freaks, the council decides to have them killed. However, one of the Pharisees, Gamaliel, who is wise and well respected, offers some sound advice to the council.

"Leave them alone," he urges with an almost insane amount of faith. "If you're wrong about this, you just might find yourself fighting against God" (Acts 5:38–39, paraphrased).

Indeed.

On the night of my anniversary, I was fighting against God and didn't realize it until I was on my knees in my bedroom at three o'clock in the morning staring at the makings of a deadly house fire.

I look back on that night—the canceled babysitter, the unexpected snow, the inability to get home for most of the night—and I see the perfect orchestration of powers I can't comprehend that saved my entire family. Our home is an old, wood-frame house built in the 1950s with mostly original wiring. In the event of a fire, it would burn fast. Change even one event that night, and I have no doubt that tragedy would have struck my family with a cruelty I don't even want to imagine. Every event that I'd raged against that night actually delivered me awake, into the perfect time and place, to detect and defuse a situation that would have destroyed my family. I'd spent the entire evening fighting against God while he was actively engaged in my life, working for the protection of my family. Just days before, I'd heard someone say, "What we sometimes perceive as a problem is often protection." Those words came alive in the moment I discovered a smoldering fire inside the walls of my home.

Oh, how many times have I fought against God's goodness because I failed to see his hand or hear his voice? How many times have I fought against what he was trying to do for my children because of my deafness, my blindness, my own ego, and an unholy desire for control?

Too often, I fear.

When it comes to our families and our kids, sometimes God is at work in their lives, trying to bless them in ways we can't imagine, and too often we are resisting the very moves he is making. We have to wake up to that fact. Instead of asking God to bless our parenting efforts, we need to join him in the plans he's already blessed. We rely so much on our own par-

> Instead of asking God to bless our parenting efforts, we need to join him in the plans he's already blessed.

enting expertise, but it's all worthless—every book we've read, every class we've taken, every life experience—if we're not walking with God in our parenting.

When it comes to helping others on their journey, counselor Leanne Payne writes, "No matter how qualified the Christian minister, physician, psychologist, or counselor, he is still one who is inadequate, apart from God, in the face of his own and others' needs."* The same can be said of parenting. We simply can't do this without God's intimate counsel.

The apostle Paul says that we see through the mirror dimly, as if looking through smoky glass. We are blind and cannot see. Indeed, we can never fully understand the heart of God and learn to predict his movements. However, that doesn't mean he doesn't speak to us and try to guide us. We just have to allow him the chance to get through to us. On behalf of our kids, we must constantly ask him—*Father, what are you doing here?*—and then give him the time and space to answer.

Comedian Lily Tomlin once asked, "Why is it that when we talk to God we're said to be praying, but when God talks to us, we're schizophrenic?"†

In most circles, if you suggest actually hearing from God, you'll get some uncomfortable stares (and far less invitations to social events—even in church communities). I know very few Christians who believe that God still speaks and they might actually hear him. They may half hope that God still *acts* in some mysterious, cosmic way, but how can we ever join him in what

---

*Leanne Payne, *The Healing Presence: Curing the Soul Through Union with Christ* (Ada, MI: Baker Books, 1995).
†"Inside the Mind of Lily Tomlin: Her Best Quotes," Biography.com, January 27, 2017, https://www.biography.com/news/lily-tomlin-quotes-sag-lifetime-achievement-award.

he's doing if we don't ask him and wait for an expected answer? He's not likely to give us the full story (we couldn't understand it all), but he won't leave us completely in the dark. That's why he first created light and declared it to be good—*You need to see what's going on here if you're going to be part of it!*

Throughout the Bible, it's not the insane, freaky people who hear from God; it's the ones we're supposed to emulate. An intimate conversation with our Father throughout life is supposed to be a given, like breathing air and learning to walk, but it's an innate skill most people abandon in life's busyness and their pursuit of personal comfort and control. Mike Yaconelli suggests that children are born with the ability to hear God's whisper, but they quickly lose their "God-hearing." The world is too loud, fast, and distracting. Spend some time with young children and watch their sense of wonder and joy—their ability to experience life in ways that we've lost along the way. I believe children do possess a type of God-hearing. It's beautiful to think we might actually come into the world with that holy aptitude (before we're forced to "grow up"). If God-hearing is something we innately possess, then it's a skill that can surely be reawakened. And we're going to need it, not only for ourselves, but on behalf of our kids so we don't end up fighting against whatever God might be trying to do for them.

When's the last time you faced a tough parenting issue and prayerfully asked, *God, what are you doing here?* and actually expected him to answer? I promise you, he will answer, but you've got to be willing to step aside, remove your own ego from the equation, and have just enough faith and folly to believe that he is not only working to bless your kids, but when asked, he'll clue you in on the path and invite you to join him on the journey. After a while, walking with God through parenting becomes as second nature as driving a car. You'll find yourself in constant conversation with him, not only asking more and more questions, but getting more and more answers. And the peace that comes with those answers? Oh, friends. The peace. The comfort. It's so life-giving. It's like you're no longer struggling just to keep your head above water, but you suddenly know how to ski and slice through the waves. And as we develop the ability to listen, our kids learn it from us; together, we join God in helping our kids navigate the unique voyages meant only for them. But to do that, we've got to keep asking, listening, and learning to see what's really out there . . . and try not to become that unsuspected floating piece of debris that will take our kids' feet out from under them.

That's what God was telling me with that boomerang story from so many years ago.

Ben is heading back to school in a few days for his junior year of college. He's been wrestling with his decision to change his major. To be completely honest, Laura and I have struggled with this. A part of me fears Ben might be making a mistake. I've not come right out and told him it's a bad idea, but I've given him plenty of information to think about, thinly veiled arguments to dissuade him.

But what if I'm wrong?

What if my young man's childlike God-hearing is still intact, just enough that he's actually hearing and following? What if the unease in my soul is not because of worry for my son, but because I'm fighting against God on this? Have I become the deadwood below the surface that might body slam my son?

For weeks, I've been praying: *God, what are you doing here? Where are you leading my son? What is it you expect from me?* For weeks, I got no answer. Then, out of the blue, Ben starts telling that boomerang story, about the "the worst day" of his life. Next came the memory of Steve's accident.

Father, you are so patient with me, so loving and good.

God speaks to us all in unique, personal ways. He often comes to me through what I call the "M&Ms" of life: music, movies, memories, and metaphors. It's not just that I love those things, but he made me the way I am, so he knows where my eyes, ears, and thoughts will be most attuned. He puts up billboards in those familiar places for me to see. I'm sure I drive by most of them without realizing it, but in the case of these two memories, I saw clearly what he was telling me about my son.

> God speaks to us all in unique, personal ways. He often comes to me through what I call the "M&M's" of life: music, movies, memories, and metaphors.

I'd once pulled a toy boomerang out of Ben's tiny hands and never allowed him the chance to throw it on his own, robbing him of whatever dreams had been placed within his heart. I'd been the hunk of wood that took him down, the face of evil beneath the disfigured Superman.

Like that arrow we discussed earlier, a boomerang can only work when it's released. Unlike an arrow, however, a boomerang thrown correctly will sail through the air and return to the one who threw it.

Through those memories, I heard the unmistakable voice of my Father saying, *Trust me with this. I'm directing his path.*

———

I recently did some research on boomerangs and discovered my incredible ignorance about them. It turns out that some of the best boomerangs in the world are designed with three blades for distance and accuracy. Me and my stupid assumptions.

Somewhat as a joke, I ordered one for Ben. When it arrived, I wrapped it up and stuck a childish birthday card on top—*Wishing a MONSTROUS birthday to a special boy!* It wasn't even his birthday, at least not literally, but it certainly felt like a birthday . . . metaphorically speaking. My symbolic gift to my son, whose life I place in the hands of the one who knows him best.

A three-legged boomerang. A perfect trinity. Father, Son, Holy Ghost. Parent, child, God.

I hear you loud and clear, Father.

Ben laughed when he opened the gift, and I saw a childlike sparkle in his bearded face. Of course he wanted to try it out immediately. We hopped in the truck and drove to the high school. Ben marched out onto the vacant baseball diamond where he'd lived so many adventures. With boomerang in hand, he coiled and then unloaded, looking much like David facing down a giant, I'm sure.

I admit that a part of me hoped it would sail off into the distance and be lost forever. That might provide me with a good laugh and some poetic justice. (Yes, I have much unhealed brokenness lingering inside of me.) But that's not what happened. The thing actually made a turn and almost made it all the way back to Ben. He tried a few more times. By his fourth throw, he was winging it like a master.

"Well, I'll be . . ." I muttered to Katie as we watched from a distance. She laughed. It was a beautiful moment.

Ben's boomerang carved through the air with a graceful arc and came flying right back into his hands. A perfect throw and catch. All I could do was smile, hearing God's voice whisper through the trees, *Ah, the beauty of someone doing what they're made to do. You can see it now, can't you?*

Indeed, I could.

There is nothing more beautiful than God's revelation of authentic strength.

CHAPTER 15

The Right Path Is Hard to Find

Friends, I want to ask some personal questions—take some time and write out your answers: *Who are you (not what you do for a living, but tell me about your heart and soul, tell me about the person inside)? How did you become that person? Were there landmark events that kept you on track or took you off course? And how much of "you" now seems like a poser (some inauthentic charade you play for acceptance or survival)?*

Headed into my fifties, I feel like I'm just now getting some of my life back on track, and I know I'm not alone in suffering a lot of "lost" years.

The sobering reality is this: in many cases, kids fail to take the path meant for their lives because their parents don't have the time, energy, or wisdom to help them find it.

That's not an accusation. That's a confession.

Years ago, we'd all gathered for Grannie's birthday. My dad, aunts and uncles, cousins . . . everyone was crammed into Grannie's tiny house, which sat at the foot of a small, wooded hill, just across a narrow bridge that spanned Fourpole Creek. I played in that creek as a child, throwing rocks and catching minnows, frogs, and crawdads. On this day, however, the creek was barely a trickle of water through moss-caked rocks and brown silt.

I suppose most families are like mine; when they get together, it's not long before they're splashing around in old memories and laughing about so much water under the bridge. Before long, Dad* became the center of attention. The baby of the family, Dad's older siblings all turned on him, the favorite child by all accounts.

"Tom could do no wrong," one of my aunts said with an eye roll.

"Oh, horsesh*t," Grannie replied. But her eloquent protest wasn't enough to slow the prosecution. The evidence was quickly produced: the times Tom snuck out of the house; missed curfew; got in trouble at school . . . Apparently, my dad had embraced a devil-may-care attitude at a young age, and there'd been no stopping him. At any rate, my aunts and uncles all agreed: their baby brother got away with murder.

"You would've whipped us raw if we'd ever tried half the nonsense Tom got away with," Aunt Jo challenged Grannie with a sincere, blue-eyed stare. "Why is that, Mother?"

Grannie nodded with an accepting grin. She didn't try to deny it.

"Because," she began, "he was the last one." She took a deep breath and snorted. "By the time we had him, I was just tired."

———

One of my favorite movies is *The Natural* with Robert Redford. Redford plays Roy Hobbs, a child prodigy baseball player des-

---

*My biological father.

tined for greatness. He catches the eye of pro scouts and soon finds himself riding the wave of his incredible talents, landing a tryout with the Chicago Cubs. Roy's notoriety grows, especially after he strikes out "The Whammer" (a Babe Ruth–type character and the top hitter in baseball) at a roadside carnival. Hobbs is set to become a legend . . . until he is lured to a hotel room by a mysterious woman. She shoots Roy before taking her own life. The name Roy Hobbs quickly fades from almost legend to obscurity.

I'm always haunted by something Roy's dad says to his son. Early in the film we see young Roy pitching to his dad. You can feel the elder Hobbs's delight in watching his son living out of something so deep and pure—so *natural*—that it's almost heartbreaking in its beauty. After several *crack*s of the ball hitting the mitt, Ed Hobbs says something to his son that lingers in my soul as a father.

"You've got a gift, Roy"—the expression on the man's face reveals a complex mix of pride, joy, and grim concern—"but it's not enough. You've got to develop yourself. If you rely too much on your own gift, then you'll fail." Not long after those words are spoken, Roy's father dies unexpectedly.

You've got to develop yourself.

I'm pretty sure Roy's dad is talking about something other than practicing his baseball skills. He's talking about something much deeper.

Roy's talent (his gift) kicks open the door to his future. His path seems secure . . . until a scandalous encounter with a damaged soul. Roy isn't strong enough to stand firm and resist the gale-force winds of evil. He could knock the cover off the baseball, confidently stare down the best players in the world, but the *self-development* his dad warns about fails to keep pace with the boy's athletic prowess. The young man's talents and skills are superstar caliber, but his character (the self) isn't developed enough to keep him on track.

> *You can enter God's Kingdom only through the narrow gate. The highway to hell* is broad, and its gate is wide for the many who choose that way. But the gateway to life is very narrow and the road is difficult, and only a few ever find it.*
>
> —Matthew 7:13–14 (NLT)

Matthew's quote of Jesus refers to following The Way, the lamb, the good shepherd, God's son, the Messiah who has come to rescue and restore us. Jesus is that narrow, difficult path; that road that leads us into the presence of our Father, a way that few ever find. However, I think these words have too often been twisted and used to pin souls down, leaving them crippled and wounded on the roadside, stifling growth rather than unleashing the power of God and setting people free. Sadly, this damage is usually done to children by their own parents, even the best *Christian* parents.

Verses like these have been used for hundreds of years as justification to put up tight guardrails to keep children *on track*. As parents, we select behaviors and attitudes we deem worthy of certain social groups or some ideal of what we think a Christian is supposed to look like, and then we convince ourselves that as long as a child stays on that narrow path we've prescribed, they'll be fine. It reminds me of the old slot-car racetracks my brother and I had when we were boys. We'd lay out

---

*Greek: "The road that leads to destruction."

the racecourse, using what limited track pieces we had—a few straightaways and turns—place our cars on the track, and then one of us would yell, "*GO!*" There was very little skill involved. You quickly learned to slow down going into the turns so your car didn't go flying off track, but beyond that, it was just a process of counting laps as our cars drove in an oval. It never took long before we grew bored. There was no adventure. No excitement for the mysteries ahead, not even if we saved our allowance money and bought new cars (which we did a few times). Every car was forced to follow the same path.

That's exactly how some of us parent our children, laying out those narrow slots while telling our kids to slow down through the turns so they don't go spinning off track. Kids are then left with two options: stay on a narrow path that goes nowhere, or put the hammer down and jump the track on purpose. Either outcome is a tragedy.

Indeed, Jesus tells us the path to the Kingdom is narrow. However, we should remember that the *Kingdom of God* is not so much a destination, per se, but a life force to discover, unveil, and unleash. In teaching us to pray, Jesus makes that clear. "Thy kingdom *come*, Thy will be done in Earth, as it is in Heaven" (Matthew 6:10 KJV).* Jesus is praying for the delivery of the Kingdom. This isn't a plea to get us into Heaven, but a longing to get Heaven into us. It is about unleashing our souls from slavery's bonds so we are free to run along a unique life path as we reflect the image of our creator in very unique and specific ways. The controlling helicopter parent says, "Here's your path, keep your pin in this slot, slow down in the turns, and when the race is over you'll get into Heaven." However, the psalmist reveals

---

*Emphasis added.

something else. "I run in the path of your commandments, for you have set my heart free" (Psalm 119:32, WEB). We have to be set free before we can find that narrow path.

A child will never be able to stay on life's narrow path until he is set free to discover it. In this case, the narrow path is the true self. And that authenticity must be nurtured and developed if we want that child to finish his peculiar, wild race.

> *The path of development is a journey of discovery that is clear only in retrospect, and it's rarely a straight line.*
> —Eileen Kennedy-Moore[*]

> *They move on. They move away. The moments that used to define them . . . are covered by moments of their own accomplishments.*
> *It is not until much later . . . that children understand; their stories and all their accomplishments sit atop the stories of their mothers and fathers, stones upon stones, beneath the water of their lives.*
> —Mitch Albom[†]

> *Let's raise children who won't have to recover from their childhoods.*
> —Pam Leo[‡]

---

[*]Eileen Kennedy-Moore, PhD, and Mark S. Lowenthal, PsyD, *Smart Parenting for Smart Kids: Nurturing Your Child's True Potential* (Hoboken, NJ: Jossey-Bass, 2011).
[†]Mitch Albom, *The Five People You Meet in Heaven* (New York: Hachette Books, 2003).
[‡]Pam Leo, "Transforming the Lives of Children," ConnectionParenting.com, http://www.connectionparenting.com/parenting_articles/lives.html.

By the time we had him, I was just tired.

—Grannie

We all laughed, but Grannie's words revealed an eternal truth of parenting: sometimes the tank is empty. I've found myself at the end of many days with nothing left, and all I want to do is check out for a while. I'm often too spent to consider who each one of my children is becoming. Heck, sometimes in the depths of frustration, I can't even remember their names.

My grandparents worked full-time industrial jobs. After slaving away in the furnaces of a glass factory each day, they came home to their other job—raising five hillbilly brats. I say that with a grin, because those brats all turned out okay. For the most part, anyway. However, that baby—my dad, the one they were just too tired to deal with—missed something along the way, I suspect. If forced to use one word to describe my dad, it would be "restless." I love and appreciate him, but also feel sorrow for a man who is still searching for something that remains beyond his grasp. Although now in his seventies, Dad is still wandering the desert like a blind man with an unquenchable thirst. Not a bad guy, just lost and hurting. Multiple marriages, homes, and jobs have come and gone over the years, but nothing can define or complete the man who can't seem to find peace with himself. I'm reminded of a line from a Bruce Springsteen song: "It's a sad man, my friend, who's living in his own skin and can't stand the company." By last count, I think Dad's been married seven times, and I'm heartbroken for him. He has drifted from woman to woman and job to job, surviving entirely on his gift: by nature, he is a charming, smooth-talking salesman. He's that guy who could sell a broken ice-maker to an Eskimo and leave them feeling good about the deal. It's a rare gift, indeed. However, it's not enough. The self has to be developed, as Ed Hobbs tells his son. Without a firm foundation in who we are and for what we stand, we lose our way. It's inevitable. Not so ironically, our talents—our very gifting—are often used to send us spinning off track, leaving us banged up and lost. I'm sure many of you know exactly what I'm talking about. And I know you want something better for your kids.

When I was a young father, I once had a conversation with Grannie about my dad.

"He's my son, and I love him," she'd said, almost apologetically, "but your dad never grew up."

I'll never forget the look on her face as she'd said those words. It was an expression that carried an odd mix of adoration and aggravation. Several years later she would admit her role in the outcome: "I was just tired."

Had my grandparents not been too tired to engage their youngest son in the difficult, messy, inconvenient times of parenthood, might Dad have found his narrow path?

We've talked about training up children in the way they should go, but let's step deeper into that mystery. We need to consider *the way they should go* in terms of finding that narrow gateway few ever find. This isn't about harnessing a child's talent. Nor is it about discipline and staying within the boundaries of what is and isn't acceptable behavior to others. As Mike Yaconelli writes, "Christianity is not about learning how to live within the lines; Christianity is about the joy of coloring."* Living out

---

*Mike Yaconelli, *Dangerous Wonder* (Colorado Springs, CO: NavPress, 2003).

of the true self brings joy, because it takes us into the heart of God's loving intentions for us.

If we can believe the outrageously preposterous idea that God made us each uniquely and for a special purpose—why else would he know the specific number of hairs on your head (Matthew 10:30), have a plan for you to prosper (Jeremiah 29:11), and have a white stone that is yours and yours alone with your name on it (Revelation 2:17)?—then we must recognize that we each have a specific journey. It's a narrow gateway because it's only meant for the individual to come to the Father in a very unique, holy way. We each carry a one-of-a-kind divine spark within us. It is core to who we are and for what we were made. Who you are—not necessarily your gifts and talents, but what psychologists call the *self*—is your unique revelation and reflection of the Father. It is a light that only you can shine. The discovery of the self is the very unveiling of *thy kingdom come*, for which Jesus prays. It's also the narrow pathway that few will find—even if they follow all of the commandments and every guideline in Scripture; even if they harness and unleash the power of their unique talents. I know a lot of talented, successful, devout Christians who are miserable and lost, even further off track than some of my atheist friends. They've followed a narrow path, all right, but it was the wrong one. The authentic self has been buried rather than developed. Meanwhile, that divine spark cries out for release, creating a chaotic roar of frustration, anxiety, and depression. We can't do that to our kids.

> The Lord says, "I will guide you along the best pathway for your life.
> I will advise you and watch over you.

Do not be like a senseless horse or mule
that needs a bit and bridle to keep it under control."
—Psalm 32:8–9 (NLT)

Parents, ponder those words in your hearts. The Lord doesn't want us to be controlled and driven. He wants us to follow his guidance. He will lead us on the best path meant only for us. But that comes from somewhere deep inside each individual as God unveils who we are and we find the courage to join him in the development of that unique, divine spark.

"You've got a gift, Roy . . . but it's not enough. You've got to develop yourself. If you rely too much on your own gift, then you'll fail."

Our number one job as parents is to stand alongside our kids and fight off the enemy while the true self is revealed. Only then will they be strong enough to find their life path, stay on course, and use their talents for whatever purpose God intends.

After a sixteen-year disappearance, Roy Hobbs reappears and winds up playing for a struggling baseball team that is mired in mediocrity. Before long, Roy's presence helps change everything about that team. Certainly, his talent—the gift his dad recognized at an early age—plays a role, but it's really the heart of the man (the self) that has the greatest impact. When Roy returns, having fully developed himself, he stands firm in the face of temptation, bribery, abandonment, and threats to his career and even his life. The man—the self—is so secure that Roy can't be compromised, and that authentic strength has an impact on others that seems otherworldly. Supernatural. Or just something *natural* that we all have, but few manage to find: *the narrow path.*

Take a long look at your kid and then ponder, *Who are you?* The answer to that question will determine everything in your child's future. No matter where they go, who they marry, what talents they have, what they do for a paycheck . . . none of that matters next to becoming the person God meant for them to be—the unveiling of the soul.

> Take a long look at your kid and then ponder, *Who are you?* The answer to that question will determine everything in your child's future.

There is a growing realization that a child's sense of *self* is more intact at birth than once believed. Children intrinsically know they are unique, special, and different from everyone else, but in our efforts to socialize them, we risk driving this out of them. It's almost like boot camp. We tear them down so we can build them back up in our own image. Unfortunately, we risk destroying the *self* that God created as we try to mold the person we'd like to see.

Children are born with a unique design, plan, and path for their lives. They are who they are because our Father made them that way. As parents, we can only foster their growth by constantly asking God his intentions: *Who is this person?* As God reveals the answer (and he will if you learn to listen), we become holy partners in the development of that true self. Too often parents become hyperfocused on what kids can do (their skills and behaviors), but completely ignore who they are as individuals. Only when adolescence hits does the question become urgent.

Who is this alien stranger that has taken over the child I thought I knew?

During adolescence (those insane teen years), a child's sense of self becomes challenged in new ways as they face massive social and biological changes. More than ever before, kids struggle with who they really are, and parents either are dragged along for the wild ride, try to take control of the whole process, or they check out completely. Some parents think their only job is to teach their kids to become self-sufficient, and once they can dress and feed themselves, then they're on their own to figure out the rest. This is both lazy and cruel. Although the identity crisis throughout the teen years is a normal experience, it's also a critical time where parents have to stay plugged in to help kids find the answer to their question: *Who am I?* But parents can't answer that question for their kids. It's a question that parent and child both have to ask our Father.

One of my teens fell into a habit of saying, "I hate people," with a sardonic smirk. It's something I'd expect from an arrogant, uncaring jerk, or one who is unsure of himself, defensive, and unable to love others out of some wounding. I went to God with the question: *Father, who is this person?* We need to have a clue about who our children really are if we are to help them along their narrow path. If you ask and wait for an answer in a posture of listening and surrender, God will drop some bread crumbs. He always does. I will warn you, though: we have to be careful about what we hope to see in our kids. Don't answer your own question and convince yourself it's from God. We have to remember that our kids are not our second (or third or fourth) chance to right our own wrongs, live out the dreams we were denied, or develop that person we'd hoped we might become. We have to risk our kids becoming people we don't expect them to be. Remember, it's their narrow path—not ours. In this case, I certainly didn't want to think my child

> **We have to risk our kids becoming people we don't expect them to be. Remember, it's their narrow path—not ours.**

was created to be an isolationist loner, but if that's who God meant for this child to become, to force anything else would border on child abuse.

God, who is this person?

What he showed me was a child who, years earlier, completely choreographed and arranged for a Christmas meal and gifts to be delivered anonymously to a classmate (a boy often overlooked and dismissed by others, whose family was destitute). God reminded me of how alive my child had been through that whole process—certainly not the behavior of someone who hates people. That sort of kindness can only shine from someone who is made to love others with selfless passion.

As a father, I realized I had to engage my teenager in rescuing a self that had somehow gone off track. But I needed to be delicate, not forceful. Something had happened along the way that had assaulted my child's heart. As we discussed earlier, the ways we're meant to reflect the heart of God are the very places evil attacks. The earlier we can start to see who our kids really are and the narrow path that's meant for them, the better prepared we are to help develop and strengthen that self against the assaults that always come.

If we neglect this early on, it's just that much harder once the teen years hit. And as many of you know, parenting teens is a constant struggle of tightrope walking. We have to give each kid space to explore, make mistakes, and test the limits of their own identity, while also remaining close enough to provide support and guidance. If we hover like helicopter parents, we make it too much about us, leading our kids around with bit and bridle because, ultimately, we don't really have much faith that God has any intentions for our kids' lives beyond our own selfish, petty desires. On the other hand, if we completely abandon our kids to the world, then the world will start to tell them who they are, and that's always a complex mess of mixed messages and lies.

> We have to give each kid space to explore, make mistakes, and test the limits of their own identity, while also remaining close enough to provide support and guidance.

Social psychologist Rollo May* suggests that most of us become lost because we let the world tell us who we are. We live our lives as a *house of mirrors*, reflecting whatever we think others expect or demand of us. Life becomes a production, and if we do this long enough, we internalize the behaviors and attitudes of whatever company we keep. Instead of shining the unique light inside of us, we are reduced to incongruent, distorted reflections of a broken world. As a result, May says, we

---

*Rollo May, *Man's Search for Himself* (New York: W. W. Norton, 2009).

become "hollow people" who are empty inside because we don't know who we truly are. The self is lost, so we struggle through life, restless souls desperate to fill a hole where the self—the divine spark—should be.

Tragic.

––––––––

I expect this to be a tough chapter for most parents to digest because of its very nature. People want clear direction. They want steps to follow. *Give me a list of ingredients and tell me when and how to add them.* As we tell attendees at the end of our retreats, unlike self-help guides, God doesn't give us the exact steps to follow in order to unleash our lives. He knows if he did that, we'd run off and do it, leaving him somewhere far behind.* As murky a concept it seems, helping your kid unearth, grow, and develop her unique self requires a faith walk on your part. You simply must remove the reins of control. That's scary for most of us, but, friends, you've got to face the reality: Parenting is a faith walk. And if you can define exactly what a faith walk should look like, then you're doing it wrong. As Mary Steen-

> **Parenting is a faith walk.**

burgen says in the movie *Parenthood*, "These are kids, not appliances. Life is messy."

But we shy away from messy. The unknown terrifies us. That's why so many have created a god in their own image, and those images are terrible distortions of the real thing.

If we want our kids to find that narrow pathway that is

––––––––

*Giving credit where it's due, I borrowed this concept from something I heard John Eldredge say. Thanks, John!

uniquely carved out just for them, then we have to embrace the mystery of the process. We have to engage our kids with prayerful wisdom to help develop the person—the self—God made them to be.

> If we want our kids to find that narrow pathway that is uniquely carved out just for them, then we have to embrace the mystery of the process.

When it comes to our kids, we can never be too tired to be present. When kids first come into the world, we thank God for the precious gift. However, we can't lose sight of the holy task we've been handed and what that means for our lives. When God delivered that bundle into your open arms, he didn't gift you so much as he handed you a lifelong mission and a message: *This is going to take some endurance, a lot of faith, and constant prayer.* We must be ready to guide and encourage, but with a prayerful, listening heart, careful not to force our own will and demand our own way.

My baby girl, Katie Jo, is a senior in high school. Since the time she was old enough to go out with friends, she's always heard the same thing from me (all of my kids have). I don't bark out a litany of rules or expectations. I don't tell her what to do and what not to do. The possible combinations of trouble are far too expansive. I'm reminded of a friend whose young son once shouted out the *F*-word in a restaurant upon dropping his fork. After being severely scolded by his father, the heartbroken, confused towhead looked up at his dad through teary eyes and said, "But, Daddy, I didn't say sh**, h***, or d***." My buddy had to admit, those were the only ones he'd told his boy not to say. A humorous reminder for this dad: I can't cover all the bases.

Or can I?

Each time my daughter walks out the door, I say the same thing: "Remember who you are. And whose you are." It's gotten to the point that I only say the first part—*Remember who you are*—and she finishes the rest:

"And whose I am."

It's only natural that she does that, because we're in this together. "Remember who you are and whose you are" is powerful in its simplicity because it reminds both of us to consider who she is . . . and that no matter where she goes or what she does, she is a reflection of not only our family, but the one who made her for something unique and special.

Remember who you are and whose you are.

Psychologists have long studied the power of groups. Why do people lose their individuality and surrender to group pressures? And not just teenagers. What leads people to act out in horrible ways that they'd never do on their own? How do people so easily lose sight of who they are?

Psychologists like Philip Zimbardo point to something called "deindividuation":

> *Deindividuation can occur when we become so caught up in events and in the feelings of the group that we lose our individuality. Once our individuality has been reduced, we lose track of who we are and what our values are. This in turn causes us to become more impulsive, more sensitive to our present emotional state, and, to some degree, more unable to regulate our own behavior.*[*]

---

[*]John P. Dworetzky, *Psychology*, 3rd ed. (Eagan, MN: West, 1988), 574.

In short, it's a surrender of self.

Parents can help protect against this nightmare by nurturing the development of each child's divine spark—the self. Alvin Price* says "parents need to fill a child's bucket of self-esteem so high that the rest of the world can't poke enough holes to drain it dry."† Indeed, the rest of the world will try to do just that.

Our kids need to know who they are and whose they are so they can navigate that very narrow path meant only for them. And they need parents willing and able to support them on that unique journey of solving for X. It's a holy task we've been given.

---

*Author of *101 Ways to Boost Your Child's Self-Esteem* and coauthor of *Discipline: 101 Alternatives to Nagging, Yelling, and Spanking.*
†https://www.goodreads.com/author/quotes/24858.Alvin_Price.

CHAPTER 16

A Wide-Angle Lens

Think of a time when you felt like a total failure, one shining moment of defeat that made you just want to quit.

While you're choosing from your many options, let me share one of my favorite loser stories from the baseball field:

Little League All-Stars. District championship game.

Bottom of the sixth inning. Tie game. Winning run on third base. Twelve-year-old Ben Fulks emerges from the dugout.

His dad has joined the other parents on a hillside above center field. The man sighs heavily, turns away from the field, and puts his head down on a friend's shoulder. Anxiety and prayer come together in a moment of desperate hope.

Please, God. Let him have this one. You know he needs it.

Ben's had several chances to be the hero in the past—those pressure-filled, game winning moments—and the wheels have always come off the bus.

"I don't know if I can watch," Ben's dad says to his friend.

"Are you kidding?" the friend laughs. "He's led the league in hitting for the past two years. This is his moment!"

His moment.

That's a lot of pressure to put on a kid: *This—right here, right now—is your defining moment. Finally, at the ripe old age of twelve, all of your hard work, thousands of swings in batting cages, rapid fire soft tosses, tee drills . . . it all comes down to this. Everyone's watching. All eyes are on you. Your team is counting on you. Complete strangers are holding their breath in anticipation of your next swing of the bat.*

Ben steps into the batter's box. He reaches out with his bat to touch the far side of home plate and then plants his feet. He lifts his bat. The boy looks in control. But his dad knows the truth: a storm is raging inside the boy.

"It will be the first pitch," Ben's dad says to his friend. "He'll go after the first one."

The pitcher looks down the runner on third. Takes the pitch call from his coach. Takes one more glance at the man on third. And then he unloads a fastball headed for the outside corner of the plate. As his dad predicted, Ben goes after it.

There's a muffled *CRACK!* The crowd erupts. After an uncharacteristic split second of hesitation, Ben explodes down the first-base line as his teammate races for home. The defense is scrambling in a confusing blur. Ben's defining moment becomes swallowed up in chaos.

Almost sixteen years earlier, I had collapsed into the chair behind my desk. End of the school day. Sitting in the quiet, staring into space, I felt like a complete failure. My first year of teaching wasn't all I'd hoped it would be, and here I was only two months into it, feeling defeated and disheartened. In my head I was replaying all the ways I'd struck out during this past week alone. Was I really prepared for a lifetime in this profession?

At some point in the midst of my self-cannibalistic reverie, my friend and mentor John entered the room. He didn't say anything at first. He must have read my body language: shoulders hunched, legs sprawled out, arms hanging limp at my sides. I felt like—and surely looked like—a man who'd been dragged around the room by the kids from *Lord of the Flies* before they dropped his lifeless carcass into the chair reserved for the man in charge. I was merely holding that guy's place.

The man in charge.

That sure wasn't me. If I'd had the energy, I would've been waving my white flag. Why did I ever entertain the fantasy that I could not only do this job, but do it with such grace and style that I might actually make a difference in the lives of kids? The idea suddenly seemed laughable. But I couldn't laugh. In fact, I felt like crying, wondering if Mom had been right all along. Had I made a mistake when I chose teaching as a career?

"So." John finally spoke up as he pulled a student desk around and then sat down to face me. "How was your day?"

He didn't need a reply. His playful grin confirmed that.

"Swell." I sighed heavily. "Just swell."

We sat in silence for few moments, haunted by echoes from the *tick-tick-tick* of the cheap plastic clock on the wall, a classroom-warming gift from Laura. My eyes scanned the room and paused on my quote of the day: "We have just one world, but we live in different ones."—Dire Straits.

Indeed.

"I don't know what I'm doing, John." I said to my friend. "I feel like I'm wasting my time and their time. I'm starting to feel like a dancing bear—I can entertain them for a few minutes, but I'm not sure I'm teaching them anything. I certainly don't feel like I'm connecting with any of them." I started to admit what I was really feeling—*I'm not cut out for this, and I'm pretty sure I'm a terrible teacher*—but I held back the thought.

"I'm going to give you two things," John said, holding up two fingers. "First, this job is hard. Period. It's even harder if you care enough to want to do it well, and I know you do. I see it in you. I know how much of yourself you pour into this. But you can't throw in the towel. You're in the first round of a prize-fight, and you're taking some early shots. I promise, it gets easier as you start to find your rhythm and style. That's just hard to do when you're too worried about getting punched in the mouth."

He laughed at that, and I joined him. I certainly felt beat up.

"The second thing is," he continued, "you have to see yourself with a long view, over the long haul. You can't look at pieces of your career under a microscope and think that one tiny part defines you. You have to view yourself with a wide-angle lens. One lesson, one week, heck—even one year!—doesn't define you. I've been doing this for ten years now. I've had my struggles, times when things didn't work out and it seemed like I was spinning my wheels and going nowhere, but if I look at my whole body of work so far, I'm comfortable saying that I'm a pretty darn good teacher. You are, too. I've heard the kids talk about you and your class. Trust me, they like you, and they're learning. But you're not going to hit the winning run every time you step up to bat. You're going to strike out a lot in this profession. If you're not striking out, that only means you're not trying—and that's the teacher you don't want to be."

I was considering John's words and realized I'd started nodding in agreement. Hope was sneaking in through the cracks in my soul.

"Take the long view," he repeated. "That's hard to do now because you're just starting out, but if you don't cut yourself a little slack, you'll never make it long enough to enjoy that view." He smiled and patted me on the shoulder.

It was some of the best advice I've ever received, and I have applied it to every facet of my life. Including parenting.

> *We put so much stress on ourselves to do everything right, but what does that mean? My experience has taught me that there is no such thing as doing everything right; it just comes down to taking it one day at a time, doing the best you can.*
>
> —Cara Maksimow, LCSW, CPC*

I've shared some not-so-pretty things about my own parents, and to leave you with some of those images would not only be unfair to them, but also a gross misrepresentation of what kind of parents they've always been. Sure, Mom made some mistakes over the years, but she never failed to love and care for us in many sacrificial ways. And although my stepdad once shook a glass jar filled with metal washers and sent me screaming in terror down a haunted hallway, he's also the one who provided much-needed structure in our home. Though it's healing to identify those parenting missteps that wounded us, I can't point out those few shortcomings and allow those to define the people who made every effort to provide my siblings and me with a future. There were many joyous moments. We never suffered any kind of want for physical needs. Church and education were always high priorities. Kindness toward others was a way of life. Illness was attacked head-on with a trip to the doctor, no

---

*Cara Maksimow, *Lose That Mommy Guilt: Tales and Tips from an Imperfect Mom* (New York: Open Door, 2015).

hesitation. To this day, I don't think of my stepdad as the "jar shaker." I think of him as the one I can call whenever I need help and he drops whatever he's doing and comes to my rescue. The same with my mother. Every. Single. Time. In short, they are incredible parents when viewed as they should be: through a wide-angle lens. They deserve that grace. Just as much as the rest of us deserve it.

Laura is prone to fall into a pit of self-loathing from time to time, commenting that she's a terrible mother. Right now she's beating herself up because she's going to miss Danny's cross-country track meet due to traveling plans. I don't want to write off her feelings of disappointment, but it's hard to not laugh at her for being so self-critical when she tells me how awful it is that she won't be there for our son. Sure, she'll miss Danny's run, but when he looks back on his life's race, he'll see his mom was always there. When I view my wife through a wide-angle lens, all I see is a woman who has always busted her tail, rearranging schedules, tearing away from work, denying her own personal needs, all so she can be there to support our kids in every possible way. Her efforts in this arena are superhuman, and to see her beat herself up over one missed athletic event tells me that she's too hyperfocused on one small thread in a beautifully woven tapestry of parenting love.

Friends, the X-Plan is much bigger than a single text message.

You're going to get a lot of things wrong as a parent. I'm not suggesting you should ignore those things and fail to learn from them, but you can't hamstring yourself over them, either. Take the long view. See yourself with a wide-angle lens. Give yourself the long-range grace to keep becoming the incredible parent you were made to be. The fact you're reading this book shows you care, that your heart is invested in doing your absolute best for your kids. Remember in whose image you were made, and embrace the truth that you carry the light and love of the universe in your soul. Even with dozens of slipups along the way, how can you *not* see yourself as a great parent with that kind of power radiating throughout your life?

> Take the long view. See yourself with a wide-angle lens. Give yourself the long-range grace to keep becoming the incredible parent you were made to be.

At the same time, we have to be extra cautious about getting too caught up in our kids' successes and failures. If a twelve-year-old kid hits the winning run in a district championship game, it's a little premature to start picking out Major League Baseball colors and second homes in spring training towns. Likewise, that kid's not a loser if he fails to hit the winning run. I've seen so many parents become so overly invested in their kids' lives that every situation their kids face seems to carry life-and-death consequences. That's just cruel. Our kids are dealing with enough just with growing up; it's not fair to pile on with your own anxieties, hopes, and fears.

Sometimes your kid will hit the winning run.

Or maybe he won't.

But what will the kid's life look like when viewed over the long run, through a wide-angle lens?

We have a picture in our family room of a twelve-year-old baseball player in midswing. A split second forever frozen in time. It was a gift from a friend, a professional photographer, who had captured the moment perfectly. Ben's final at-bat in that district championship game. There is so much detail in the picture. The determination in his young eyes. The sweat on his royal-blue jersey. The fine blue lines of his pinstriped pants. The swing is textbook perfect as the bat makes contact with that outside fastball the pitcher had tried to sneak past my son to get ahead in the count. Ben went after that first pitch, just as I had predicted, and did absolutely everything right.

However, the picture also captured one other heartbreaking detail.

That *CRACK!* we'd all heard from beyond center field was not a perfectly swung bat crushing the laces off of a fastball.

The picture in our family room reveals the truth of that heartbreaking moment. The head of Ben's bat snapped off at the point of contact. His bat broke at the worst possible time, in a moment when he was completely in the zone, in his groove, running along his narrow path.

The head of the bat went flying through the air, having absorbed too much of the ball's energy. What, by all accounts, would have been a walk-off home run ended up bouncing past the pitcher and rolling toward second base. Ben took off for first base and his teammate headed for home.

The shortstop collected the ball and fired it to the catcher for the play at the plate.

"You're out!" screamed the umpire.

Our boys ended up losing.

I now look at that picture of my son in that beautifully heartbreaking moment and refuse to let myself focus on the broken bat. It's one small detail, an unfortunate hiccup in an otherwise awesome display of who my son was becoming in that season of his life.

Friends, we talked earlier about seeing though God's eyes, and that certainly applies here as well. While the details can certainly matter, the story God has been telling for thousands of years only starts to make sense and reveal its beauty when viewed through a wide-angle lens. The same is true when it comes to how you view your kids and yourself as a parent. If there's one word that should remain part of our parenting lexicon, it's "relax." Don't get so caught up in all of the little things. Do the best you can. Invite healing and growth where needed. And back up and take the long view. We've all got a long way to go. Allow yourself and your kids the grace and space that are needed for the journey.

CHAPTER 17

Never Alone

How is God moving in your child's life right now? Is he calling you to step in with authority, or urging you to back off? Who has he placed in your life to help you along this stretch of the journey? I hope my kids come to realize the times I've failed them have been the result of my own distance from God, lonely times I've swallowed the lie, *I'm on my own here, and this is completely up to me.*

Let's return to the adulterous woman of the Bible.

Jesus tells her, "Go and sin no more."

Remember what Jesus is actually saying here: *Don't turn away from God.*

Why is that so hard?

I've always tried to imagine what it must have been like to experience Jesus, the man—to stand in his presence in these stories that have become so common we risk missing their true essence and power. If we linger in these stories just long enough, we start to see Jesus in his full humanity and what that means for us. I often try to insert myself into these stories and let my heart and mind wander . . . and wonder.

What if I'd been there?

Would I have been one of the faces in the mob, calling for

the woman's stoning? I'm afraid I've probably been that a time or two.

Would I have been a disinterested passerby who just went about his business and completely missed the physical presence of God in my midst? Yep. Been there, done that.

What if I were Jesus in this story? How might I have handled that bloodthirsty crowd? It seems silly for me to even consider it. I lack the strength and grace. If Jesus is God in flesh, appearing in God's fullest intention of humanity, then I am certainly less than human. That at least permits some hope for growth, because the thought of becoming divine is laughable for this covetous old sinner (to use a Dickens phrase).

However, what if I'd been in the woman's position? How might I have handled that?

If I am completely honest, I think a part of me would have wanted to throat punch the mercurial rabbi for his flippant "Go and sin no more." Though few would admit it, I think most Christians would've felt the same.

"No one else knows about this," my friend said to me, "and they never will. You know how people talk, and I just can't have my daughter living with that stigma."

He'd come to me because he needed a sympathetic ear, and someone who would pray for and with him. I'm honored to have friends willing to share their pain and struggles with me. I'm humbled they trust me with their open hearts. Beyond that, I'm blessed with tremendous insights into a dark reality of parenting: most parents suffer heartbreaks and struggles completely alone for fear that even their closest friends will judge them. That's tragic.

I'm not suggesting your life (or the lives of your children) should be an open book for the world to see. However, you simply must share a fellowship with someone who will listen and pray with you through the darkness. And when it comes to raising kids in this postmodern age, there is plenty of darkness to suffer.

Trouble hits. Assaults come against your kids, your spouse, and your own heart. Sometimes evil tips its hand and you know how to fight it; sometimes not so much. Other times it's not even evil at work, but just bad luck or rotten circumstances. Whatever it is, when trouble hits your family, you're usually too deep in it to recognize what's really going on and how you should handle it. It's during these times you need some allies of the heart: a small, tribal group with whom you can share the grit of your life with no concern for judgment or scorn. Friends like that are, indeed, rare; but I urge you to pray about it and ask God to reveal the people you can trust with your heart. And then reach out to them!

> Ask God to reveal the people you can trust with your heart. And then reach out to them!

You simply cannot raise strong, healthy kids by the sweat of your brow with no support for your own heart. As a sometimes renegade loner who tends to struggle with control issues, I know this all too well. Thankfully, God has placed a handful of men and women in my life with whom I can drop my fig leaf and they're not afraid to tell me what I need to hear. Though they handle it with beautiful tenderness and grace, they hold my heart with honesty, love, and accountability. For that I am thankful. I pray you have those people in your life.

Too many don't, and that's just devastating. Holy fellowship is a more critical weapon in the parenting arsenal than any parenting book ever written (including this one).

Holy fellowship is a more critical weapon in the parenting arsenal than any parenting book ever written.

A friend called me just this afternoon, needing a sounding board for something he's wrestling with regarding his teenager. Though it's become something of an expected joke, I said to him what we always say to each other during these types of discussions, "Well, did you pray about it?"

The funny thing is, sometimes we haven't! Trouble hits, and we start scrambling as we prepare to fight whatever battle lies ahead. It's almost as if we're duped into believing that once we get our lives in order, we'll be able to afford the time to talk with God, as if he just wants us to keep him up to speed on new developments and how our lives are going. Thankfully, I have friends who remind me that I must always look to God first, or else whatever trouble has come my way has already beaten me.

If you ever feel like raising kids is a constant struggle just to catch your breath, I'm going to suggest you pay attention to that feeling, because it's telling you something. Consider it a wake-up call. Parenting is like working as a deep-sea diver. You're at the bottom of the ocean, and you have a job list to complete each day. Too many of us wake up and attack the job list without first connecting the umbilical that delivers the breath of life. We make some unholy agreement that once we get the job done, then we'll have some extra time to plug up to our lifeline. Meanwhile, we're starving for air. Our vision becomes cloudy as the mind gets hazy. Friends, when we're in this condition, we provide little good for our kids.

Go . . . and don't turn away from God.

What if I were that woman?

Jesus looks down at me. My accusers have departed. Stones dropped haphazardly are scattered around me in the dust.

"Go," Jesus says to me, "and sin no more."

For a moment all I can do is stare at him. Only moments ago death was clawing at my naked body, and now here I am in the temple square, covered in blood-soaked dirt from being dragged through the street. My face, bruised, bloodied, and tearstained. My hair tangled into filthy knots.

And all he can say to me is, "Go and sin no more"?

I open my mouth to speak to this man, who now looks at me with eyes that haunt me with their kindness. He did just save my life, didn't he? Perhaps that's enough. He got me out of this mess. He got my "X" and showed up. I should just be grateful for that.

But I can't. Not entirely.

Go and sin no more . . .

"Really?" I say to him, my voice full of mockery and growing rage. " 'Go and sin no more?' Is that all you've got? Where exactly shall I go? Those men you ran off, do you think they'll actually leave me alone? They're probably waiting for me outside the wall. And you suggest I should just . . . *GO?* Shall I go home to my husband now? Do you think I'll be welcomed back into his bed? Is there any place at all in this town I can ever GO again? IS THERE? Or perhaps you mean GO, as in go to another town and try to start over with my life. Is that what you're suggesting, Jesus?"

By now I have risen and I am screaming at him, spittle flying from my lips. He lets me continue as I pour out all of my frustrations, fear, and anxiety on him.

"You haven't helped me here! You've only prolonged the inevitable and made it worse! 'Go and sin no more'? Are you freaking kidding me?"

I stop just long enough to catch my breath, and that's when he reaches out to me, puts his arms around me, and I collapse into his arms and sob. Only later will I realize the depth of his simple words to me.

Go and sin no more.

Go . . .

"I know it's going to be hard," he says to me with that simple word, "but you have to keep going. And don't ever give up. Even when you feel defeated and exhausted, keep going. No matter what others do or say, no matter what comes against you, keep going. You are more than you realize—if you could only see what I see—and you are needed more than you realize. So . . . go . . . don't give up . . . ever. . . . Keep going . . ."

. . . and sin no more.

" . . . and don't ever turn away from God."

Friends, I told you earlier that this is one of my favorite stories, and this is primarily why. There is so much truth and beauty behind those simple words: *Go and sin no more.* They have carried Laura and me through many parenting storms.

When I first penned that X-Plan piece, this story of the adulterous woman was dancing in my head. A woman who'd gotten herself into a mess, and Jesus handles it with such incredible strength and grace. He doesn't condemn her. Doesn't punish her. Doesn't shame her. He simply extracts her from the trenches, brushes her off, and tells her the secret of finding a life worth living:

> *Keep going . . . and don't ever turn away from God.*

Keep going . . . and don't ever turn away from God.

This is Jesus's beautiful way of telling us that we're never alone. He's promised he will never forsake us, and that gives me great comfort, especially in the midst of my most epic screwups. How could I not want my kids to feel that same assurance?

Keep going . . . and don't ever turn away from God.

We need to live out those words with everything we have if we truly want a life worth living. And our kids need to see that attitude in us.

That alone is the best parenting advice I can offer. Everything else in these pages is merely a reflection of that (at least I pray it is).

I often jokingly say, "Kids are resilient. They'll survive in spite of what we do to them." We just have to remember that parents aren't well-oiled machines and kids aren't well-designed products that get spit out when everything is functioning correctly. Parenting is a journey we take with our kids. That's why I've tried to write this not to be a handbook or a manual, but as a challenge—I hope you walk away from this book not satisfied with concrete answers, but wrestling with new questions that stir your heart. Your kids need you to be willing to grow alongside them. I say again—this is a journey you take together.

Whatever challenges you and your kids may face, just remember that some problems can't be solved, some wrongs can't be righted, and some mistakes can't be unmade. Unfortunately, that's simply the way of this broken world. But that doesn't mean we can't live with hope, forgiveness, and joy. And—oh!—what a joyous, adventurous, authentic life our kids might find with those words echoing in their young hearts:

Keep going . . . and don't ever turn away from God.

―――――――

I'm at the far corner of the roof, down on my knees, wiring up a new antenna. The morning sun is climbing fast, and the rooftop is already heating up. In another hour, it will become a furnace up here. I have to hurry or risk being baked alive.

I hear a scuffling sound somewhere behind me, and I glance over my shoulder. Across the roof I see Ben—my eleven-year-old who is afraid of heights, the one I left stranded halfway up the ladder. Somehow he found the courage to climb just a little bit higher than he once thought possible. His body is slowly moving over the edge of the rooftop. It reminds me of the gelatinous monster from the old creature feature *The Blob*.

I watch, but I say nothing. I want to encourage him, but I don't want to distract him and cause him to lose his balance. It's about a twenty-foot drop to the concrete below. *Come on, Ben*, I'm silently rooting for him, *you've got this*. After a few tense moments of positioning and repositioning his hands and feet, Ben rolls himself onto the roof. He takes a deep, cleansing breath, pushes himself up onto his knees, and then stands. From my angle, the boy somehow looks taller than he was earlier this morning.

Ben turns in a tight circle, surveying the view, slow enough to let himself take in all that his young eyes can see. Then I notice his hands balling up into tight fists. Slowly, those fists lift toward the sky.

"This. Is. Awesome!" he cries out, his voice echoing off the hillside as if the trees are shouting back in agreement.

———

The summer after Ben's freshman year of college, he took a job working construction. I had to laugh when I learned he was spending most of his time doing grunt work on a roofing job. In this case, "grunt work" consisted of hauling eighty-pound bundles of shingles up a ladder. Ben still wasn't comfortable with heights, but he was doing it.

How far the boy had climbed.

How far we'd climbed together—all of us.

How far we still have to go.

Friends, good parenting isn't about having all the answers, getting it right every time, and producing that perfect child. It's a climb up a ladder, one rung at a time. It's a journey into the unknown, searching for the ways Jesus is moving and following his lead.

It's an adventure, a treasure hunt to unearth your child's beautiful, priceless, authentic strength. It's a journey you must take together.

And *X* always marks the spot.

Acknowledgments

I would be quite a scoundrel if I failed to thank my loved ones whose stories fill these pages. To give the world a glimpse into our lives takes a crazy kind of courage. I pray it encourages others to be honest and vulnerable with their own stories. Ben, Katie, and Danny; Mom and Dad (Dads—both of you!); Tom and Jennie—I love you all. We're nowhere close to perfect—no family is—but my life is better because of you. Our love is stronger than anything the enemy can throw at us.

Special thanks to my agent, Wes Yoder: Wes, your patient guidance and care for this knucklehead has been Christlike. And to the best friend I've still not met in person, Matt Mikalatos: Matt, your kindness, suggestions, and support made this book a reality. I'll never forget that. To my editor, Becky Nesbitt, and the entire team at Simon & Schuster's Howard Books—wow! Just wow! You couldn't have made this adventure any easier or more fun. A huge "Thank you!" also goes to the dear ones who slogged through early drafts of this book (and others) and offered advice and encouragement. Special thanks go to Marie Manilla for her nudges that kept me moving, and David Hermon, who was crazy enough to listen to God and relay the message. To my Empty Stone compadres—your friendship has rescued me more times than you know. And I must give a shout-out to my Colorado brothers (you know who you are): you men have helped fill my bucket and remind me of what matters. To my Dos-3-Guise bandmates—there, I mentioned you . . . now get off my back. (I really do love you! You guise reflect God's loving heart in the most unexpected ways.)

Just a few more . . . and I simply must set these apart.

To Laura: Who could have imagined our first date in tenth grade would lead us here? You, my love, have challenged me, inspired me, consoled me, and always walked beside me—even when I've stumbled off track. To steal a line from one of your favorite movies: "You make me want to be a better man."* I obviously couldn't have written this book without you.

To you, dear readers—you have embraced and shared my work (quite literally) millions of times. You breathed life into this book, and I'm so grateful that you're with me on this journey.

And the best for last . . .

Years ago, I felt God's calling, and I resisted with everything I had. But he persisted. He's like that, you know. Finally at the end of my rope, I offered a deal (I know, I know—never try to make deals with God). I said, "Okay, Father, I'll do what you want on one condition—I won't take credit for anything that goes right as long as I don't have to take the blame if this thing crashes and burns." I was shocked when he took me up on my offer . . . but that's given me the freedom to risk, to follow his lead without hiding from potential failure. So, for everything in these pages that touched your heart, you know who to thank.

My God, thank you for loving me and all the ways you continue to father me. You are the author of my story.

---

*As Good as It Gets (Culver City, CA: Sony Pictures Home Entertainment, 1998), DVD.

Scripture References

Index